MW01010604

Carlos A. Schwantes

In Mountain

University of Nebraska Press

Lincoln & London

Shadows

A HISTORY OF

Idaho

Manufactured in the United States of America

⊖ The paper in this book meets the minimum requirements of American

National Standard for Information Sciences—

Permanence of Paper for Printed Library Materials, ANSI Z39.48–1984.

First Bison Books Printing: 1996

Most recent printing indicated by the last digit below:

10 9 8 7 6 5 4 3 2 1

Preparation of this book was aided by the

John Calhoun Smith Memorial Fund of the University of Idaho and spon-

sored by the Institute for Pacific Northwest Studies.

Maps and charts supervised by Allan Jokisaari

at the University of Idaho Cart-O-Graphics Laboratory, Moscow, Idaho.

Library of Congress

Cataloging in Publication Data

Schwantes, Carlos, 1945–

In mountain shadows: a history

of Idaho/Carlos A. Schwantes.

p.   cm.   Includes bibliograph-

ical references and index.

ISBN 0-8032-4213-1 (cl. alk. paper)

ISBN 0-8032-9241-4 (pa.)

1. Idaho—History.   I. Title.

F476.S38   1990   979.6–dc20

90-12838   CIP

Dedicated to Siegfried Rolland and Merle Wells

Idahoans love the land—the mountains,

the deserts, the prairies, and the waters.

They are hunters, anglers, and huckleberry

pickers, truly emulating their ancestral

food-gatherers; Idahoans are a satisfied lot,

generally non-affluent, who can travel the

nation and the world and come home with-

out envy.—from the *Idaho Almanac* (1977)

Contents

Illustrations

Preface

During the past several years I have received many requests for a concise history of Idaho that captures the essence of the state's heritage. "Idaho history in a nutshell," one person called it. That is what I seek to provide in this volume, a relatively brief book that traces main themes yet keeps in mind that history is about people, not just dates and facts, abstract forces and movements. Hence, everyday life receives special attention.

In narrating, analyzing, and instructing, I try to offer something useful not only to those who are already well versed in the subject but also to every reader who simply wants to know how Idaho evolved into the state it is today. What follows is in some ways an extended essay on the character of Idaho.

My hope is that *In Mountain Shadows: A History of Idaho* will inspire readers to seek out books and articles mentioned in the Suggestions for Further Reading and to pursue special subjects in depth. Of particular value are the articles in *Idaho Yesterdays,* a quarterly journal published by the Idaho State Historical Society since 1957, and *Pacific Northwest Quarterly.*

I have profited from the advice of many people, but I alone must take responsibility for the topics covered and any errors of fact or judgment that may appear in the following pages. For the various forms of help they gave me, I want to thank Terry Abraham, head of Special Collections at the University of Idaho, and Lois Ackaret, also of Special Collections; Craig Harline, my colleague in the Department of History; Lawrence Merk, director of the University of Idaho's Center for Business Development and Research; Gerald A. Willett, Jr., Department of Civil Engineering, University of Idaho; David Crowder, Judith Austin, Elizabeth Jacox, and Larry Jones of the Idaho State Historical Society; Blaine Bake, archivist at Ricks College; Arlan Call of the Twin Falls Public Library; A. J. Simmonds of Utah State University; Nancy Gale Compau of the Northwest Room of the Spokane Public Library; Edward Nolan of the Eastern Washington State Historical Society; David Nicandri and Elaine Miller of the Washington State Historical Society; Susan Seyl of the Oregon Historical Society; Lory Morrow of the Montana Historical Society; Dorothy Dahlgren of the Museum of North Idaho; Julie Roy Jeffrey of Goucher College; Don Snoddy of the Union Pacific Railroad Museum, Omaha; Virginia Ricketts of Jerome, Idaho; Cort Conley of Cambridge, Idaho; George and Kay Simmons and her mother, Jo Walker, all of Moscow, Idaho.

The students in my classes on Idaho and the Pacific Northwest were an enormous help and an unfailing inspiration. At the University of Idaho, the history department chair Kent Hackmann; current dean of the College of Letters and Science Kurt O. Olsson; the academic vice-president Thomas O. Bell; and President Elisabeth Zinser provided vital support. I am also indebted to William S. Greever, Doyle E. Anderegg, Elizabeth Madison, Marjorie Whitten, Dennis W. Baird, and Nancy L. Dafoe for a variety of important reasons. Special thanks go to Orval and June Hansen and to James W. Asaph, all of whom helped to defray the cost of final preparation of *In Mountain Shadows*. I feel very fortunate to have Carol Zabilski of the *Pacific Northwest Quarterly* as editor of the manuscript. As always, I am impressed with her skills.

Siegfried Rolland played a key role in this project. He not only was instrumental in getting me to move to the University of Idaho but also succeeded in imparting to me his love for Idaho history, a subject he taught for thirty years. He became a good friend and confidant. In fact, I believe the last book Sig read was an early version of this manuscript. He was characteristically generous with his time. Merle Wells, former state historian, has always been willing to share his incomparable fund of knowledge with me. More than anyone else, Merle is Mr. Idaho History. These two men showed me the way, and it is appropriate that *In Mountain Shadows: A History of Idaho* should be dedicated to them.

CHAPTER 1

And here we have Idaho, Winning her way to
fame, Silver and gold in the sunlight blaze,
And romance lies in her name. —from "Here
We Have Idaho," official state song

Essential Idaho
More than Famous Potatoes

"I love your famous potatoes, but tell me is Idaho located east or west of the
Mississippi River?" The middle-aged man who refueled my car in Pennsylvania posed a question that took me by surprise. Yet, according to a tale
often told in the Gem State, a person visiting the East Coast introduces himself as being from Idaho, and is politely informed by his host, "Yes, but back
here we pronounce it Iowa."

Such incidents remind us that Idaho—despite the claims of "winning her
way to fame" in the state song—is one of the least known of the fifty states,
even to residents of neighboring states, and even to many Idahoans themselves. Divided by geography, religion, transportation patterns, and history,
Idahoans often know less about distant parts of their own state than they do
about nearby portions of Utah, Montana, Wyoming, Nevada, Oregon, or
Washington. Small wonder: by highway the distance from Bonners Ferry, in
the north, to Boise and on to Montpelier in the southeast is 790 miles, only
slightly less than from New York City to Chicago. Even today only a single
paved road, U.S. 95, winds its way across the welter of mountains that sepa-
rates the northern and southern portions of Idaho.

Divided We Stand

During the heyday of railway passenger service, from the 1880s through the
1920s, it was impossible to travel from the panhandle to Boise without leaving Idaho and in most cases changing trains. Not surprisingly, at the turn of

No. 4 MAIN STREET, RIGGINS, IDAHO.   NORTH AND SOUTH HIGHWAY

1. The Salmon River canyon, the community of Riggins, and Idaho's sole highway link between north and south as it appeared in the late 1920s or early 1930s. Courtesy Oregon Historical Society, 34144.

the century it took residents of far northern Idaho longer to reach their own state capital than the capitals of either Washington or Montana. Of the forty-eight contiguous states, only California and Texas extend a greater distance north to south.

Perhaps it is a curious commentary on the physical and psychological distances dividing Idaho that panhandle residents typically describe the state's ten northern counties as "north Idaho"—as in North Dakota or North Carolina. These people typically speak of *eastern* Oregon or *eastern* Washington or even *southern* Idaho, but most often they say *north* Idaho.[1] The common usage has a separatist connotation that dates from a century ago when panhandle residents attempted to join either Washington or Montana. Today a good many people living in southern Idaho have never traveled north of McCall or New Meadows and apparently have no compelling reason to do so. In short, if there is one point above all others that explains the essence of contemporary Idaho it is the state's divided character.

Divisive matters were so much a part of its early history that it is a wonder Idaho survived long enough to become a state in 1890. When Congress created the territory in 1863, it sprawled across an area one-quarter larger than

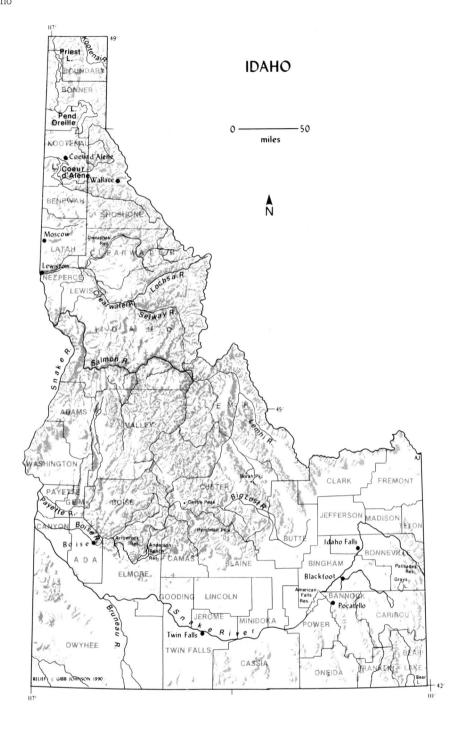

IDAHO

0 —————— 50
miles

N

Texas and seemed little more than a temporary holding facility for land that no one else wanted or knew how to govern. Within boundaries that encompassed not only present-day Idaho but also all of Montana and all but the southwestern corner of Wyoming lived a non-Indian population of 30,559 men and 1,089 women. These hearty souls were scattered among a hodgepodge of mining camps so remote that scarcely a trail connected them.

Nothing during those early years suggested that the vast and largely treeless Snake River plain in the south and the densely forested mountain north would someday be part of the same state. Even before the whites—or Euro-Americans—arrived, the Indians of the interior plateau north of the Salmon River and those of the Great Basin desert south of it developed two different cultures. The Euro-American newcomers seemed likely to perpetuate those differences by the way they initially drew their boundary lines. When, for example, Washington became a territory in 1853, it encompassed the northern portion of future Idaho, leaving Oregon with the southern portion.

The division of early Idaho between Union and pro-Confederate factions during and after the American Civil War further complicated matters. In many ways, Idaho was as much Confederate as Union territory. Its remote location coupled with the appeal of mining camp bonanzas made it a haven for people on both sides who sought to escape the horrors of war. Their differences engendered lively discussions and flag-waving demonstrations that led to an occasional mining camp brawl. Conflict between Unionists and Secessionists seemed especially violent in the Boise Basin. In the Idaho legislature also, a large contingent of pro-Confederate lawmakers battled for their cause.

These and several other divisive matters will be discussed in detail in later chapters. It is sufficient to observe here that even as the state approaches the twenty-first century it appears destined to confront yet another division, the serious economic gap that is widening between have and have-not counties. In 1988 the Boise area experienced unprecedented prosperity; yet more than half of Idaho's forty-four counties were worth less by the end of 1988 than they had been a year earlier.[2] The old natural resource–based enterprises—the mining that began with the Clearwater rush of the early 1860s, commercial farming that dates from roughly the same era, and logging that first boomed with the opening years of the twentieth century—were clearly not prospering to the same degree as the high-tech industries that clustered in the Boise-Nampa area. How the "two Idahos" resolve their differences will form another chapter in the saga of a state that should have as its motto Divided We Stand.

One modest note of caution should be sounded: it is all too easy to concentrate on the divided nature of Idaho and thereby miss the obvious things that Idahoans share. Central Idaho's rugged Salmon River country affords the same recreational opportunities to hunters, fishermen, and backpackers whether they live in Lewiston to the north or Boise to the south. North or south, easy access to the out-of-doors contributes to the state's open, friendly life-style. In addition, for well over a century, north and south have shared a natural resource–based economy. Through the years Idahoans have learned to live with the divisions in their state, to curse them, to joke about them, and somehow to surmount them.

The Face of the Land

The history of Idaho cannot be understood apart from the prominent geographical features that contribute so much to the divided nature of the state and are thus essential to every Idahoan's sense of place. The state's southern boundary stretches along the 42d parallel for 305 miles, and its northern boundary along the Canadian border at the 49th parallel for 45 miles. The distance from north to south is 479 miles. Between the two parallels lie 83,557 square miles of land compressed by a contorted eastern boundary into an oddly shaped piece of real estate that on the map resembles a hatchet or a pork chop.

Except for the Snake River plain, Idaho is one vast sea of mountains, some eighty ranges in all, broken only by infrequent islands of farmland, such as the Camas Prairie and the Palouse hills of the northern panhandle. The highest point is Mount Borah at 12,662 feet; the lowest is Lewiston at 738 feet. The average elevation of Idaho is approximately 5,000 feet above sea level; only four states are higher. If its vertical surfaces could be rolled flat, one wit has observed, Idaho would become the largest state in the union. But who can conceive of Idaho without its mountains?

It is the mountains that contribute most to the irregularity of Idaho's natural and human landscapes. Unlike the prairie states, where neat rectangular fields of corn and soybeans extend to the horizon and impose a manmade pattern on the land, Idaho still appears largely rough and unfinished. Except for state and international boundaries, city streets, and an irrigated portion of the Snake River plain, straight lines are not a common feature of the Idaho landscape. In south-central Idaho the land is uplifted into a series of jagged peaks aptly named the Sawtooths, and sinuous hills that stretch away to the horizon give the Palouse country in July and August the appearance of a swelling ocean of wheat. The rugged, nearly inaccessible terrain of the state—especially in the Bitterroot and Sawtooth ranges—is one reason why a defining quality of life for Idahoans is the opportunity to commune with nature much as it existed before humans attempted to reshape it. That is not possible in most of the trans-Mississippi East.

Mountains that border the Salmon River divide Idaho into north and south and prevent easy communication and transportation. This problem grows worse during the winter months when snow makes highway travel difficult and an occasional avalanche may block Whitebird grade on U.S. 95 and force motorists to make a lengthy detour through neighboring states.

All of Idaho, even the flat places, can be described as lying within the mountains' shadow. Few areas are situated so that mountains are not readily visible on the horizon, and even those anomalous places still experience the influence of mountain ranges on weather patterns, vegetation, and economic activities. Challis, for example, at 5,175 feet, receives an average of only 7.5 inches of precipitation a year—less than Tucson, Arizona; Wallace, at 2,770 feet, receives 46.1 inches. Accounting for much of the difference is the way nearby mountain ranges influence weather patterns.

The typical climate of northern Idaho is maritime, and that of southern Idaho is continental. During the winter months moist air from the Pacific Ocean often blankets the panhandle. Summers, by contrast, are relatively dry, and in places like Moscow and Lewiston people must water their lawns to keep them green. August is a time of forest fire danger. Summer temperatures have climbed as high as 118 degrees, a state record set in July 1934 in the northern community of Orofino.

From the Washington border across the panhandle to the Rocky Mountains, the amount of annual precipitation increases until it almost equals that in parts of Puget Sound and the Willamette Valley, enabling stands of western white pine, red cedar, and Douglas fir to thrive. Forests cover 82 percent of the land in the north, but only 28 percent of the much drier southern portion of the state. Here is a highly varied landscape of hills, eroded slopes, mountains, sagebrush-covered plains, and sandy deserts, all underlaid with basalt, the product of volcanism. Summer thunderstorms may occur in southern Idaho when moist and unsettled air occasionally flows north from as far away as the Gulf of Mexico or the Gulf of California. But truly violent weather that takes the form of a tornado or hurricane is rare.

Idaho, which has more extensive water resources than any other state in the mountain West, receives nearly a hundred million acre-feet of water each year in the form of rain and snow.[3] Water is probably Idaho's single most important natural resource. Because the state lies entirely west of the Con-

2. Sheep graze in the Stanley basin of the Sawtooth Range in August 1955. Courtesy Forest Service Collection, National Agricultural Library.

tinental Divide, almost all of its nearly sixteen thousand miles of rivers and streams and more than two thousand natural lakes eventually drain into the Pacific Ocean through the Columbia River. The one notable exception is the Bear River, which flows through extreme southeastern Idaho into Utah's Great Basin desert. Thus most of Idaho's annual precipitation either evaporates or returns to the ocean, but not before a series of dams harness it to generate electric power and irrigate crops. Eight percent of the total irrigated land in the United States is within Idaho.

Of all the state's many rivers—from the Boise, Bruneau, and Blackfoot in the south to the St. Joe, Clark Fork, and Kootenai in the north—none serves Idaho in a greater variety of ways than the Snake, the thousand-mile-long waterway that drains more than a hundred thousand square miles of land before it joins the Columbia River in south-central Washington. In volume of water carried and in area drained, the Snake ranks sixth among the rivers of the United States.

The waterway has been called the Nile of Idaho, and half the state's population lives within fifty miles of its banks. In fact, except for the northern

3. Shoshone Falls of the Snake River, a tourist attraction near the community of Twin Falls, as depicted in the late 1920s. Courtesy Oregon Historical Society, 40043.

portion of the panhandle and the extreme southeast—the only parts of the state that lie beyond the reach of the great river—Idaho could aptly be described as the Empire of the Snake.

Originating in a remote canyon spring just south of Yellowstone National Park, the Snake traces a crescent-shaped course across southern Idaho where it transforms an empire of aridity and stone into more than three million acres of irrigated land. Then, as the river approaches the Oregon border, it swings abruptly north and plunges into Hells Canyon, the continent's deepest gorge. Thirty miles long and in places seventy-nine hundred feet deep, one-third of a mile deeper than Grand Canyon, Hells Canyon compresses the Snake River into a maelstrom of white water that terrorized early explorers and effectively blocked river communication between northern and southern Idaho.

Once the entire Snake River ran free, its waters boiling over a series of scenic cataracts and rapids as they dropped from an elevation of more than 7,000 feet, where the river originated, to a little more than 700 feet, where it left the state at Lewiston. The most impressive of the cataracts was Shoshone Falls, 212 feet high, approximately the same height as Niagara Falls, and not inappropriately called the Niagara of the West by early settlers.[4]

Shoshone Falls is still there, and when the river runs high, the cataract resembles its former self. But with so much water impounded and diverted for irrigation, the Snake River seldom runs high any more. It is now cribbed and confined by more than fifteen irrigation diversion and hydroelectric dams along its 570-mile course through Idaho, and most of its tributaries are also dammed. Beginning with Swan Falls, a hydroelectric dam built across the river south of Boise in 1901, dam building continued and would have eventually tamed even the waters of Hells Canyon had not a lengthy series of protracted legal battles culminated in victory in 1975 for those who wanted to preserve the scenic wonder.

Because of its rugged terrain and divided character, Idaho is a state that continues to defy easy geographic classification. The well-watered panhandle with its lakes, extensive forests, and fields of grain, blends readily into eastern Oregon and Washington, with which northern Idaho has many ties of commerce and communication; the arid south is often indistinguishable from neighboring portions of Nevada, Utah, and Wyoming and from the Oregon desert. Not surprisingly, some Idahoans perceive their state as oriented toward Oregon, Washington, and the Pacific rim, while others consider it part of the intermountain West. It has often been said that Idaho is the only

American state with three capitals: Boise, Salt Lake City, and Spokane. It is also one of the few states divided into separate time zones north and south.

Naturally Idaho

Fundamental to the Idaho character is the fact that much of the state remains uninhabited or only lightly populated. This means that even the state's largest cities lie on the edge of the outback. There is a great deal of credibility in Idaho's recent promotion of itself as the Great Getaway—and not just for out-of-state visitors but also for residents of Boise and Pocatello. When Idaho's population reached the one million mark in 1985, it only equaled that of the Salt Lake City–Ogden metropolitan area.

Giving the million residents of the Gem State plenty of elbowroom is Idaho's size, an area equivalent to the six New England states plus New Jersey, Maryland, and Delaware. Or to compare it another way, Idaho encompasses almost as much land as the United Kingdom of Great Britain and Northern Ireland. It might also be noted that, as large as Idaho is, the federal government still owns 64 percent of the land, and some 40 percent lies within the boundaries of national forests.

Perhaps because so much of the state is off limits to permanent settlement, Idaho will likely remain more rural than its two neighboring states to the west. As late as 1990 it had only three cities of thirty thousand or more—Boise, Pocatello, and Idaho Falls, and all three were situated on the Snake River plain. Idahoans living in urban areas—communities the federal census defines as having twenty-five hundred or more residents—comprised 54 percent of the population; nationally, urban dwellers averaged 74 percent. Two separate urban complexes centering on Boise and Pocatello contained half the state's population. In 1985 the federal Census Bureau reported that Idaho ranked first in the nation in percentage of residents living outside standard metropolitan statistical areas: 81 percent as compared with less than 5 percent in California and New Jersey.

In 1990 the population density of Ada County—site of Boise, the state's largest city with 125,000 residents—was 195 people per square mile. Yet some counties in central Idaho contain fewer than 1 person per square mile. This pattern of settlement means that even urban residents maintain a strong attachment to their natural setting. Historically, low population meant that settlers struggled with a challenging natural environment. Not surprisingly, Idahoans have commonly believed that the difficulty of settling the land determined the type of people who put down roots. That is, rugged

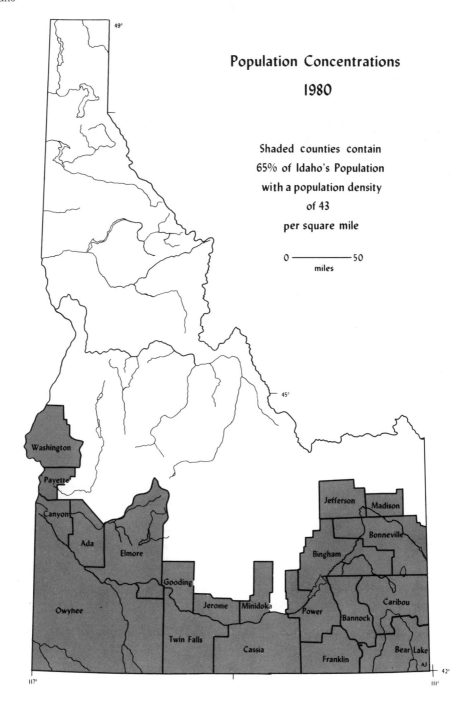

Population Concentrations

1980

Shaded counties contain
65% of Idaho's Population
with a population density
of 43
per square mile

4. A familiar scene in a state that largely defines itself by out-of-doors activities: a party of fishermen in the mountains north of Boise in 1915. Courtesy Library of Congress.

mountains and forbidding sagebrush plains called forth strong-willed, self-reliant men and women to match them, or so Idahoans like to believe.

Even if this romantic form of geographic determinism is impossible to prove, it remained central to the thinking of a generation of pioneer settlers and helps to explain why so many Idahoans once defined progress as taming nature by logging, mining, or irrigating the land. Perceptions of nature waiting to be subdued still shape public discussions of how best to treat Idaho's land, mineral, timber, and water resources. Today, however, a growing number of residents have come to realize that this natural heritage, especially in its untamed state, defines the character of Idaho, and they are reluctant to see it exploited and sacrificed to short-term economic considerations.

CHAPTER 2

The pleasure I now felt in having triumphed over the Rocky Mountains and descending once more to a level and fertile country where there was every rational hope of finding a comfortable subsistence for myself and party can be more readily conceived than expressed, nor was the flattering prospect of the final success of the expedition less pleasing.
—Meriwether Lewis, entry for September 22, 1805, after surmounting the Bitterroot Mountains on his way to the Pacific Ocean

1805
Year of First Contacts

"I reflected that I had as yet done but little, very little indeed, to further the happiness of the human race, or to advance the information of the succeeding generation." Ironically, the young man who penned these melancholy words on his thirty-first birthday was Meriwether Lewis, co-leader of one of the most dramatic and significant expeditions in American history.[1]

Just a week earlier, on August 12, 1805, Lewis and an advance guard of three other explorers had hiked through what is now Lemhi Pass into future Idaho, the last of the fifty states to be entered by whites. There (about seventy-five hundred feet above sea level), where the Lewis and Clark expedition crossed the Continental Divide, they also crossed a major divide in the history of Idaho's Native Americans.

Before 1805, contacts between Euro-Americans and the Indians of the interior Northwest had been at best indirect. As early as 1781, a smallpox epidemic struck the Nez Perce tribe when white traders transmitted the disease to Indians of the East, and it spread across the Great Plains to devastate the Nez Perces and their neighbors. The trade goods of Euro-Americans had also reached the interior. But now two peoples, Indian and white, stood face to face for the first time, and neither side could have predicted with accuracy the long-term consequences of their encounter.

Indians; or, "the People"

President Thomas Jefferson instructed Meriwether Lewis to compile detailed information about the Native Americans he encountered during his odyssey.

Although the explorers were unable to obtain firsthand knowledge of all Idaho tribes, they did make contact with peoples who represented the two distinct Native American cultures that anthropologists today label Plateau and Great Basin. The two cultural regions divided roughly along the Salmon River, much as modern Idaho splits between north and south. Although members of the two cultural regions differed dramatically in language and to a lesser extent in customs, they had in common a seminomadic hunting and gathering way of life. That is, none of the Indians of future Idaho practiced agriculture. And all of them lived in tribes, bands, and families scattered along separate river valleys and lake shores.

Through the Shoshones who lived in the vicinity of Lemhi Pass, Lewis and Clark were introduced to the Indians of the Great Basin, the forbidding high desert country of southern Idaho, eastern Oregon, Nevada, and Utah. Living among the Shoshones were the Bannocks (who called themselves *Panakwate* but which Euro-Americans heard as "Panak" or "Bannack"), a small band of Northern Paiutes who moved from southeastern Oregon into Shoshone territory. Collectively the native peoples of southern Idaho were known as the Snake Indians, a name apparently derived from claims that they frightened Plains Indians with sticks having snakes painted on them.

Given the meager resources available in the Great Basin, a land of dry soil, low rainfall, and high evaporation, the Shoshone-Bannocks were relatively well-off, utilizing salmon, game animals, birds, and edible plants of the Boise and Salmon river drainage systems in their diet. Salmon ascended the Snake River as far as Shoshone Falls in early summer, and bison were common in parts of southern Idaho until the late 1830s.

Indians of the Great Basin spent much of the year foraging for food in small and dispersed groups, although several families might come together for a communal rabbit drive or to dig for camas bulbs. It was common for Shoshones to name their subgroups after the food most abundant in their customary dwelling grounds: thus among the Shoshones were groups whose names translated as "seed eaters," or "fish eaters," or "mountain-sheep eaters."

The Shoshones acquired numerous horses after 1700 and used them to travel to the Great Plains, where they hunted buffalo and traded with the tribes living there. Curiously, although the Shoshones were the first of the northern tribes to obtain horses, they were one of the last to acquire firearms. Thus when their neighbors the Blackfeet, Cheyennes, Arapahos, and Utes acquired guns, they harassed the Shoshones and sought to drive them back

5. A "Sheepeater" band
of Shoshones as photo-
graphed by William H.
Jackson around 1871.
Courtesy Smithsonian
Institution.

into the mountains and restrict their mobility. Perhaps one reason why first contacts between Euro-Americans and the Indians of Idaho were so peaceable is that all the Indians needed help defending themselves against marauding Blackfeet, who claimed a vast western domain as their own.

The Northern Paiutes inhabited a large territory that included the southwestern corner of Idaho. It was an arid domain where even in the best of times the small scattered Paiute bands, which lacked permanent villages and complex social organization, spent their days traveling on foot from one oasis to another in a never-ending search for water, firewood, and food. Although individual bands occasionally cooperated with one another, there was no tribal unity. Usually only a few families remained together for any length of time, for the supply of rabbits, birds, pine nuts, and other foodstuffs was simply too small to feed many people.

The Indians of the Great Basin held an annual intertribal rendezvous near the confluence of the Boise and Snake rivers, near present-day Weiser. Here

they celebrated the opening of the fishing season and traded with one another. Nez Perce visitors from the north came to trade their fine ponies; Indians of the Columbia River might swap prized shells from the Pacific coast for the buffalo hides and dried meat brought by the Shoshones. The Paiutes offered arrowheads fashioned from obsidian. For a month or two the Indians traded, gambled, and held ceremonial dances. This yearly custom apparently lasted until the early 1860s.

When Lewis and Clark left the land of the Shoshones, they traveled north to that of the Flatheads and then west across the Bitterroot Mountains into the valley of the Clearwater, where they encountered the Nez Perces and the culture of Idaho's Plateau peoples. The Plateau cultural area extended from the Cascade Range to the Rocky Mountains and from central Idaho to central British Columbia. Living in northern Idaho were the Kalispels (whom French-speaking trappers called Pend d'Oreille), the Kutenais (sometimes spelled Kootenai), and the Coeur d'Alenes (so named by French-Canadian fur traders but called *Skitswish* in their own Salish language). All three of these groups lived in an area that lay north of the route followed by Lewis and Clark.

In a homeland that stretched south from the Clearwater region to the Wallowa Mountains in present Oregon were an estimated four thousand to six thousand Native Americans called Chopunnish by Lewis and Clark and Nez Perce by French-Canadian fur traders, though these people did not pierce the septum of their noses. They were known in their own Sahaptian tongue as *Ne-Mee-Poo*, "the people."

When European and American fur traders and explorers first reached the Plateau cultural area in the early years of the nineteenth century, the Indians there lived in small semipermanent fishing settlements along major streams and tributaries. Each settlement was usually an autonomous unit with its own leaders, most of whom had gained their standing by democratic means rather than by heredity. The Nez Perces, for example, were divided into perhaps as many as sixty small independent bands. Prior to the coming of whites, they had a permanent governing council, a political organization that could speak for all of them, but they had no head chief to sign away their lands in treaties. On occasion, villages or bands (several villages that associated voluntarily because of common bonds) came together to trade, fish, hunt, gather roots in a communal harvest, socialize, or wage limited warfare against a common enemy.

When the Nez Perces experienced conflict, it was usually with their closest neighbors to the north, the Coeur d'Alene and Spokane peoples. But their oldest and most bitter enemies were the Shoshonean-speaking people to the south. The Nez Perces occasionally taunted the Shoshones and drew them into ambushes in the canyons of the Salmon and Snake rivers, and the Shoshones made daring raids into Nez Perce territory. Each side generally observed a truce during the summer months.

Indians of the Plateau, like those of the Great Basin, spent many hours of the day obtaining and preserving food. Their diet was rich in the salmon that made annual runs up all the major rivers of the interior. Depending on the season, the Plateau people engaged in various types of food gathering and storing. During the salmon run of May and June, they used scoops, nets, spears, and other devices to catch the fish, which they dried and ground into a nutritious meal for later use and for trade. From June to September the Nez Perces lived in temporary camps on the camas grounds, where they harvested and prepared the starchy bulbs for winter food. The bulbs of the camas—second in importance only to fish in their diet—resembled small onions and were eaten cooked or raw. The annual gathering of the camas

Indian Groups

Kutenai

Kalispel

Coeur d'Alene

Nez Perce

Shoshone
Bannock

Northern
Paiute

0 ————— 50
miles

RELIEF © GIBB JOHNSON 1990

was a time when members of different Nez Perce bands got to know one another.

Indians of the Plateau also dug several other kinds of vegetables including the bitterroot and the biscuit root, harvested berries in season, and hunted deer, elk, mountain sheep, and other game. Some natives hunted the bison that once roamed southern Idaho.

Before the coming of the horse and extensive contact with tepee-dwelling Plains Indians, Plateau dwellers spent their winters in protected valleys housed in circular, earthen-roofed structures built partly underground. During the summer they moved to cooler elevations and lived in rough pole lodges covered with mats of tule or cattail. Plateau dwellers were ideally situated to borrow and give freely through contact with their neighbors, especially after they acquired horses in the early 1700s. Before the horse, the people of the plateau traveled entirely by foot or water.

The horse had an impact on Indian society and culture not unlike that of the automobile on twentieth-century America. The Nez Perces used horses to make regular trips to the Great Plains to hunt bison and exchange trade goods. Through contact with those Indians they adopted such innovations as skin tepees, buckskin clothing, and feathered headdresses for festive occasions. Their diet—once consisting of approximately 80 percent fish—also changed after the coming of the horse, acquiring a greater reliance on buffalo, elk, deer, and antelope. The Nez Perces first obtained horses from the Shoshones of the Great Basin around 1710, the latter probably having acquired them from the Comanches of the southern plains, who in turn got them from Spaniards, who had introduced horses in the New World. Large herds flourished on the abundant natural grasses of the Plateau, and the natives of the region became skilled horsemen. They traded surplus horses to other tribes and to Euro-American fur traders who followed in the wake of Lewis and Clark.

Lewis and Clark: The Corps of Discovery

The epic journey of Lewis and Clark lasted twenty-eight months and covered nearly eight thousand miles from the valley of the Mississippi River to the mouth of the Columbia River, and back to St. Louis. But of the many strange and unknown lands they crossed, none proved so wild or so formidable as Idaho.

In many ways the Lewis and Clark expedition marked the culmination of a dream that had long fired the imagination of Thomas Jefferson. Only months after becoming president, Jefferson commenced laying the groundwork for a great overland odyssey. In January 1803, shortly before the United States completed purchase of the sprawling Louisiana Territory and doubled the nation's size, Jefferson sent Congress a secret message requesting an appropriation of twenty-five hundred dollars to finance an expedition up the Missouri River and thence to the Pacific Ocean.

The president spoke of the need to extend the external commerce of the United States and to learn more about the unknown lands of North America. Commerce and curiosity were inextricably part of the Lewis and Clark expedition, and not mere idle curiosity, but carefully planned scientific reconnaissance. Jefferson, it must be noted, had no explicit territorial ambitions in the far Northwest, although the expedition's accomplishments would bolster future United States claims to the area.

To command the party, Jefferson selected his private secretary, Captain Meriwether Lewis. With the president's approval, Lewis invited an old friend and frontiersman, William Clark, to be his co-leader. Lewis left Washington, D.C., on July 5, 1803, and made his way to Pittsburgh and then down the Ohio River to the falls near the future city of Louisville, where Clark joined him. The Corps of Discovery, the expedition's official title, commenced the main phase of its historic journey up the Missouri River from its winter camp near St. Louis on May 14, 1804. In addition to Lewis and Clark, the corps included twenty-seven young unmarried soldiers, the mixed-blood hunter George Drouillard, and Clark's black slave, York. A few other soldiers accompanied the expedition up the Missouri to winter quarters called Fort Mandan (in present-day North Dakota) and then returned the following spring with its first year's records and scientific specimens.

Lewis and Clark had anticipated a relatively easy portage across the Rockies from the navigable headwaters of the Missouri River to those of the Columbia. Instead, when they reached the Continental Divide at Lemhi Pass, they gazed west upon range after range of mountains stretching as far as their eyes could see. When they attempted to follow the Salmon River through the mountains, that wild stream forced them back.[2]

The explorers then turned north and in the company of their Shoshone guide, Old Toby, struggled across the Bitterroot Mountains. From Lolo Pass, Toby led them down an old fishing trail to the headwaters of the Clearwater River instead of crossing to the ridgetop and following an old Indian route, the Lolo Trail. Their food almost gone and game practically nonexistent, the Corps of Discovery had no choice but to kill and roast one of their colts in the vicinity of the present-day Powell Ranger Station on U.S. 12. Sergeant Patrick Gass called the horsemeat "good eating."[3]

To return to the main trail, the Corps of Discovery labored up Wendover Ridge, a route so steep that some of the horses gave out, others slipped and were injured, and one rolled down the mountainside, smashing Clark's field desk, which it carried, although the animal itself somehow escaped injury. The explorers finally reached the top, where at an elevation of more than seven thousand feet they slogged west through a snowstorm unanticipated in mid-September. Thirty-three cold, wet, and hungry people were reduced to making a meal of a few pheasants and another of their colts.

For nine days they struggled across the Bitterroot Range, "this horrible mountainous desert," as Gass described it in his journal. Clark complained that he had never been so wet or cold in his life: "Indeed I was at one time fearful my feet would freeze in the thin mockersons which I wore."[4]

Their situation grew so desperate that on September 18 they "dined," in Lewis's words, on a few canisters of dehydrated soup, an unpalatable army experimental ration Lewis had obtained in Philadelphia, a little bear oil, and about twenty pounds of candles. Hunger and fatigue nearly broke the men's spirits. Several of them became ill with dysentery and broke out in skin sores. Never would the expedition come so close to failure as it did in the snows of Idaho.

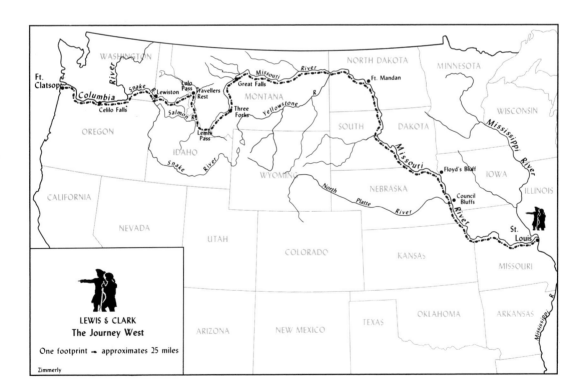

Clark took a party of six hunters and scouted ahead of the main group for game. Two days later this advance guard descended to the Weippe Prairie and made its first contact with the Nez Perces. Having endured several days of near starvation, the explorers indulged in such a hearty meal of salmon, buffalo, berries, and roots that Clark confessed in his journal, "I find myself verry unwell all the evening from eateing fish & roots too freely." [5]

The Corps of Discovery survived its ordeal in the Bitterroots, but severe and lingering bouts of gastritis afflicted several members, including Lewis and Clark. After entrusting their horses to the Nez Perces and constructing five dugout canoes on a riverbank near present-day Orofino, the explorers continued down the Clearwater, Snake, and Columbia rivers. When on November 7, 1805, they reached the long-sought waters of the Pacific, Clark rejoiced in his notebook, "Ocian in view! O! the joy." A few days later the men erected a small stockade on the southern bank of the Columbia River and named it Fort Clatsop after the nearest Indian tribe.

After enduring an exceedingly damp and disagreeable winter (only twelve days were free of rain) and failing to secure a hoped-for ship home, the Lewis and Clark expedition headed east again on March 23, 1806. Once more the explorers faced the daunting prospect of having to retrace their steps across the Bitterroot Mountains. And again Idaho's rugged land thwarted their plans. Although they reached the vicinity of present Kamiah in mid-May, deep snow in the Bitterroots blocked their way until late June. They remained in camp for twenty-seven days while waiting for the snow to melt. Once over the mountains, the corps made remarkably fast progress and returned to St. Louis on September 23, 1806.

Adding a noteworthy chapter to the history of exploration is not all that Lewis and Clark accomplished. They revealed that the far Northwest was rich in beaver and other furbearing animals, and this information lured a generation of trappers and traders to the new land. The explorers' journal entries, and their drawings, maps, and artifacts, contributed greatly to knowledge about terrain, native peoples, and the flora and fauna of the West. The Lewis and Clark journals are among the treasures of the nation's written history. Nearly two hundred years later, perhaps more than any other exploratory venture, the Corps of Discovery still captivates the interest of scholars and fires the imagination of ordinary American citizens.

Envision a person camped today along the trail of Lewis and Clark in the Bitterroot Mountains: at dusk when the stars first come out and only mountain profiles are visible in the distance, the camper will see almost exactly what Lewis and Clark saw nearly two hundred years ago. Along few other stretches of their route from St. Louis to the Pacific Ocean is that still true.

The Real Sacagawea

The Corps of Discovery spent the winter of 1804–1805 near the villages of the Mandan and Hidatsa Indians, about fifty miles north of present Bismarck, North Dakota. Accompanying Lewis and Clark when they resumed their progress in early April 1805 were an interpreter named Toussaint Charbonneau, his young Shoshone woman, Sacagawea, and their baby, Jean Baptiste, affectionately nicknamed Pomp by Clark. No one associated with the expedition has been more thoroughly romanticized than Sacagawea. Over the years writers have made extravagant claims for her as expedition guide and American heroine. The result is many disagreements about her life.

Not one shred of evidence of a romantic bond between Sacagawea and Clark exists, though some novelists have imagined such a connection. Nor was Sacagawea the expedition's guide in any usual sense of the word. Only once did she provide guide services: in late July and early August 1805, she recognized important topographical features indicating that the expedition had entered Shoshone territory. But she did not accompany Lewis's advance party when it made contact with her people. Sacagawea did help the party secure packhorses for the arduous climb ahead from her brother (or cousin) Chief Cameawait.

Lewis once wrote of Sacagawea, "If she has enough to eat and a few trinkets I believe she would be perfectly content anywhere." This is perhaps too harsh an assessment, and one that does not take into account Sacagawea's role as translator. Moreover, her physical presence and that of her child evidently reassured Indians that the Lewis and Clark expedition was not a war party. Sacagawea died on December 20, 1812, at Fort Manuel in present South Dakota; Clark became the guardian for her young son, Jean Baptiste, and educated him.[6]

From a global perspective, the Lewis and Clark expedition was only one more act in an ongoing drama of imperial and commercial competition. President Thomas Jefferson hoped that Lewis and Clark would find a way to redirect the fur trade of the far Northwest away from British markets and south into the United States, but well before that happened, preliminary reports from the Corps of Discovery stimulated further British and Canadian exploration and trade on the Pacific slope.

After some time spent in reflections and solemn mourning, we left the place and proceeded down the [Salmon] river, and encamped near Bonneville's Fort, which he has abandoned and which is situated in a small pleasant vale. This place would be favourable for fur business, was it not that it is on ground where conflicting tribes often meet.—Samuel Parker, *Journal of an Exploring Tour beyond the Rocky Mountains* (1838)

Contested Terrain
The Quest for Furs and Souls

After Lewis and Clark returned to St. Louis in 1806, Idaho remained contested terrain for the next several decades. Euro-Americans from the United States competed with British and Canadian interests, first for its fur wealth and then for the land itself. Protestants and Catholics competed with one another to convert Indians to Christianity. Indian traditions competed with the new way of life offered by Euro-Americans.

Fur Empires

Among the world's business enterprises in the early nineteenth century, few were more important than the fur trade. The hat-making industry alone used a hundred thousand beaver pelts each year to supply fine headwear to European aristocrats and a rising commercial class. American fur merchants would not concede so lucrative a trade to their British and Canadian counterparts without a spirited contest.

In the vanguard of fur traders and trappers who responded to Lewis and Clark's discoveries was David Thompson, who in 1807 undertook the first of several journeys that led him through the labyrinth of mountains and valleys that composed the upper reaches of the Columbia River system in British Columbia, Idaho, and Montana. A talented surveyor, map maker, and trader for the North West Company of Montreal, Thompson is remembered for his explorations and for the several important fur-trading posts he established, including Kullyspell House in northern Idaho. Here on the shore of Lake Pend

Oreille, on September 9, 1809, he and two Indians built a simple house for trading. Kullyspell House lasted about two years.

Even as Thompson and his fellow Nor'westers extended the reach of Montreal's fur merchants, the first American traders probed the Rocky Mountains from another direction. When Lewis and Clark neared the Mandan villages on their return journey to St. Louis, they released Private John Colter to head west in search of beaver. His wanderings took him to the upper Yellowstone country and the Teton Valley of Idaho. Also released early from the expedition was George Drouillard. Both men eventually ended up as employees of the merchant and trader Manuel Lisa. Excited by information gathered by Lewis and Clark, Lisa dispatched parties of traders up the Missouri River to channel the fur wealth of the new land through his St. Louis–based enterprise.

Andrew Henry, Lisa's partner in the Missouri Fur Company, and a group of trappers entered Idaho after a battle with the Blackfeet forced them to cross over the mountains in search of less dangerous country. In 1810 on a fork of the Snake River near modern St. Anthony, they built a temporary winter post called Fort Henry. Although it amounted to little more than a few log cabins and a dugout, Fort Henry was among the first American habitations in future Idaho. Lack of game forced the trappers to subsist that winter largely on beaver and horsemeat. After they broke camp the following spring and fanned out through the Rocky Mountain country, one of the parties met another group of American traders and trappers heading west. These were the Astorians.

John Jacob Astor was a German-born businessman who dreamed of making a fortune in the fur trade of the far Northwest. Encouraged by reports of the region's natural wealth, he laid plans for a vast new business empire. From a post he proposed to build near the mouth of the Columbia River, his traders and trappers would travel across the Northwest collecting the furs they would ship to markets in China. To turn his dream into reality, Astor dispatched two expeditions, one by land and another by sea, to the North Pacific coast.

Heading the overland party was Astor's field marshal, Wilson Price Hunt, a twenty-seven-year-old St. Louis fur merchant woefully inexperienced for an undertaking of this complexity. Assisting him was Donald Mackenzie, formerly of the rival North West Company. The Hunt party departed St. Louis in October 1810, a month after the seafaring Astorians left New York.

Assigned to reconnoiter an overland route and to seek sites for a string of trading posts extending from the Missouri to the Columbia, members of the Hunt party—consisting of a small group of company officials and about fifty

The Struggle for Survival in Snake River Country

Washington Irving penned a vivid account of the Astorians' trouble-plagued crossing of Idaho late in 1811. He left no doubt why the French Canadians described the Snake River as the "accursed mad river":

"Mr. Hunt and his companions followed along the right bank of the [Snake] river, which made its way far below them, brawling at the foot of perpendicular precipices of solid rock two and three hundred feet high. For twenty eight miles that they travelled this day they found it impossible to get down to the margin of the stream. At the end of this distance they encamped for the night at a place which admitted a scrambling descent. It was with the greatest difficulty, however, that they succeeded in getting up a kettle of water from the river for the use of the camp. As some rain had fallen in the afternoon, they passed the night under the shelter of rocks. . . .

"On the 19th of November, Mr. Hunt was lucky enough to purchase another horse for his own use, giving in exchange a tomahawk, a knife, a fire steel, and some beads and gartering. In an evil hour, however, he took the advice of the Indians to abandon the river and follow a road or trail, leading into the prairie. He soon had cause to repent the change. The road led across a dreary waste, without verdure; and where there was neither fountain, nor pool, nor running stream. The men now began to experience the torments of thirst, aggravated by their usual diet of dried fish. The thirst of some of the Canadian voyageurs became so insupportable as to drive them to the most revolting means of allaying it [drinking their own urine]. For twenty five miles did they toil on across this dismal desert, and laid themselves down at night, parched and disconsolate beside their worm wood fires; looking forward to still greater suffering on the following day. Fortunately it began to rain in the night to their infinite relief; the water soon collected in puddles and afforded them delicious draughts."
—Washington Irving, *Astoria; or, Anecdotes of an Enterprize beyond the Rocky Mountains* (1836), 205ff.

employees—were plagued by blunders, Indians, and scheming rivals. They meandered needlessly. Hunger, thirst, sickness, and death accompanied them as they crossed the rugged and barren wilderness.

The seagoing members of Astor's enterprise fared no better. After a series of disasters, they reached the Columbia River several months ahead of Hunt's group, and on the south bank of the river near present-day Astoria, Oregon, they built Fort Astoria. An advance party of overlanders finally arrived at its log palisades in January 1812, and others straggled in during the next several days and weeks. From their main base at Fort Astoria, traders and trappers canoed up the Columbia and established several additional posts, including one each on the Clearwater and Boise rivers later that year.

In the contest for survival in the Pacific Northwest, the Astorians waged a heroic but ultimately futile struggle. In October 1813, in the midst of the War of 1812, they sold out under duress to their Canadian rivals, the North

West Company of Montreal. The Nor'westers were in turn absorbed in 1821 by the Hudson's Bay Company, an old and powerful British fur enterprise headquartered in London.

Snake Brigades

The Hudson's Bay Company had confined its operations mainly to north-central Canada until the merger, but it became a transcontinental giant when it acquired the seven Pacific Northwest posts of its erstwhile Montreal rival. Among these was Fort Nez Percés, located near the confluence of the Snake and Columbia rivers and a main jumping-off point for the Snake River country of southern Idaho since 1818.

Donald Mackenzie, the former associate of Wilson Price Hunt, returned to the ranks of the Nor'westers after the Astoria venture fizzled and led the Canadian company's first three expeditions into the Snake country. A great bear of a man whose inexhaustible fund of energy earned him the nickname Perpetual Motion, he established the pattern for all future expeditions. Instead of seeking to trade with the Indians, as was the customary practice, Mackenzie and teams of experienced trappers went after the furs themselves. Living off the land, they roamed over a large area before returning with their booty to Fort Nez Percés.

The Hudson's Bay Company continued the Snake brigades from 1821 until the early 1830s and in the process learned much about the geography of the interior Northwest. The jumping-off point changed over time, but one thing never changed: life in the Snake country was always dangerous. Finan McDonald, another veteran of the old North West Company and leader of the 1823 expedition into the Snake country, lost six men in a fatal encounter with Indians. An unnerved McDonald thanked God when he reached home safely and prophesied that he would return to the Snake country only when the beaver there grew skins of gold.

Alexander Ross, who headed the Snake brigade in 1824, inadvertently opened a new chapter in the history of the fur trade when members of his party met seven St. Louis–based trappers near the present-day community of Blackfoot. The chance encounter with Jedediah Smith and six other Americans surprised Hudson's Bay Company men. During the decade that had elapsed since Astor's ill-starred West Coast venture, few Americans entered the Oregon country, although they possessed as much right as the British to trap its streams. As the result of a treaty signed in 1818, Great Britain and the United States held the region jointly.

Unaccountably, Ross bragged to Smith and the Americans that during the

7. In many places the Snake River lies at the bottom of sheer cliffs that frustrated Astorians and others seeking an easy way to cross southern Idaho. Courtesy Idaho State Historical Society, 73–221.370.

previous four years the Hudson's Bay Company had taken eighty-thousand beaver pelts. That was a great exaggeration, but it whetted Smith's desire to pursue such riches for himself. The persistent Americans even accompanied the Hudson's Bay men back to their base of operations that year at Flathead Post on the Clark Fork River, much to the displeasure of Ross's superior, George Simpson, who had already resolved to replace him as head of the Snake brigade. Only a short time earlier Simpson had blasted Ross as "a self-sufficient, empty-headed man" whose "reports are so full of bombast and marvelous nonsense that it is impossible to get at any information that can be depended on from him."[1] When Ross allowed Americans to accompany him deep into territory the Hudson's Bay Company considered its own, he seemed to confirm Simpson's acerbic judgment.

The man who replaced Ross was Peter Skene Ogden, who led the Snake brigades for the next five years beginning in late 1824. This burly, ruthless veteran of the old North West Company was well qualified to carry out Simpson's order to trap the animals of the Snake country to the point of extinction. Ogden was supposed to turn the area into a "fur desert," to implement a "scorched earth" policy that would keep Americans out of the Columbia River region and thereby bolster British territorial claims in anticipation of the day when an international boundary would divide the Oregon country.

Ogden had not entered the fur trade out of economic necessity. He grew up in a rich and respected Montreal family and could have lived a comfortable life pursuing a legal career in the St. Lawrence Valley. Ogden, however, had an innate love of adventure and while still in his midteens entered the rough-and-tumble world of the fur trade. Like his predecessor, Perpetual Motion Mackenzie, Ogden was a man of phenomenal physical energy. He explored an enormous amount of Great Basin country new to Euro-Americans, and not without reason is the city of Ogden, Utah, named for him.

Ogden was, in the words of one associate, a humorous, honest, eccentric, law-defying "terror of the Indians."[2] The latter point was surely an exaggeration, for he enjoyed uncommonly good relations with Native Americans. Ogden even took as his common-law wife an Indian woman, Julia Rivet, who was his equal in wilderness survival skills and resourcefulness. She and their young children accompanied him on several of his six expeditions into the interior West.

In the vast and dangerous Snake country, the Hudson's Bay Company risked encounters with both hostile Indians and American competitors. When Ogden reached the Henry's Fork area of eastern Idaho in 1825, he found thirty American mountain men already there ahead of him, busily trapping whatever beaver remained. To Ogden's chagrin, several of the self-employed trappers attached to his expedition soon defected to the Americans. In the Snake country, too, nature added additional torments—driving sleet, deep snow, bitter winds, and barren landscape—that prompted Ogden to describe the country as cursed.

During an expedition in 1826 several of Ogden's men suddenly became ill while trapping along the Raft River in south-central Idaho. One man dropped unconscious near his traps, and others complained of severe pain in the head and limbs. Soon half the brigade was too weak to move. Ogden attributed the mysterious affliction to their eating tainted beaver meat and used himself as a guinea pig in a successful effort to confirm his diagnosis. He thereupon prescribed for himself the same remedy he gave his men: pepper mixed with gunpowder and water. Whatever the medicine's value, the Snake brigade was soon back on its feet. Ogden concluded that the beaver had eaten poisonous water hemlock that grew in abundance along the Raft River.

Mountain Men

Ogden trapped the furbearing animals of the Snake country as ruthlessly as he could, but he never achieved his object of discouraging Americans from entering the region. A Missouri businessman, General William Henry Ashley, dispatched his first expedition of fur traders up the Missouri River in 1822 and thereby launched a new phase of American activity in the mountain West. Most of Ashley's men were not salaried employees like the *engagés* who signed contracts to work as boatmen or trappers for the Hudson's Bay Company; they were instead free trappers or mountain men, colorful individuals like Jedediah Smith and Jim Bridger, whose explorations acquainted Euro-Americans with vast areas of the West.

Ashley popularized the "rendezvous system" in 1825, a scheme that replaced permanent trading posts and thereby saved money. The trappers associated with Ashley and his successors in the Rocky Mountain Fur Company and similar enterprises, along with their Indian allies, gathered at an appointed place each summer to trade pelts for a year's supply of goods sent west by pack animals and wagons from St. Louis. This arrangement dominated the Rocky Mountain fur trade until 1840, when the last major rendezvous was held.

The rendezvous was a combination fair, circus, and rodeo. It was a time for feasting, drinking, carousing, and contests of skill. Although often held on the Green River, in future Wyoming, in 1828 it took place at the southern end of Bear Lake, and in 1829 and 1832 in Pierres Hole, near present-day Felt and Tetonia, Idaho.

The Pierres Hole rendezvous of 1832 began in typical fashion: approximately two hundred mountain men—some associated with the Rocky Mountain Fur Company, some with John Jacob Astor's American Fur Company, and some independents—came together with about two hundred lodges of Nez Perce, Flathead, Shoshone, and Bannock Indians to await the annual supply caravan from St. Louis. But on July 18 the gathering erupted into the Battle of Pierres Hole when a large band of Blackfeet entered the campsite. Old quarrels caused a Flathead warrior to shoot and instantly kill an approaching Blackfeet chief and thus spark a general mêlée. When the fight ended, as many as ten Blackfeet, seven Nez Perces, and six trappers lay dead. The remaining Blackfeet escaped to take revenge on trappers and their Indian allies in the upper Missouri country for several more years.

Dr. John McLoughlin, who for two decades supervised Hudson's Bay Company operations in the Pacific Northwest, estimated that between 1832 and 1838 there were from five hundred to six hundred Americans annually in the Snake country. That figure, however, exaggerated American influence in the far Northwest.

Although American trappers in the Rocky Mountains greatly outnumbered the men of the Snake brigades—perhaps they even outnumbered the entire Hudson's Bay Company work force in the Pacific Northwest—they represented more of a nuisance to the "Honourable Company" than a significant competitive threat. Most Americans trapped their furs in the mountains east of the Oregon country. Moreover, the Hudson's Bay Company had the advantage of greater capital, superior organization, more knowledge of the terrain, and better relations with the Indians.

The typical American trapper, though often romanticized as a free-spirited individual who enjoyed the freedom of the hills, was in fact a person who lived a tenuous life of privation. He endured often unprofitable hunts and occasional harassment by Indians. Whether as an independent trapper or as an employee of one of the St. Louis–based fur companies, the American mountain man was often at the mercy of poorly capitalized merchants who were inclined to strike sharp bargains. As a result he seldom felt loyalty to an employer, and he rarely enjoyed the security of a large organization in dealing with the Indians.

American trappers incurred the wrath of Indians far more often than did employees of the Hudson's Bay Company. During the two trading seasons of 1824–26, Indians killed a total of thirty-two Americans in the Snake country, and though the Hudson's Bay Company was not immune to attack, its losses were substantially less. Occasionally one party of American trappers committed an outrage against Indians, who in turn wreaked vengeance on the next mountain man to come along. Indians who might not hesitate to attack a small band of American trappers were likely to think twice before setting upon parties associated with the powerful Hudson's Bay Company.

Nathaniel Wyeth: The Ice Man and Fort Hall

Most American fur traders confined their activity to the eastern fringe of the Oregon country, and none of the handful who ventured farther west to the Columbia River was successful. For five years beginning in 1832, a Boston ice merchant named Nathaniel Wyeth attempted to revive the old dream of John Jacob Astor by establishing a fur-trading business on the lower Columbia. After repeated failures there, he expanded his economic horizons to include the Rocky Mountain country, where he obtained a contract to supply trade goods to the 1834 fur rendezvous to be held that year on the Green River.

Unfortunately for Wyeth, when he finally reached the rendezvous site, he found that St. Louis suppliers had arrived first and stolen his customers. His contract was unenforceable, and so he was stuck with a large supply of merchandise a thousand miles or more from the nearest market. Wyeth's best alternative was to build a trading post on a site north of present-day Pocatello, Idaho. On August 5, 1834, after a month of construction, Wyeth named his post for a senior partner in his enterprise and ordered a celebration. The next morning a homemade American flag was raised over Fort Hall and saluted. Stocked with bacon, flour, beans, whiskey, and other goods, the post was ready to cater to fur traders and Indians.

The Hudson's Bay Company responded to Wyeth's invasion of the Snake country by subsidizing the operation of Fort Boise, which was built in August 1834 near the confluence of the Snake and Boise rivers, close to the annual Indian rendezvous. The two forts ended the need for the Snake brigades and eventually evolved into major outposts along the Oregon Trail.

As for Wyeth, his fortunes continued to sag until he returned to Boston and reentered the ice business in 1836. Two years later he sold Fort Hall to the Hudson's Bay Company, which now regained its near monopoly in the region's fur trade. Despite his hard luck, Wyeth had nonetheless stirred further interest in Idaho and the Pacific Northwest when in 1834 he lured the first American missionaries and scientists to the region.

Fort Hall supplied goods to travelers along the Oregon Trail for nearly two decades and even gained some unexpected regular customers with the arrival of the first party of Mormons in the Salt Lake Valley in 1847. American emigrants were good customers, but they were also agents of change. The desire of overland travelers for meat made it more profitable for Indians and mountain men around Fort Hall to hunt antelope rather than trap beaver, and by 1850 the former Mormon customers stocked stores of their own and undersold the Hudson's Bay Company post. The loss of profit, the changing nature of the fur trade, and growing Indian unrest in the Snake River country combined to cause the Hudson's Bay Company to abandon Fort Boise in 1855 and Fort Hall in 1856.

A generation of fur traders and trappers revealed to the world some of nature's treasures in the Pacific Northwest, yet their contribution to settlement of the region was at best indirect. They knew only too well that population growth and commerce in furs were incompatible. Wherever farmers appeared, fur trappers and traders retreated into an ever-shrinking domain.

Idaho's fur trade era lasted about forty-five years—from the days of Lewis and Clark until the mid-1850s. Changing fashion, notably the switch from top hats made from beaver pelts to those of silk, as well as overtrapping took a toll on profits. During the decade after the division of the Oregon country in 1846, the Hudson's Bay Company gradually withdrew from the American Northwest. A few Idahoans, it should be noted, found trapping profitable even in the late twentieth century, but by then the age typified by great fur companies, the rendezvous, and the mountain man was long past.

The Mission Era

An incident in 1831 initiated missionary activity in Idaho and the far Northwest. In that year an Indian delegation consisting of one Flathead and three Nez Perce men journeyed to St. Louis seeking the superintendent of Indian affairs, William Clark, a tribal hero since the days of the Lewis and Clark expedition. Conversing only in sign language they requested the "book" and the "black robes" for their people. They may have meant the Holy Bible and the Jesuits, but it is equally possible that they wanted a portion of the white man's power that seemed to reside in his printing and religion.

In any case, word of their arrival spread across the East from pulpit to pulpit, and a call went forth for all good Protestants to help those they regarded as poor misguided pagans. First to answer the prickings of conscience was Jason Lee, a young Methodist minister, who traveled with Nathaniel Wyeth from New England to the Willamette Valley in 1834. Two years later a second Protestant venture commenced when the American Board of Commissioners for Foreign Missions, an ecumenical body representing Congregationalist, Presbyterian, and Dutch Reformed believers, sent two missionary couples, the Whitmans and Spaldings, to the Oregon country.

The four missionaries journeyed west in 1836 with a small party of helpers. Marcus and Narcissa Whitman built their station among the Cayuse Indians near future Walla Walla; Henry and Eliza Spalding chose a site farther inland, about thirteen miles east of present-day Lewiston. At a post called Lapwai they pursued the twin goals of Christianizing and "civilizing" the Nez Perce Indians.

The Spaldings built a schoolhouse and church and developed the first irrigated farm in Idaho. They taught the rudiments of Christianity to a people who seemed to practice no formal religion. In fact, though, the Nez Perces did claim a spiritual link with nature and regarded the spirits of natural forces around them as guardians that gave them a special kinship with their surroundings.

Another missionary couple, Asa Bowen Smith and his wife, Sarah, operated an American Board mission post sixty miles farther up the Clearwater River among the Nez Perces at Kamiah from 1839 to 1841. Smith, who was more of a scholar than he was a frontiersman or a missionary, selected the site because it lay close to the heart of Nez Perce country. As a linguist he sought to learn the native tongue in its purest form, and he eventually compiled a Nez Perce dictionary and grammar.

Missionaries inevitably faced problems of how best to work with Indians. Should they induce these nomadic hunters and gatherers to become farmers in order to settle them around a mission station? Should they instruct Indians in English or in their native tongue? Could stations be self-supporting and still allow missionaries enough time for religious work?

Spalding resolved these dilemmas by urging the Nez Perces to abandon their migratory ways and adopt an agrarian life-style that he considered better suited to their survival in a world ever more dominated by Euro-Americans. Some Nez Perces did abandon the annual buffalo hunt in 1837 in order to raise potatoes and other crops. Spalding soon had a blacksmith shop and gristmill in operation, and in 1839 he imported a small printing press from Hawaii. On this, the first printing press in the Pacific Northwest, he was able to publish the Gospel of John and other materials in the Nez Perce language. A water-powered sawmill and flour mill followed in 1840.

All this technology could be seen as evidence of steady progress, but in his attempts to Christianize the Nez Perces, Spalding actually experienced many setbacks and frustrations. Unconverted young men sometimes used his fence rails for firewood or danced around the mission school to the amusement of students and the annoyance of Spalding. Yet if he chastised the troublemakers, they might retaliate by cutting the tail off one of the mission cows, or worse.

Another of Spalding's problems was that he and his colleagues did not get along well with one another. Several years earlier he had unsuccessfully courted Narcissa Prentiss, now Marcus Whitman's wife, and the past created tensions between the two couples.

Then there was Spalding's fellow missionary on the Clearwater, Asa Bowen Smith, who was highly critical of Spalding's attempts to convert Nez Perce Christians into farmers and who ridiculed him in letters to American Board superiors back east. Smith's acerbic tongue alienated other missionaries as well and may have been one reason why he built his mission at so remote a site as Kamiah. His numerous complaints finally caused the board to order the Whitmans to take over the Lapwai post and both the Spaldings and Smiths to return home. Only a personal appeal by Whitman, who undertook a daring ride east during the winter of 1842, caused the board to change its mind.

When Whitman returned in 1843, the first large contingent of white settlers accompanied him. Indians, who believed that the missionary doctor had gone east to gather reinforcements of American farmers and soldiers, viewed the changes with apprehension. Nearly five thousand whites made their way west to Oregon in 1847. Although the main trail bypassed the Whitmans' station after 1844, those who were sick and destitute turned their wagons north to the mission, bringing with them an epidemic of measles and dysentery to which the Indians had no natural immunity. An estimated 50 percent of the Cayuses died in less than two months. With rising anger, they observed that white children treated by Dr. Whitman usually recovered, but not Indian children. On a cold, foggy day—November 29, 1847—shortly after the last wagon departed, the Cayuses attacked the mission at Waiilatpu. In the ensuing struggle, they killed Marcus and Narcissa Whitman and eleven others.

The tragic events of late 1847 concluded a chapter in the history of Protestant missions. As a result of the Whitman massacre, the Spaldings hastily relocated to the Willamette Valley where they lived for several years. At the time they abandoned it, the Lapwai mission had forty-four acres under cultivation, and 164 horses, cattle, and hogs. For all its zeal, the Oregon Mission during its heyday from 1836 to 1847 recorded only twenty-one Indians baptized into the Presbyterian church (six adults and fifteen children). Among these was old Chief Joseph, converted at Spalding's Lapwai station.

The era of Roman Catholic missions in the Pacific Northwest dates from 1838 when two Franciscan priests from Canada, Francis Norbert Blanchet and Modeste Demers, responded to a call from French-Canadian employees of the Hudson's Bay Company who had retired to farms along the Willamette River. Roman Catholic missions continued with Pierre Jean De Smet, a Jesuit missionary from Belgium, who journeyed from St. Louis to the Oregon country in 1840 with an American fur-trading caravan. A year later he founded St. Mary's Mission among the Flathead people at what is now Stevensville, Montana.

During the six years that De Smet remained in the Pacific Northwest, he and Anthony Ravalli, Nicholas Point, and other Jesuits established several missions in the Rocky Mountains, including one among the Coeur d'Alenes. Point founded the Mission of the Sacred Heart on the banks of the St. Joseph River (now the St. Joe River) on December 4, 1842. Periodic flooding required

8. Pierre Jean De Smet, S.J., pioneer Roman Catholic missionary in the Pacific Northwest. Courtesy Eastern Washington State Historical Society, 441.

that the post be relocated to a site on higher ground in 1846, where two years later Father Ravalli began building a permanent church.

To construct the Greek Revival church, Ravalli used only a broadax, an auger, some ropes and pulleys, a penknife, and the labor of unskilled Indians. Catholic priests, including Joseph M. Cataldo (whose name became most closely identified with the structure), labored at the Sacred Heart Mission from 1846 to 1877, converting Indians to the new religion and an agricultural way of life. In time two-thirds of the Coeur d'Alene Indians were baptized into the Catholic church. Today the mission at Cataldo is the oldest standing building in Idaho.

Unlike the Protestant missionaries, who were Americans and blatantly ethnocentric, the Catholics tended to be immigrants, strangers in the land themselves. This is no doubt one reason why Protestants regarded them with such suspicion. Catholics and Protestants have historically differed on many tenets of Christian faith, even as Protestant denominations and sects differed among themselves. Catholics were suspicious of Protestants, too, believing that, while they pretended to spread their faith, their true mission was to foster trade and commerce. Protestants responded that Catholic accommodations to native traditions showed too great a willingness to compromise with sin in all its blackness.

The intense rivalry between Catholic and Protestant missionaries is perhaps revealed most clearly in the giant illustrated charts, or ladders, that each used to teach Indians the way to heaven. Essentially maps of the road to salvation, some charts were six feet long; they usually began with Creation and extended through the Christian era to the time of modern Indian missions. One Catholic ladder showed Protestants as tortured pilgrims falling into hell. Eliza Spalding responded with a Protestant version in which she reversed the roles: Catholics, including bishops in miters, were shown pitching headlong into the flames.

Idaho's mission era saw the establishment of two American Board posts, a Roman Catholic mission, and a Mormon (Church of Jesus Christ of Latter-day Saints) mission. In response to a call from Brigham Young, twenty-seven Mormons made a four hundred–mile trek north from Salt Lake City in May 1855 to a remote fork of the Salmon River. There they built a fort of planks and mud and named it Lemhi after a king in the Book of Mormon. The Salmon River mission was not a success, however, and was abandoned three years later on orders from Young during a time of rising tension and violence between Mormons and Indians and the United States Army. Fort Lemhi was never reestablished.

Idaho's mission era lasted little more than two decades (1836–58). By 1860 all of the early posts had been abandoned except for the Catholic mission among the Coeur d'Alene people. In the work of Christianizing Indians, the missionaries left behind a mixed record: their ideals were lofty, their motivation generally sprang from the best of human qualities, but in too many cases the missionaries were unable to surmount cultural and religious biases. However history may judge their successes and shortcomings, they did play a role in better defining the Pacific Northwest in Euro-American minds and thereby helped to encourage pioneer settlement of a distant corner of North America.

I learned then that we were but few, while the white men were many, and that we could not hold our own with them. We were like deer. They were like grizzly bears. We had a small country. Their country was large. We were contented to let things remain as the Great Spirit Chief made them. They were not; and would change the rivers and mountains if they did not suit them.—from Joseph, *Chief Joseph's Own Story* (1879)

Defining the Land

Whether they were conscious of it or not, fur traders, missionaries, overland trail pioneers, and other agents of Euro-American settlement contributed at least informally to defining the land that became Idaho. The United States government reentered the process in the late 1830s and early 1840s when it launched the first official exploratory expeditions since Lewis and Clark. Soon a new generation of maps, descriptive documents, and artwork provided federal officials and a curious public a more precise image of the far Northwest than ever before.

The work of definition also took the form of diplomacy and a treaty in 1846 that divided the Oregon country between Great Britain and the United States along the 49th parallel. Finally, in the 1850s when Euro-Americans and Indians of the Pacific Northwest negotiated their first formal treaties, they defined not just the land but also a relationship between two races and cultures.

Overland to Oregon

The words "Oregon Trail" invariably conjure up images of pioneer families plodding west by covered wagon. Along the two thousand–mile route to the Pacific, emigrants faced the dangers of violent winds, quicksand, floods, buffalo stampedes, disease, and, on rare occasions, Indian attack. The odyssey to Oregon represented the longest overland journey that American settlers attempted. Each mile was hard won, but few stretches of the trail were less hospitable than that across the Snake River plain.

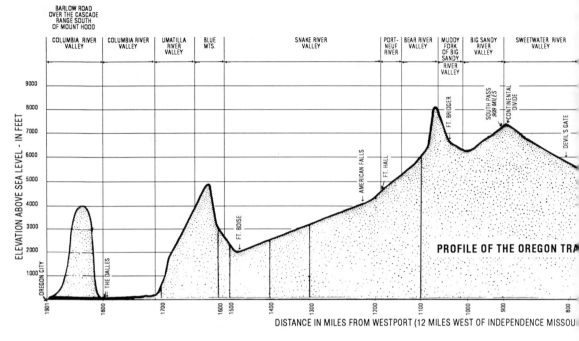

The Oregon Trail extended to the Willamette Valley from several jumping-off places along the Missouri River—the favorite site prior to 1850 being Independence, Missouri, located on the river's great bend near present-day Kansas City. Council Bluffs, Iowa, became a favorite starting point after 1850. On a map the trail resembled a badly frayed rope, with strands originating in several locations and alternate routes bowing out at intervals. Until the building of Fort Hall in 1834, there had not been so much as a cabin along the route, and even ten years later the situation had improved only slightly.

The Oregon Trail originated with a series of accidental discoveries by Astorians returning east from the Columbia River in 1812 and by the mountain man Jedediah Smith, who after 1824 publicized South Pass (in future Wyoming) as an easy crossing of the Rockies. In 1836, when the missionary women Narcissa Whitman and Eliza Spalding made it safely through South Pass, they provided a precedent for family travel over the trail. They got a flimsy two-wheeled cart as far west as Fort Boise; within a few years Oregon-bound pioneers would drive heavy wagons to the Columbia River and eventually all the way to the Willamette Valley.

More than a hundred persons and eighteen wagons rolled west in 1842 in what was the first wagon train chiefly composed of families. That year marked the beginning of covered wagon migration to Oregon. Two years later the number of emigrants gripped by "Oregon Fever" reached nearly fifteen hundred, and by 1845 it grew to twenty-five hundred. Those pioneers

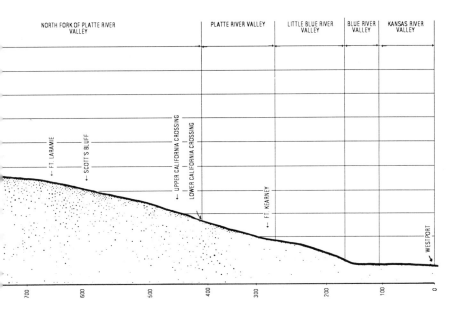

9. A profile of elevation along the Oregon Trail. Courtesy Special Collections Div., University of Washington Libraries, 6356. Redrawn.

traveled not in one great caravan but in several smaller groups departing at intervals sufficient to allow the native grasses to replenish themselves along the route. Migration became an annual event, an estimated four thousand emigrants heading west along the trail in 1847.

Between 1840 and 1860 some fifty-three thousand people completed the journey from jumping-off points along the Missouri River to Oregon. The Oregon Trail remained the major highway to the Pacific Northwest until a railroad line paralleling its route through southern Idaho was completed in 1884. The trail also served as a route for cattle and sheep drives east.

During the early years a typical overland journey required seven months. Starting in April, emigrants made their way west from the Missouri Valley across the Great Plains. On reaching the Platte River, they turned upstream until it forked to become the North Platte and then the Sweetwater. Beyond South Pass they continued to the Green River, then west to the Hudson's Bay Company oasis at Fort Hall. From there Oregon-bound travelers crossed the Snake River plain to Fort Boise, then proceeded on to the Grande Ronde Valley, the Blue Mountains, and the Whitman mission. Finally they followed the south bank of the Columbia River to the maelstrom of white water called the Grand Dalles. Beyond there they usually portaged downriver to the Willamette Valley, reaching their destination in October.

Emigrants timed their departure from the Missouri Valley so that livestock could feed off the lush plains grasslands at their peak. They plodded along in

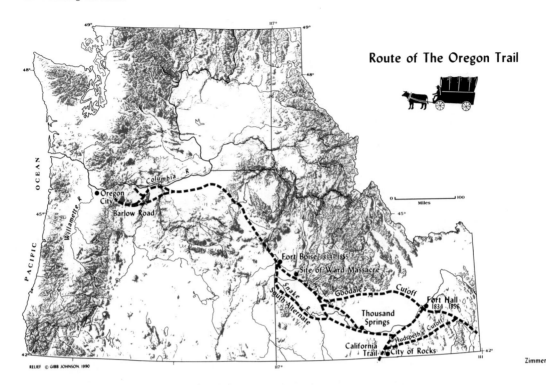

Route of The Oregon Trail

Zimmerly

4-by-10-foot canvas-topped wagons, often walking to lighten the load on the draft animals. Compared to what followed, the physical obstacles posed by the Great Plains proved relatively unimportant; the main dangers were thunderstorms, flooded rivers, and quicksand. A far more difficult obstacle was the Snake River plain. Overlanders reached there during the hottest part of summer, having already endured nearly thirteen hundred miles on the trail. Animals were tired and thirsty, but the cool waters of the Snake lay far below the canyon rim, tantalizing and yet impossible to reach. Moreover, the sharp-edged basalt lacerated the hooves of draft animals.

Early travelers' descriptions were seldom favorable to southern Idaho, which they often portrayed as nothing more than a desert of sage and sand. During the heyday of the Oregon Trail, from 1840 to 1860, few if any emigrants stopped short of the Willamette Valley to establish a permanent home on the semiarid Snake River plain. Few Euro-Americans would attempt to settle there until irrigation transformed the land.

Indian attack was an overlander's primary fear, yet in actuality it seldom occurred. The majority of early travelers saw few Indians along the trail, and later travelers could take some comfort from the forts that the War Department built along the route. Only in the mid-1850s, when Indians began to worry about encroachments on their lands, did they become hostile and aggressive, especially in the region beyond South Pass. Even so, most emigrants got to Oregon with little or no difficulty from Indians.

Statistics indicate that the most likely site for an Indian attack was on the Snake River plain. Here some bloody incidents were recorded, one of the worst being the massacre of the Alexander Ward party on the Boise River in 1854. Only two young boys who hid in the underbrush survived out of a party of twenty-three overlanders. The last major conflict with Indians on the trail occurred in 1862.

Why did emigrants undertake the long overland journey to Oregon? Their motives were varied, and no doubt many people would have been hard pressed to explain their real reasons for moving west. Some hoped to improve their health; others relished the challenge and excitement of starting a new life out West or wanted simply to escape the virulent passions associated with race and slavery at home. Record floods in Missouri, Iowa, and Illinois in 1836, 1844, and 1849 inundated and destroyed farms, and the receding waters left sickness in their wake, causing desperate people to seek alternatives.

Standing out most clearly was the desire for economic improvement. In an agrarian society that measured wealth in landholdings, the belief that Oregon contained an abundance of fertile land that was easily acquired under federal laws was compelling, especially after the panic of 1837 caused many midwestern farmers to sink hopelessly into debt. For whatever reasons, many of the Oregon-bound pioneers were impoverished farmers from the Mississippi Valley, and predominating in the 1840s migrations were Missourians.

During the first two decades of movement along the Oregon Trail, many people passed through Idaho on their way to new homes in the Willamette Valley. Though they did not settle the Snake River plain, the first generation of overlanders together with fur traders, trappers, and missionaries made an impact on the land and its native peoples, if only wagon ruts across the landscape and an occasional exchange with Indians. Certainly when compared with the profound and lasting changes that followed the discovery of gold in the Clearwater Valley in 1860, this impact was slight indeed. Nonetheless, in a very real sense these vanguards of the frontier prepared the way for the many Euro-American settlers who followed in their wake.

Official Exploration: The Second Phase

Captain Benjamin Louis Eulalie de Bonneville, a French-born officer in the United States Army, took a leave of absence in 1831 ostensibly to enter the fur trade of the West. Many historians now believe that he was actually sent to spy out the frontier, to search for a route across the Rocky Mountains to California. If so—and the proof is elusive—Bonneville was the first American since Lewis and Clark to undertake official exploration of the far Northwest.

Given a two-year leave of absence, Bonneville actually spent the next five years probing the West. On one of his trips, he traced a route from western Missouri to Idaho's rugged Salmon River country, where he established winter quarters in 1832. The next spring his party retreated to the annual fur traders' rendezvous at the Green River, then headed west again across the Snake River plain, eventually reaching Fort Walla Walla and the Columbia Valley in 1834. It was Bonneville who took the first wagons through South Pass.

In the 1840s the federal government officially re-entered the business of exploring the far Northwest with a burst of activity that lasted more than two decades and later became known as the Great Reconnaissance. Federal exploration proceeded from two different directions: from the west, members of a navy expedition probed the waters of Puget Sound and the Columbia, Snake, and Clearwater rivers as far upstream as Spalding's mission station at Lapwai; from the east came army explorers led by John C. Frémont.

Frémont was a new type of explorer, a member of the United States Army's Corps of Topographical Engineers. Most members of this elite unit (though not Frémont himself) were West Point graduates trained in such skills as engineering and map making. They brought a new degree of sophistication to the exploration of the West. The army commissioned Frémont to map and survey the trail to Oregon. He and thirty-nine men set out from Independence, Missouri, in May 1843 on a "secret" mission to Oregon. The party pushed past the Hudson's Bay Company outpost of Fort Hall, across the Snake River plain, and west along the Columbia River, where it turned south.

Frémont was the first explorer to recognize and name the Great Basin that encompassed parts of southern Idaho, Utah, and Nevada. His cartographer, Charles Preuss, completed a detailed map of the Oregon Trail. The Preuss map was a veritable gold mine of information that gave would-be emigrants precise distances and information on landmarks, river crossings, and Indian tribes. When Frémont presented his report to Congress, it created a sensation and was widely printed and distributed. His being married to Jessie Benton, daughter of Senator Thomas Hart Benton, helped to assure the success of Frémont's western endeavors, for the influential Missouri lawmaker was a key spokesman for development of the Oregon country.

Perhaps the most impressive of army reconnaissance ventures in the West was launched in 1853 when Congress approved funding for the Topographical Corps to search for the best railroad route to the Pacific Ocean. The leader of the northern survey was Isaac I. Stevens, the new governor of Washington Territory (of which northern Idaho was then a part). Assisting him was George B. McClellan, the future Civil War general. The men of the Stevens survey reconnoitered several possible railroad routes across the Idaho panhandle.

John Mullan, a young topographical engineer from West Point and a member of the Stevens party, remained in the field to oversee the work of surveying and building a military road across the northern Rocky Mountains in the late 1850s and early 1860s. Concluding the major federal efforts to explore portions of Idaho were the surveys of Clarence King (1867–72) along the 40th parallel and Ferdinand V. Hayden (1867–78), both of whom probed mainly the territory's southeastern fringes.

The Great Reconnaissance left a rich scientific and artistic legacy. Accompanying the Stevens survey were the artists Gustavus Sohon and John Mix Stanley, who produced an outstanding series of two- and three-color lithographs. When the railroad surveys were completed, the resulting maps, descriptive observations, and artwork were compiled into thirteen volumes that represented the most comprehensive body of information about the West at that time.

Accompanying the King survey was the pioneer photographer Timothy O'Sullivan, who made a side trip to Shoshone Falls in 1868 and recorded an early view of the natural wonder. Another pioneer photographer, William Henry Jackson, a member of the Hayden survey, captured some of the first images of southeastern Idaho.

John Mullan's Road

One result of the Great Reconnaissance of the 1850s was the Mullan Road, a wagon route funded by Congress to connect Fort Benton, head of steamboat navigation on the Missouri River, and Walla Walla, near the navigable waters of the Columbia River. The road was 624 miles long and cost the War Department $230,000.

Starting at Walla Walla, John Mullan's road builders worked their way east until they reached the southern end of Lake Coeur d'Alene in the summer of 1859. The Idaho portion of the road would prove unexpectedly difficult to build. The land south of the lake was swampy; the climb over the Bitterroots meant hacking a trail through thick stands of timber. Even before the road was completed, repeated flooding made it necessary to relocate a part of it to high ground north of Lake Coeur d'Alene. On July 4, 1861, Mullan and his men blazed their mark on a white pine near the bottom of what is now called Fourth of July Canyon.

Although a troop of soldiers followed the half-completed trail in 1861, the route never fulfilled its destiny as a military road. Mullan sought to encourage civilian travel by issuing a detailed guide in 1865. For the fourteenth day east from Walla Walla, for instance, he offered this advice on the way from Wolf Creek Lodge to the old Jesuit mission:

> Move to the Coeur d'Aléne Mission; distance, seventeen miles; road hilly at one or two places, but not bad; wood, water, and grass at the mission. Good place to rest animals for a day or two, and which is by all means advisable, as you now enter the timber, where camp-grounds have to be specially selected, and the animals should be well rested. Vegetables may be had at the mission.[1]

By 1866 some twenty thousand people and an unknown number of animals (including at least seven camels) had passed over the Mullan Road, most of them going from west to east, primarily from Missoula to Fort Benton. Packers occasionally used the route during the mining rushes of the 1860s, as did cattlemen who drove livestock west to the Columbia River during the years of the open range in the 1870s and 1880s. But spring flooding and lack of congressional funds for maintenance inevitably took their toll. The road fell into disrepair. Not until the federal road program of the 1920s was the route regarded as part of a transcontinental highway. Today Interstate 90 closely follows Mullan's route across the Idaho panhandle.

Treaty Troubles

The work of defining the land probably had its greatest impact on Idaho's first inhabitants when treaty negotiations reduced their once vast domain to a few widely scattered reservations. The process began in the mid-1850s. Northern Idaho was part of the newly created territory of Washington (formed in 1853), and Washington's brash young governor, Isaac I. Stevens, energetically pursued a policy of forcing Indians onto reservations and opening the land to white settlers. From Puget Sound to the Rocky Mountains, Stevens redefined the land through the agreements he negotiated.

The treaty-making process was a very complex matter that extended over several decades and involved several of Stevens's successors. Some treaties were never ratified by Congress; occasionally a reservation was established through executive order of the president. Only the highlights of the process can be summarized here.

In the Walla Walla Valley in 1855, Stevens secured one of the earliest treaties negotiated between whites and Indians of the Pacific Northwest. This hastily constructed document, which Indians of the interior signed only reluctantly, allowed the Nez Perces to keep intact their 11,000-square-mile homeland in central Idaho, Oregon, and Washington. But in 1863, following the discovery of gold in the Clearwater and Salmon river watersheds, whites negotiated a new treaty with Lawyer, a pro-American Nez Perce leader, that reduced the reservation to approximately 1,100 square miles, or one-tenth its original size. Other Nez Perce leaders rejected the document, and this gave rise to treaty and nontreaty factions within the tribe and led to an epic conflict with whites in 1877.

The work of defining the land continued in southern Idaho, where the treaties of Fort Boise in 1864 and Bruneau River two years later attempted to provide a reservation for the Boise and Bruneau Shoshones, but the two documents never came before Congress for ratification. President Andrew Johnson by executive order set aside the Fort Hall Reservation for Boise Shoshone exiles; Fort Hall Shoshone and Bannock peoples were allowed to join them in 1869.

The Colville reservation in Washington was established by executive order in 1872 for Kutenai, Pend d'Oreille, Colville, and Spokane Indians, a portion of whom resided in Idaho. A year later President Ulysses Grant created the Coeur d'Alene Reservation. This measure forced Indians to abandon three-quarters of their huge holdings in northern Idaho, move away from the mission at Cataldo, and relocate on a 600,000-acre reservation to forestall white encroachments. The Senate, however, did not formally ratify a treaty with the Coeur d'Alenes until 1891, when the tribe ceded 2.4 million acres for $600,000 that was to be divided among its members. The Duck Valley Reservation that straddles the Idaho-Nevada border was set aside by presidential proclamation in 1877 for western Shoshones and Paiutes. Idaho's last and smallest reservation, consisting of 4,105 acres of land near Bonners Ferry, was created in 1895 for the Kutenais.

The treaty-making process had tragic consequences for the Indians. Trouble arose from a number of sources: Idaho Indians utterly unacquainted with agriculture found the transition from a hunting and gathering way of life difficult; greedy federal agents occasionally pilfered or redirected supplies intended for the Indians; and white miners and settlers continued to encroach on Indian lands. Forced onto ever-shrinking holdings, some bands accepted their new status only reluctantly. The Lemhi reservation that President Grant set aside in 1875 for Shoshone and Bannock peoples consisted of hills and mountains so sterile that farming them was impossible. Tendoy, chief spokesman for the Lemhi people, was taken to Washington in 1880 to arrange a treaty whereby the band eventually moved to the Fort Hall Reservation (in 1907).

It is hard to imagine that Euro-Americans did not fully comprehend what they were doing when they redefined the land: the former governor and one-time United States senator W. J. McConnell used strong language to describe the process in his memoir-history of Idaho:

> As the crickets and jack rabbits sometimes over-run and destroy the crops in these valleys today, without asking leave, so we of the Anglo-Saxon race in those days over-ran and destroyed the hunting grounds of the original owners, and without asking leave took forcible possession thereof. Not having the time to spare from our other pursuits to sufficiently punish the Indians for presuming to bar our progress, we appealed to the government to support us in holding the country we had entered.[2]

It should not be surprising that warfare erupted in the interior Northwest only months after the 1855 Walla Walla council concluded its work, and that Indian hostilities continued to flare up at intervals in Idaho until 1879. Conflict over the newly defined land is examined in detail in Chapter 6, which looks at the many troubles that overwhelmed the young territory of Idaho in the 1860s and 1870s.

CHAPTER 5

On the 1st of Oct. [1860] commenced our labor. Found gold in every place in the stream,
in the flats and banks and gold generally dif-
fused from the surface to the bed rock. I never
saw a party of men so much excited. They
made the hills and mountains ring with
shouts of joy. —E. D. Pierce, describing a
gold discovery on Orofino Creek, from *The
Pierce Chronicle* (n.d.)

The Emergence of Idaho

From 1805, when the first whites entered the land destined to become Idaho,
until the 1860s, the inhospitable terrain and the Indians were of little interest
to anyone except a few trappers, explorers, and missionaries. Most white
pioneers, in fact, had a very low opinion of Idaho, regarding it as only a
barrier to be crossed, not a land to be settled. The rugged mountains brought
Lewis and Clark to the brink of ruin, and the desiccated Snake River plain
drove thirsty Astorians nearly insane. Similar torments awaited later explorers and fur traders.

Settlers bound for Oregon in the 1840s and 1850s dreaded the Snake
River country. They feared both the Indians and the waterless, treeless land.
Not until 1860 did Idaho get its first town, although the pioneers who
founded Franklin insisted that they were in Utah until a formal survey of the
boundary in 1871 forced them to concede that their settlement was indeed
within Idaho Territory. Only after the discovery of precious metals did Euro-
Americans show much interest in settling the land that became Idaho.

Gold Fever

Gold! That single word lured thousands of fortune seekers into the remotest
parts of Idaho. It all began on August 12, 1860, when Elias Davidson Pierce
and twelve men left Walla Walla and moved quietly and illegally across the
Nez Perce Reservation. Not long after the illicit prospectors found some

10. This panoramic view of Lewiston, Washington Territory, in 1862, shows it to be a town still fashioned mostly of tents. Courtesy Oregon Historical Society, 485.

promising diggings on Orofino Creek, word of the discovery leaked out, and the Clearwater rush was on.[1]

By midsummer 1861, a jerry-built collection of tents and nondescript structures fashioned from hand-hewn logs and whipsawed lumber grandiloquently called itself Pierce City. And why not? The booming community was now the seat of the most populous county in Washington Territory. Soon a second collection of stores, hotels, and saloons took the name Oro Fino City. Located about three miles from Pierce, Oro Fino boasted six restaurants, two hotels, two bakeries, four meat markets, twenty whiskey shops, ten gambling saloons, one watchmaker, one bookshop, one barbershop, three doctors' offices—about seventy-five buildings in all. During the high-water season, an army of gold seekers traveled by steamboat up the Columbia and Snake rivers from Portland to Lewiston, where they obtained saddle and pack animals to push on into the interior. Some miners walked to the diggings. Provisions were packed into the Clearwater country from the booming town of Walla Walla or bought from the Nez Perces, who began trading with the miners shortly after the first prospectors arrived. Indian farmers living along the fertile bottomlands of the Clearwater, Snake, and Salmon rivers provided eggs, corn, and cattle to the newcomers.

Early Lewiston was little more than a haphazard assemblage of tents. A local army officer refused to let merchants erect permanent structures because this was still Nez Perce country, but so many newcomers arrived each

day that stopping them proved hopeless. In fact, Lewiston and the mining camps of Pierce City, Oro Fino, Elk City, Florence, and Warren were all located on Nez Perce land.[2] Despite the obvious injustice done to them, the Indians did not retaliate with violence, as they sometimes did in other parts of the West. The Nez Perces desired to maintain peaceable relations with Euro-Americans.

Many of the first gold seekers were depression-ridden farmers from Oregon's Willamette Valley who left for the Idaho diggings despite the protests of Portland newspapers. The ranks of miners included churchmen, merchants, laborers, and lawyers, virtually anyone capable of handling a pick and shovel. The argonauts came from all over the United States as well as from Mexico, Canada, Great Britain, Italy, France, China, and the Hawaiian Islands. The typical miner wore a beard and had a look in his eyes that contemporaries described only as gold crazed. In this group a gray-haired man was a rarity, though many of the gold seekers were already veterans of earlier rushes to California, British Columbia, and Colorado.

Express companies transported some three million dollars' worth of gold dust down the Columbia River in 1861. Gold dust was legal tender, and every miner carried some in a buckskin pouch. Merchants and hotelmen kept a pair of small brass scales handy to weigh the precious metal. Gold dust was worth sixteen dollars an ounce ordinarily—less than that in some districts. A scoundrel occasionally tried to mix heavy yellow sand with the dust to cheat the unwary. Because at this time banks were practically unknown, frugal miners sometimes buried gold dust in baking powder cans in or about their cabins.

Inevitably some prospectors reached the diggings too late to claim the choicest ground. Their continuing search led them farther south, where they discovered rich placers at Elk City and Florence in the rugged and remote Salmon River country, and still farther south into the Boise Basin, where they discovered gold on Grimes Creek, August 2, 1862.

Arrastras and stamp mills in the Boise Basin seldom stopped as they methodically ground the gold-bearing quartz to powder. At the peak of the excitement, sawmills ran day and night, and lumber was purchased to build houses or sluice boxes as fast as it could be manufactured. Collections of small buildings fashioned from rough lumber that took the names of Centerville, Placerville, Idaho City, and Pioneerville went up as if by magic. The Boise Basin yielded twenty million dollars worth of gold by 1866.

Within three years of its founding in 1862, Idaho City surpassed Portland as the most populous city in the Pacific Northwest. It featured opera houses and theaters, music stores, tailor shops, breweries, bowling alleys, bakeries, and other urban amenities, not to mention the numerous saloons found in every mining camp. Idaho City in the summer of 1863 had 6,275 residents, 5,691 of them male.

In the Idaho mining country, as in California and other regions during earlier booms, towns sprang up like mushrooms and vanished when miners stampeded to new diggings. Thousands of disappointed gold seekers followed each new rush. An estimated eight thousand people were in Florence in late June 1862; two weeks later six thousand of them had departed. Oro Fino City was soon abandoned, and the place burned to the ground in August 1867. A few of the mining towns, notably Pierce and Idaho City, survived in scaled-down form; most communities of this type did not.

Miners worked hard and had little time for play. In the summertime when the water was running, some men labored feverishly seven days a week. Hour after hour they hauled and shoveled, dug ditches, and built sluice boxes and flumes. In the process they transformed clear mountain streams into muddy rivulets.

Never mind the damage to the environment; excitement was in the air. The miners were participants in a giant lottery, and none could predict who would find the elusive pockets of gold that would make a poor man a king. Driving them on were stories of men like Jacob Weiser, who recovered five hundred pounds of gold in two days at "fabulous Florence," an amount worth about $260,000 today. The arrival of packtrains laden with all sorts of mer-chandise enlivened the miners' existence. On the streets the braying of mules mixed with fiddle music from the saloons and the hammering of car-penters. The din of construction occasionally grew so loud that it interrupted conversations.

Recreation consisted of gambling, drinking, dancing, and the theater. Al-most every town had a Bella Union saloon, a What Cheer hotel, or a California theater. A common frontier name for a saloon was the Bank. Saloons were community social centers. In early mining camps there were no restrictions on liquor sales. Whiskey was the favorite drink, taken straight and at a gulp. Familiar names for whiskey included tangle-leg, lightning, and tarantula-juice.[3]

At intervals, theatrical troupes reached the camps, where they usually played to a packed house. Performances were boisterous affairs: patrons let loose a lot of animal passion in the form of whistling and stomping of feet, especially after they visited the adjacent bar during intermission. Books, magazines, and newspapers were also a part of some miners' lives. Men might spend their evenings reading or in serious discussion or recollection of experiences from back home. Sometimes talk of the classics occurred around a campfire. One miner in Oro Fino City spent winter evenings read-ing Sir Walter Scott's novels to his comrades.

Sunday was a time for washing and patching clothes, cooking up food for the next week, and mending broken tools. It was also the liveliest day of the week, dance halls, saloons, gambling houses running full blast. All other businesses were open as well. Churches sprang up early in mining camps. Churchgoing or not, miners were noted for their charity.

Food prices varied. In Oro Fino City in 1861, the cost of such staples as bacon, beans, and sugar averaged four times higher than in Portland. During the winter of 1861–62, some Oro Fino residents packed in potatoes on their backs through fifteen to twenty miles of deep snow. Uncooked potatoes sliced up and soaked in vinegar provided a remedy for the dreaded disease of scurvy.

Besides creating considerable excitement and some personal wealth, the mining boom of the 1860s gave birth to the new territory of Idaho. It also infused the Union economy with badly needed gold during the Civil War. In addition to the boom of the 1860s, Idaho experienced another decade of min-ing excitement in the 1880s that had equally far-reaching consequences (see Chapter 8).

11. Brigham Young, the inspiration behind numerous Mormon settlements in early Idaho. Courtesy Church Archives, Church of Jesus Christ of Latter-day Saints.

Saints in Search of a Promised Land

While mining booms were attracting people to the northern and western parts of Idaho, Mormon farmers were entering the southeastern corner as they moved north from the Salt Lake Valley. Members of the Church of Jesus Christ of Latter-day Saints have been prominent in Idaho history since the 1850s and 1860s. Commonly called Mormons or Latter-day Saints, they constitute by far the largest religious group in the Gem State, and no state or territory outside Utah has a larger percentage of Mormons in its population than Idaho.

The first Mormon pioneers traveled west in 1847 from Illinois to the Great Salt Lake to build a Zion free from the religious persecution they had previ-

The Paris Tabernacle

The Paris, Idaho, Stake Tabernacle served as an ecclesiastical headquarters for Mormon settlers living within a fifty-mile radius of the settlement. This stake was the first permanent organization of its type outside Utah. Construction of the tabernacle began in 1884. Volunteer labor used local materials that included red sandstone and timber; a shipwright fashioned the ceiling from wood by adapting a style of construction used in seafaring vessels in New England.

The Paris Tabernacle was dedicated in 1889 and is today on the Register of Historic Places in the United States.

ously encountered. They likened their migration to "the gathering" of ancient Israel, and some seventy thousand church members undertook the trek to the Great Basin during the next twenty-two years. Some of the poorer lugged their belongings on handcarts.

Their leader, Brigham Young, envisioned the proliferation of Mormon communities throughout the Rocky Mountain West. Church members planned to establish more than three hundred communities beginning with Salt Lake City and extending from southern California to Canada.

On April 14, 1860, a band of thirteen colonists founded Franklin, Idaho's first town. They built a common corral and arranged their wagon boxes for protection while a fort was constructed; they also designed their first log cabins to provide shelter from Indian attack. The Mormon pioneers surveyed a townsite, dug a ditch for water, and on May 26 planted their first gardens and fields. This marked the birth of agriculture in southeastern Idaho. Brigham Young visited the fortified village and approved. A sawmill, gristmill, and store soon added vitality to community life.

Young wanted the Bear Lake valley to serve as a northern outpost of Mormon colonization. Thus on September 15, 1863, General Charles C. Rich and thirty to fifty colonizers crossed the mountains from Franklin and chose a site eight miles north of Bear Lake. Their new town, Paris, was modeled after Salt Lake City. When Young visited in May 1864, he instructed Rich to assign lots one block at a time and encouraged settlers to build substantial houses so that the new community would have a neat, orderly appearance. Over the next several years, crude log cabins gave way to attractive frame homes.

Young named several of the Mormon settlements of southeastern Idaho: Montpelier, Ovid, Bennington, Bloomington, St. Charles, and Fish Haven. Many of the people who settled these towns were Scandinavian and English converts eager to help build the new Zion.

Although the valleys were fertile, pioneer life could still be harsh. For the

Denomination	Washington	Idaho	Oregon	Utah
Roman Catholic	♔♔♔♔♔♔♔	♔♔♔♔	♔♔♔♔♔♔	♔
Presbyterian	♔♔	♔	♔♔	♔
Methodist	♔♔♔	♔♔	♔♔♔♔	
Baptist	♔♔♔	♔	♔♔♔	
Disciples	♔♔	♔	♔♔	
Lutheran	♔♔♔	♔	♔	
Congregational	♔♔	♔	♔	
Episcopal	♔	♔	♔	
Latter-Day Saints		♔♔♔♔♔♔♔♔♔♔	♔	♔♔♔♔♔♔♔♔♔♔♔♔♔♔♔♔
Adventist	♔		♔	
Eastern Orthodox		♔		♔
United		♔		
Friends		♔		
Evangelical		♔		
All others	♔	♔	♔	♔

Percentage of Communicants, 1910, by Denomination
(Each symbol approximates 5 percent)

first several years, grasshoppers routinely destroyed crops in the Bear Lake valley. Flour had to be hauled in from Logan or Brigham City, Utah. During the winter months, mail had be to carried twenty-five miles over the mountains from Franklin on snowshoes; Charles C. Rich sometimes performed the feat.

All of the Mormon settlements developed in a similar way. Each was to be a self-contained community that centered on family and religion. Church authorities presided over a highly organized society. Colonists united to construct schools, meetinghouses, irrigation canals, roads, and bridges. Mormon settlements could be identified by their wide streets, landmark tabernacles and other church structures, and general air of prosperity. Homesteads clustered closely about the church, and fields lay on the outskirts of town. Faith, morals, crops, and irrigation were all regarded as matters of community concern.

Such key businesses as the general store and creamery were likely to be cooperative enterprises. The Paris Co-Operative engaged in the manufacture of leather, boots, shoes, harnesses, lumber, shingles, and cheese and operated a general store and printing office before closing down in the early 1890s. Only rarely did large numbers of non-Mormons attempt to settle in these towns. One exception was Montpelier, which Mormons established in 1864 but which gained a substantial non-Mormon population in the 1880s when it developed as a railroad center.

Other Mormon pioneers pushed north into the upper Snake River valley, although their settlements (unlike those along the Utah border) were not church sponsored. Mormons steadily increased in number until by 1877 Idaho had thirty-one distinct Mormon settlements and by 1890 about twenty-five thousand Mormon residents. Mormons constituted about one-quarter of Idaho's total population at that time and perhaps as many as one-half of all its churchgoers. It was a religious division unique in American history.

Origins of Idaho

When Lewis and Clark entered Idaho in 1805, the United States had no formal plans to extend its boundaries west of the Rocky Mountains. That changed in 1818 when Great Britain and the United States agreed to joint occupation of the sprawling territory known as the Oregon country. After lengthy negotiations enlivened by threats and bluster on both sides, the two countries finally reached an agreement in 1846 to divide the region at the 49th parallel, the present international boundary between Canada and the United States.

12. Mormons maintained a trim and efficient ward meetinghouse in Bancroft, seen here in the early 1930s. Courtesy Oregon Historical Society, 32194.

Two years later Congress established the Territory of Oregon, which included future Idaho. In 1853, federal lawmakers separated Washington Territory from Oregon and divided the land destined to become Idaho between them.

When Oregon became a state in 1859, the immense but sparsely settled eastern segment of the former territory was attached to Washington, thus creating a geographical monstrosity that stretched from the Olympic Peninsula to the crest of the Rocky Mountains and included all of future Idaho and portions of Montana and Wyoming. The great distance that separated its capital at Olympia, on the southern edge of Puget Sound, from several new mining settlements in the interior complicated the governing of Washington Territory.[4]

From the perspective of Olympia, the situation grew worse after the discovery of gold on the Clearwater and at several other inland locations. The frontier village of Walla Walla emerged as a major supply point for the mining camps. It soon grew to be the largest settlement in Washington Territory and a dangerous rival to Olympia, which feared that Walla Walla might displace it as capital. The discovery of gold on Washington's eastern frontier (in future Montana) further complicated political life in the sprawling territory. Olympia, in short, was only too glad to have Congress combine Washington's remote mining regions into a sprawling new territory called Idaho, created on March 4, 1863, when President Abraham Lincoln signed the bill into law.

That July, citizens met in Lewiston to organize Idaho. By then, thirty-five states had already entered the Union, three generations had passed since the Declaration of Independence, and sixteen men had served as president of the United States. At the time Idaho was created, the United States had just fought two of the bloodiest battles in its history—Gettysburg and Vicksburg—to ensure the survival of the Union, yet it would take Idahoans nearly two weeks to learn of the outcome. Idaho's first telegraph link with the rest of the country and its first transcontinental railroad lay several years in the future.

At the time of Idaho's creation, New York City had one million residents and was the nation's largest urban center. The fledgling territory, by contrast, had a total of 32,342 residents who were scattered across an expanse of land almost seven times larger than the entire state of New York.

The new territory was not only geographically remote from the East Coast, it was chronologically distant from the mainstream of American history. Tales of the American Revolution were part of Idaho's heritage, but not part of its immediate experience. Early Idaho was forged from the interaction of Indi-

That Curious Name Idaho

When the United States House of Representatives voted to create the new territory, the bill carried the name Montana. In the Senate, Henry Wilson of Massachusetts moved that the name be changed to Idaho because "Montana is no name at all." Defeated at first, Wilson renewed his argument, which Benjamin Franklin Harding of Oregon supported, saying, "I think the name of Idaho is much preferable to Montana. Montana in my mind signifies nothing at all. Idaho, in English, signifies 'Gem of the Mountains.'" After only a few more moments of deliberation, senators assented to the new territory of Idaho by a vote of twenty-five to twelve.

One of the steamboats that transported gold seekers up the Columbia River was named the *Idaho*. Its owner apparently got the name from a Colorado mining man who said that it meant Gem of the Mountains. Indeed, Colorado had almost been named Idaho, and it was a Coloradan who coined the word Idaho, claiming that it was of Indian derivation. Until research in the late 1950s rediscovered the truth that Idaho was an invented word, several generations of Idahoans had been taught that it came from the Indian words *E Dah Hoe* and meant Gem of the Mountains.

—*Congressional Globe*, 37th Congress, 3d Session, March 3, 1863, p. 1509.

For an extended discussion on the origin of the name Idaho, see "Footnotes to History," *Idaho Yesterdays* 8 (Spring 1964): 33–36; "New Notes on the Word 'Idaho,'" ibid. 2 (Spring 1958): 26–28.

ans, missionaries, miners, and explorers, not Pilgrims, planters, seafarers, and Revolutionary War heroes. Idahoans had no creation myths of their own, like those central to the history of the original thirteen colonies; they had fought no epic battles for their independence; and they had no shrines comparable to the Alamo or Plymouth Rock.

The emergence of Idaho was thus more a product of chance than the outcome of any long-term historical trend. In a real sense Idaho would have to be "invented" during the next several decades, unlike some of the original American colonies that had evolved over generations from first settlements along the Atlantic seaboard and had spread inland only gradually, often along a single river valley. Idaho, a wholly arbitrary creation, would never experience that kind of historical or cultural unity.

It would, in fact, be difficult to develop any kind of emotional attachment to a place called Idaho when Congress kept rearranging the boundaries: without moving an inch, a person living on the upper Missouri River would have been a Nebraskan in early 1863, an Idahoan in late 1863, and a Montanan by mid-1864. No one present at the creation could have predicted with any accuracy how the boundaries of Idaho would look in ten years, much less a century later. Neither could anyone predict whether Idaho would even survive long enough to become a state.

CHAPTER 6

Those who endeavor to comprehend the circumstances under which that first legislature
met will find their minds bewildered by the
effort. Legislative bodies usually have as a
guide the enactments of former sessions, their
duty being to amend laws already in force or
enact such new ones as experience has suggested. But these men came to a little frontier
town [Lewiston] where many of the inhabitants were lawless and where the accommodations were of the most primitive character,
and entered with energy and intelligence
upon the duties which were new to most of
them.—from W. J. McConnell, *Early History
of Idaho* (1913)

Trials of a New Territory

The formation of Idaho Territory in 1863 was only a beginning, and not a very promising one at that. Members of Congress drew boundaries on a map and gave the enclosed space a name, but it would require the people who now called themselves Idahoans to breathe life into the federal lawmakers' new creation. During the five decades bracketed by the Civil War and the First World War, the men and women of Idaho would build new towns, new institutions, and a new economy. Theirs was seldom an easy task, but in the process of confronting adversity and overcoming it, they forged the basis for a viable state.

A Time of Trouble

A common belief in Idaho is that the state's eastern boundary would have followed the Continental Divide through what is now Montana had not drunken surveyors got lost and followed the wrong range of mountains north from Lost Trail Pass. In fact, the official survey of the Montana-Idaho border was completed in two sections, the northern panhandle in 1899 and along the Bitterroots and Continental Divide between 1904 and 1907. That was more than thirty years after Congress last adjusted Idaho's boundary. More-over, because the surveyors began at the Canadian border and worked their way south, it would have been impossible for them, drunk or sober, to make the wrong turn and head north again at Lost Trail Pass.

This often-repeated myth implies that a survey error was responsible for

	OREGON	WASHINGTON	IDAHO
1848 to 1853			
1853 to 1859			
1859 to 1863	Statehood 1859		
1863 to 1864			
1864 to 1868			
1868 ...		Statehood 1889	Statehood 1890

From Territory to Statehood

Territory

State

Idaho's odd-shaped boundary, when in fact it was a product of the cavalier manner in which politicians often treated territorial matters. According to the federal Constitution, Congress retained supreme power over all territories. It could, for example, determine the length of territorial legislative sessions and the number of legislators, and it might veto their enactments. Congress could also alter territorial boundaries, as Idahoans learned all too well. As it is in any colonial system, the potential for tyranny was great, but Uncle Sam generally remained too indifferent to territorial affairs either to tyrannize or to guide them with a firm hand.

Idaho's original boundary reflected mainly the desire of Olympia politicians to jettison their territory's eastern counties in order to create a more compact Washington that would not jeopardize the status of Olympia as capital. Congress responded by stretching the boundary of the new territory to include present-day Idaho, Montana, and all but the southwestern corner of Wyoming. Legislators from the upper Missouri River area found it nearly impossible to reach the capitol at Lewiston, and territorial officials faced a similar challenge when they sought to administer the vast domain. Thus it should not be too surprising that members of Idaho's first legislature, when they finally assembled in Lewiston in December 1863, unanimously petitioned Congress to divide the territory to make it easier to govern.

Even after the creation of Montana on May 26, 1864, greatly diminished Idaho's size, it still encompassed a portion of future Wyoming west of the Continental Divide. Alas, Congress was not yet done tinkering with the shape of Idaho: on July 25, 1868, federal lawmakers shrank Idaho to its present contorted dimensions by carving away what would become the southern portion of Yellowstone National Park, all of the Grand Tetons, and a portion of the oil- and coal-rich Green River country, an area that could today be pumping tourist and energy dollars into the Gem State's treasury instead of Wyoming's.

Idaho's early territorial years can only be described as a time of trouble. The territory was too sprawling to govern effectively, especially since communication and transportation were so poor, and its administrators—nonresidents appointed in Washington, D.C.—commanded so little respect that Idahoans often derided them as carpetbaggers. Financial woes made the situation even worse. Normally Congress provided most of the funds needed to run its western territories, but at the time of Idaho's creation, the nation was split by the bloody and costly Civil War. Fighting for its survival, the Union had little money to spare. Gold fever and epidemic gambling and liquor consumption added to the problems in Idaho caused by distance and poor administration. The ingredients for turmoil were all too obvious.

Yankees and Rebels

Although Idaho was a long way from the battlefields of the East and South, Civil War tensions still threatened to destroy it. The territory's first legislature adopted a strong antislavery resolution, yet supporters of the South were so common in its mining camps that Idaho was in many ways a Confederate territory. Some pro-Southerners were draft dodgers and some were civilians who only wanted to escape the horrors of war, yet all were hostile to the federal government. Idaho's majority Democrats divided between avowed supporters of Southern secession and those who wanted only peace and accommodation between the two warring sections.

During 1863 large wagon trains rolled west from Missouri and Arkansas and brought to Idaho entire families desperate to escape the guerrilla warfare that threatened to destroy their home states. Emigration from the border states not only swelled the ranks of Southern sympathizers but also brought prospective brides to the overwhelmingly male territory. Scarcely had the first wagons creaked to a halt in Boise before men from the nearby stores, billiard halls, and saloons lined the sidewalks for a look at the ladies. "'Goo-goo' eyes were seen on the Boise streets for the first time that day," recalled Governor William J. McConnell. "Of the marriages resulting from those speedy courtships I have yet to learn of a divorce."[1]

Almost every American in Idaho's mining camps had a friend or relative fighting on either the Union or Confederate side. Thus they anxiously awaited the arrival of the stagecoach and with it the latest newspapers. Because there were never enough copies for everyone, little groups formed around the fortunate individuals to learn the latest news from the battlefields around Atlanta or Richmond.

When the Confederacy was victorious, jubilant men publicly cheered for Jefferson Davis and the Rebel cause. They filled the saloons, all clamoring for liquor and predicting speedy recognition of the Confederacy by foreign governments. When the news was of a Union triumph, Yankee supporters cheered Abraham Lincoln and gathered in the saloons to toast success by singing "We'll Rally 'round the Flag, Boys" or some other Northern song. Occasionally the two sides spilled into the streets where they battled one another with their fists.

Rebel sympathizers were generally law abiding, but in January 1867 a majority of the members of Idaho's fourth territorial legislature refused to

---

Names on the Land: A Civil War Legacy

A map of Idaho reveals several names that are a legacy of Civil War tensions. Southerners platted the mining town of Leesburg (Lemhi County) in 1866 to honor Robert E. Lee. The great general's namesake eventually absorbed the rival town of Grantsville, established by Union sympathizers. Atlanta (Elmore County) was a stronghold of pro- Southern miners, who chose the name to commemorate the Battle of Atlanta in 1864. There are also the Secesh Basin (Idaho County) and the Secesh River (Idaho and Valley counties), *secesh* being a term once associated with the secessionist or Rebel cause.
—Adapted from Lalia Boone, *Idaho Place Names* (1988).

---

take a loyalty oath to the Union as required by the Reconstruction Congress. When S. R. Howlett, territorial secretary, punished the protestors by withholding their per diem and mileage money, they proceeded to break up furniture and throw it out the window. Idaho's staunchly pro-Union governor, David W. Ballard, requested federal troops from nearby Fort Boise, and within an hour blue-jacketed men ringed the building. Chastened by the show of force, Idaho's rebellious lawmakers sullenly took the oath and received their pay.

President Andrew Johnson dismissed Ballard from office no fewer than four times, but the Tenure of Office Act passed by the Reconstruction Congress kept him from being replaced without congressional approval, which was not forthcoming. Though he received no salary until the federal government resolved the impasse between its executive and legislative branches, Ballard continued to run the territory. He supported himself by working as a physician in Boise.

During the years of greater Idaho Territory, law enforcement was difficult. Living in the mining camps were men like Cherokee Bob, Dutch Fred, and Boone Helm, fugitives from justice in other states and territories, whose names became synonymous with lawlessness. When government officials proved unable to deal with such pressing crimes as horse stealing, highway robbery, and the passing of bogus gold dust, vigilance committees arose in Payette, Lewiston, and nearly a dozen other communities.

In remote Virginia City, in the portion of Idaho soon to become Montana, a rising tide of lawlessness caused angry and frustrated citizens to conclude that Sheriff Henry Plummer headed a gang of thieves. In January 1864 they organized as vigilantes and hanged Plummer and two associates. Occasionally vigilance committees left the body of an evildoer hanging from a tree as a warning to others tempted to break the law. From 1861 to 1866 vigilance committees in Idaho and Montana were reputed to have executed no fewer than 200 alleged outlaws.

Carpetbaggers

Idaho's territorial governors were for the most part an odd lot of scheming or incompetent carpetbag politicians who seemed to serve the territory best by leaving it, or not arriving at all. Save for a nonvoting delegate in Congress, a territory had little or no say over its own affairs or boundaries, which federal lawmakers could alter as they saw fit. Governors, secretaries, supreme court justices, and most other territorial officials were appointed by the president, confirmed by the Senate, and paid from the federal treasury. The territorial governor of Idaho received twenty-five hundred dollars a year, a salary apparently too low to attract competent men to the job. Gilman Marston of New Hampshire is alleged to have resigned in haste upon learning that his annual pay was twenty-five hundred dollars—not the twenty-five thousand he had expected.

Federal appointees who arrived in Idaho from the Pacific Coast were warmly received, but when an easterner came to assume office, he was usually labeled a carpetbagger. Increasing the potential for name-calling and mismanagement was the fact that all but one of the appointed governors were Republicans, though Democrats often dominated the elected legislature.

Abraham Lincoln appointed an old friend, William H. Wallace, Idaho's first territorial governor. When the new governor traveled to Idaho from Washington, D.C., he went by ship to the Isthmus of Panama, crossed it, and then boarded another ship to San Francisco and Portland. The trip took four months. Wallace served for less than a year, from March 1863 until January 1864, then got himself elected to Congress and thereby increased his annual salary to six thousand dollars.

Caleb Lyon, a faithful Republican appointed by Lincoln as the territory's second governor, had a reputation as a New York art and literature critic. Being something of a dandy, he never fit in with the rough-and-tumble miners of Idaho and was ill suited to govern the raw territory. Because he insisted on styling himself Caleb Lyon of Lyonsdale, Idaho pioneers twitted him as Cale of the Dale. It is said of Lyon that he came into office in a storm and left it in a cyclone.

Only a few months after he arrived in the territory, Lyon added his signature to legislation moving the capital from Lewiston to Boise and thereby embroiled himself in a bitter conflict. Lewiston residents argued that the

13. Caleb Lyon of Lyonsdale, Idaho Territory's eccentric second governor. Courtesy Idaho State Historical Society, 544.

move was illegal and got a local judge to enjoin temporarily the transfer of the territorial seal and archives. Lyon evaded a summons to appear in court by slipping out of town on a duck-hunting trip that took him down the Snake River into the safe haven of Washington. In Lewiston an infuriated public denounced him, and the sheriff assigned an armed guard of six local citizens to keep Boise partisans from stealing the seal and archives, which they attempted to do on December 31, 1864. Meanwhile the egotistical and ambitious governor quietly departed for the more promising environment of the national capital. For two months Idaho had no governor at all.

The acting governor, the territorial secretary Clinton Dewitt Smith, took eight months to reach Idaho when Plains Indians blocked overland travel and

forced him to detour by way of Panama. Smith leaped into the ongoing capital controversy when he managed to transport the seal and archives out of
Lewiston to Boise, but after only seven months on the job, he drank himself
to death. Meanwhile, the Boise County treasurer embezzled fourteen thousand dollars in revenues he had collected for the territory, nearly bankrupting
it. The next de facto governor, Horace Gilson, was a thief who quietly looted
the treasury of forty-one thousand dollars before absconding to Hong Kong
and Paris.

As for Caleb Lyon, after an eleven-month absence, he unexpectedly returned in 1865 to finish his term. To his credit, he did try to curb settlers'
attacks on Indians, and he negotiated what he regarded as an important
treaty with the Shoshones (but the Senate never got around to ratifying it).
His Indian policy, however, made Lyon even less popular with white residents: J. S. Reynolds of the *Idaho Statesman* warned that nothing less than
a "military escort could preserve him from violence, if not from death."[2]

When he left for good in 1866, Lyon was suspected of having stolen forty-
six thousand dollars in Indian funds that he was responsible for distributing
as Idaho's superintendent of Indian affairs. He lamely claimed that he had
tried to return the money to Washington but, while en route on a sleeping
car, a thief had stolen it from under his pillow. Some of Lyon's successors
contributed additional chapters to this tale of incompetence.

During the twenty-seven years of the territorial era, sixteen men were
appointed and confirmed as Idaho's governor. Four of them failed to take
office, and six remained in the territory less than a year—and some only a
few days. Thomas Bennett, who was governor from November 1, 1871, until
December 4, 1875, was absent twenty-three months of his term. Only eight
men served a year or more. Because governors were so frequently absent,
territorial secretaries served as acting governors during eight of the twenty-
seven years. Such lengthy absences did not decrease significantly until 1885
when an Idaho resident, Edward Augustus Stevenson, was appointed
governor.

The territorial phase of government and politics lasted nearly three decades and had few redeeming features. Idaho seemed forever to totter on the
brink of insolvency or administrative incompetence, and larcenous carpetbag
governors helped themselves to public funds. But that was only part of the
problem. Among the other types of crime that plagued early Idaho were
jumping good claims, salting poor claims, passing bogus gold, crooked
games of chance, theft, and gunplay resulting in mayhem.

14. The law comes to the mining frontier. Hawley and Puckett's law office in the camp of Thunder Mountain around 1900. Courtesy Idaho State Historical Society, 60–73.30.

Law and Disorder

Perhaps because of its sprawling size and the uncertain nature of its government, early Idaho territory was beset by occasional outbursts of violence. Most shocking of these was the grisly murder of Lloyd Magruder in 1863 on the Nez Perce Trail that connected Lewiston and the Virginia City diggings beyond the Bitterroots. Hill Beachy, a friend of Magruder, tracked the four highwaymen and had them returned from California to Idaho. After a short trial, three of the four men were hanged, though not before Idaho discovered that it actually had no criminal law.

In 1863, when Congress established Idaho, federal lawmakers failed to provide for a criminal or civil code. And because the new territory encompassed lands taken from the jurisdictions of Washington, Dakota, Utah, and Nebraska, it was not sufficient simply to consider that the laws of Washington still applied, as some people did. In 1866 the territorial supreme court freed two convicted murderers, declaring that Idaho had had no criminal law from March 4, 1863, until January 4, 1864, the date when the territory's original laws were adopted. Despite this technicality, few if any Idahoans regret-

ted the "illegal" hanging of the murderers of Lloyd Magruder. But this case did not end early Idaho's law-and-order difficulties.

Legal minds concluded that the 1864 code was so poorly drawn that a new one was needed. The legislature of 1866 obliged, but after Horace Gilson stole all the money that Congress had appropriated to run Idaho's government, the territory could not pay the printer and he refused to release the volumes. Idaho's civil and criminal code thus remained in San Francisco for three more years, during which time Idaho lawyers and courts were forced to rely on less than satisfactory newspaper copies of the laws.

Vigilance committees arose to deal with the worst troublemakers. But once local and territorial laws became effective, "popular tribunals" tended to disappear, though vigilantism reappeared in the mid-1880s when five Chinese were hanged for murder near Pierce. From 1863 to 1896 only eleven men were legally hanged in Idaho for murder, though it is estimated that some 250 murders were committed during those years. Many lawbreakers were never caught; others went to prison for a short time and were pardoned.

Idaho's early jails were about as primitive as its laws. One local observer noted that the prison in early Shoshone consisted of nothing more than a hole in the ground with a guard patrolling the rim. All criminals were lodged in county jails. Then the federal government provided Idaho forty thousand dollars to build a territorial prison, which opened two miles east of Boise in

15. The tragic results of a saloon shoot-out in the mining community of Gem about 1899. Courtesy Eastern Washington State Historical Society, L86–962.

16. Three guards and a cell block in the old Idaho State Penitentiary, probably in the early twentieth century. Courtesy Idaho State Historical Society, 70–57.17.

1872. Inmates did most of the work of quarrying stone and building the walls. Federal officials turned the Boise prison over to Idaho when it became a state. The penitentiary operated until 1974 and is now open to the public as a museum maintained by the Idaho State Historical Society.

To Fight No More Forever: Renewed Conflict

The years of the fur trade saw a few minor conflicts between Euro-Americans and Indians but no sustained warfare. That changed with the Whitman massacre of 1847, after which the Pacific Northwest endured three decades of conflict between whites and Indians.

During the 1850s warfare erupted on the Rogue River of southern Oregon, in eastern Washington, and in the Seattle area. In the first of several struggles that involved the Indians of future Idaho, the Coeur d'Alenes joined with other tribes of the Columbia plateau to battle the United States Army in 1858. In retaliation Colonel George Wright marched a troop of 570 soldiers through their land and destroyed their stores of food and hundreds of their horses.

An exceptionally vicious struggle took place in southeastern Idaho in January 1863. In the "Battle" of Bear River, Colonel Patrick E. Connor and California volunteers sent to protect settlers at Franklin virtually annihilated a band of Shoshone men, women, and children. During the wild struggle, the California force suffered 22 deaths; Connor's official tally listed 224 Indian casualties. Utah citizens who visited the battlefield the next day counted 368 slain Indians, including almost 90 women and children. That ranks as one of the worst slaughters of Indians in the American West.

Far better known, despite fewer casualties, is the so-called Nez Perce War of 1877. In 1855 the Nez Perces had acceded to one of Isaac Stevens's treaties confining them to a large reservation. But in 1863, after trespassing whites discovered gold within its boundaries, the federal government renegotiated with the Indians and reduced the 7.7 million–acre reservation to about one-tenth that size. Some Indian leaders consented and accepted the land bordering the Clearwater River east of Lewiston. About one-third of the Nez Perces (the nontreaty group) disavowed the agreement. They claimed not to be bound by the 1863 treaty, although federal agents maintained that a majority of leaders had spoken for the entire tribe. In any case, the nontreaty Indians continued to make their homes elsewhere. White Bird's band of Nez Perces remained on the lower Salmon River south of the new reservation, and Chief Joseph's people lived west of the Snake River in Oregon's majestic Wallowa Valley.

Hin-mah-too-yah-lat-kekht ("Thunder Traveling to Loftier Mountain Heights"), young Chief Joseph, inherited his father's leadership role in 1871. Young Joseph insisted from the first that his four hundred people were not bound by the treaty of 1863 because his father had never signed it. The federal government initially agreed, and in 1873 President Grant ordered part of the Wallowa Valley set aside as a reservation. But after protests from land-hungry whites, the government changed its mind and two years later insisted that Joseph and his people move to the Clearwater reservation. Since the valley was opened to white settlement at the same time, the nontreaty Nez Perces appeared to have little choice but to obey the government's ultimatum.

In mid-May 1877, General Oliver O. Howard gave Joseph's band thirty

17. Chief Joseph, made famous by the "war" of 1877. Courtesy Historical Photograph Collections, Washington State University Libraries, 70–0149.

days to leave the valley, to cross Hells Canyon and the Snake and Salmon rivers dangerously swollen by spring runoff, and to settle on the reservation. The Nez Perces began relocating when on June 13 and 14 three young warriors, including one whose father had been murdered by a local white man, killed four settlers known for their hostility to Indians. War inevitably followed.

The events of mid-1877 cannot actually be described as warfare. Eight hundred Indian men, women, and children, with a herd of more than two thousand horses, made a desperate flight across the Bitterroot Mountains to the plains of Montana where they hoped to find safety among their friends the Crows. Failing that they planned to seek sanctuary in Canada. Theirs was less a retreat than a flight to safety, a tragic odyssey in which they were pursued by Howard and his soldiers. Curiously, the man who commanded the army's Department of the Columbia was a one-armed Civil War hero, a friend of freed blacks, and a man known as the Christian or praying general because he delivered sermons to the garrisons he inspected.

At the Battle of the Big Hole River, August 9 and 10, the Nez Perces lost thirty warriors and forty other men, women, and children. The army suffered twenty-nine men killed and forty wounded. The desperate Indians headed south, winding through Yellowstone Park where their presence frightened and scattered tourists, and then north toward the international border.

On September 30 in the Bear Paw Mountains just forty miles short of their goal, the Nez Perces were overtaken by Colonel Nelson Miles and 383 troopers from Fort Keogh. The cavalrymen, who were still smarting from the Custer disaster the previous year, attacked almost immediately. In the ensuing battle, 53 officers and enlisted men were killed or wounded, while the Indians lost 22 men, women, and children. At times the soldiers seemed dazed by the Indian defenders, but after a day of intense fighting followed by five days of siege in bitter cold weather, the army prevailed. Many Indians fled across country in hope of still reaching Canada. Some made it, but others died of exposure or hunger or were murdered by Indians of other tribes.

Joseph surrendered on October 4. In words recorded by Howard's aide, he concluded a brief speech with the now famous promise, "Hear me, my chiefs! I am tired. My heart is sick and sad. From where the sun now stands I will fight no more forever." After fifteen hundred miles and eighteen engagements, including four major battles, the flight was over. In the end a total of 418 Nez Perces were taken captive: 87 men, 184 women, and 147 children.

The prisoners were exiled to Oklahoma and not allowed to return to the Pacific Northwest until 1885. Then the trip home was not a joyous one. Increasing tensions marked the seven-day journey by rail: at Pocatello a military escort had to be secured before the train could proceed on across Idaho. Because of continuing ill will in the Clearwater Valley, Joseph and a band of 150 followers settled on the Colville reservation in north-central Washington, where Joseph died in 1904 and was buried. The conflict of 1877 cost the federal government $930,000 and the lives of approximately 180 whites, mostly soldiers, and 120 Indians—65 men and 55 women and children—and it drastically curtailed the freedom of the Nez Perces. Joseph was more politician than military leader, but when whites glorified his military genius, their difficulties in capturing him seemed more plausible.

Friction with settlers provoked an uprising of Bannocks and Paiutes in southern Idaho in 1878. After several engagements, General Howard and his troops drove the fugitives back onto their reservation. A year later the last resisters, a few Shoshone families known to whites as Sheepeaters because they ate mountain sheep, surrendered to Howard's persistent troops and were moved onto the Fort Hall Reservation. The government soon diminished the size of the reservation by three-fourths when it opened the best land to white settlement. The newcomers built a town they named for the Shoshone leader, Pocatello. If nothing else, whites could always afford to be generous in the names they gave their settlements.

Pocatello was destined to become one of Idaho's major population centers, but not because of any connection with the Indian wars. The town would be the hub of an expanding network of railroads. Not long after Idaho experienced the last of its Indian conflicts, a new era dawned as railroads commenced writing their signatures in steel across the old frontier.

CHAPTER 7

While the early settlers in Idaho had a hard struggle to get people to come and help develop the resources of the country owing mainly to her isolated location, being so far from railroad and water transportation, at last the railroads came, then the people came and soon after the development of the many natural resources commenced in earnest. —from John Hailey, *The History of Idaho* (1910)

Ties That Bind
Forging Early Transportation and Communication Links

Idaho's early settlers endured a degree of isolation unimaginable today. They were not only remote from the nation's economic and population centers but also isolated within their own borders. Rugged terrain and distance between settlements hindered efforts to improve territorial communication and transportation. Messages, people, and goods moved no faster than the speed of a horse or canoe.

Even after completion of the nation's first transcontinental railroad at Promontory, Utah, in 1869, tracks did not extend beyond the southeastern corner of Idaho until the 1880s. Until then, merchandise crossed the southern part of the territory by stagecoach and freight wagon from Central Pacific Railroad stations at Kelton, Utah, or Winnemucca, Nevada. In the panhandle, steamboats brought goods from Portland to Lewiston where freight wagons and packtrains distributed them to interior settlements.

There was neither incentive nor money to improve transportation and communication links during the 1870s when Idaho's economy and population growth were sluggish, but a dramatic change occurred during the early 1880s. Important new discoveries of gold and silver in the Wood River valley of south-central Idaho and the Coeur d'Alene River valley in the panhandle revived both the mining industry and the economy. By the end of the decade, miles of new railway line had significantly reduced the cost of transporting passengers and freight. With the coming of railroads, heavy machinery could be brought in to tackle ever bigger mining jobs, and lower grade ores could

18. A train of freight wagons connected Silver City to the outside world in the 1890s. Courtesy Idaho State Historical Society, 76–138.96.

be moved out profitably to distant markets. The trains also brought settlers and tourists and thereby further stimulated Idaho's economic and population growth.

The Stagecoach and Packtrain Era

How much it once meant all over Idaho to hear the cry, "Stage!" In isolated camps and villages the one great event of the day was the arrival of the stage with its load of mail and passengers. Like the locomotive engineer of a later era, the stage driver was a popular and respected man.

The earliest form of transportation to Idaho's booming mining camps was "Foot and Walker's Transportation Line," as some people jokingly called the long hike overland. Next came saddle trains, freight wagons, and then stage-coaches. Steamboats brought gold seekers up the Columbia River as far as Umatilla and Wallula, jumping-off points for the interior camps, and if the

Snake River was high enough, all the way to Lewiston, trail head for the northern mines. Wells Fargo opened its first express office in Lewiston in the summer of 1861.

Pack- and saddle trains brought passengers and freight into the Boise Basin from steamboat landings on the Columbia River. One train might include as many as one hundred animals, each carrying 250 to 400 pounds of freight. It took thirteen days to cover the three hundred miles from Umatilla to Boise City, which soon became the transportation hub of southern Idaho. Ten to twelve packtrains arrived in Boise each day during the summer months, along with half that number of wagons, each loaded with merchandise. Some gold seekers, however, simply strapped packs to their backs and hit the trail.

Mail service began in 1864 with an overland stage that linked Salt Lake City and Boise City, from where a series of wagon roads fanned out to Idaho City, Walla Walla, and Umatilla. Some stage lines that utilized the new roads featured fancy Concord coaches that carried nine to sixteen passengers and were pulled by four to six horses.

Ben Holladay, popularly known as the Stagecoach King because he operated the West's largest network of lines, secured a contract in mid-1864 to carry the United States mail from Salt Lake City across southern Idaho to The Dalles in Oregon. This change brought triweekly federal mail service to the Boise Basin and put the pony express out of business. The coaches on Holladay's Overland Stage line regularly covered the distance from Salt Lake City to Boise in four days, and travel time was further reduced when John Hailey inaugurated a stage line from Kelton to Boise, covering a distance of 232 miles in forty-two hours. Wells Fargo acquired Holladay's stage empire in 1866.

Express companies like Wells Fargo often had a messenger accompany the stage to guard large shipments of gold and silver. Armed with a six-shooter or sawed-off shotgun, he rode atop the coach with the driver. One of Idaho's last stagecoach robberies took place in 1884 on the Kelton-to-Boise line between Hailey and Albion.

After the coming of the railroad in the 1880s, there were fewer holdups, and road agents turned to cattle rustling, a more lucrative activity for a time on the Snake River plain. Stagecoaches and pack animals did not disappear entirely, however, even after a network of railway lines extended into many parts of Idaho. They continued to serve remote communities until the early 1930s when motorized transportation became common.

Travel by stage was never without its trials. Early roads were dirt, and

The Language of Freighters

Freighters who drove mules were called mule skinners, and those who used ox teams were bullwhackers. Carrie Strahorn, who accompanied her husband on numerous journeys across Idaho, left this account of their colorful language:

"A freighter is not necessarily a bad man; he is often generous to a fault, but his language will not bear repeating here. . . . A freighter accumulates a vocabulary that would start almost any balky horse. His oaths pour through his lips like water down a hill. With every crack of the whip as it cuts into the sage-brush, or into the flank of the leader, or the wheelhorse, there is an accompaniment of profanity long, loud, and strong that dies away in mutterings of the same hot stuff, until Rock, or Pete, or Jim, lags a bit behind the other sturdy pullers, then he begins anew his oration of oaths as he snaps the whip on the ears or haunches of the delinquent animal."

—Carrie Adell Strahorn, *Fifteen Thousand Miles by Stage* (1911), 2:209–10.

rain turned them to mud. Passengers might be required to walk through a knee-deep quagmire to lighten the load, or they might have to push the coach until a better stretch of road could be reached. In dry weather the dust engulfed passengers. The alkali made their skin sore and rough and burned their eyes and noses. Perhaps even more alarming were the roads that wound down steep hillsides, such as those from Winchester into Culdesac and from the Palouse prairie into Lewiston. Winter weather so increased the problems of transportation that many stage lines simply quit running.

Stages made periodic stops at stations to change drivers and give passengers a chance to eat. Carrie Strahorn recalled a stage station on the Snake River plain where over the door hung this sign: "Hotel de Starvation, 1,000 miles from hay and grain, seventy miles from wood, fifteen miles from water, but only twelve inches from hell."[1] Unmarried men usually kept these houses. A typical meal of bread, beans, bacon, and black coffee cost one dollar.

For most of Idaho, the only alternative to the stagecoach was travel by horseback or by foot. A few fortunate places had the option of water transportation.

Steamboats 'round the Bend

Idaho is blessed with numerous rivers, but steamboats were unable to navigate them except for relatively short distances. And yet this form of transportation still played an important role in early Idaho, and in several places it complemented travel by stagecoach and packtrain.

How different the history of Idaho might have been had the Snake River been navigable through Hells Canyon and thus formed a water highway from

19. The *Spokane* and *Lewiston* were two of the steamboats that provided transportation up the Snake River to Lewiston. Courtesy Spokane Public Library.

Boise to Lewiston. The fur trader Donald Mackenzie explored Hells Canyon in 1819 when he led one of the Snake brigades. He even ascended the river in a barge manned by six French-Canadian voyageurs, but his journey did not indicate that the river could ever be a transportation artery. Forty years later, the first steamboats appeared on the waters of the inland Northwest and probed up the Snake as far as Lewiston and even beyond, but it was obvious that they could navigate only a few stretches of Idaho's most important waterway.

The first steamboat to ply Idaho waters was the *Colonel Wright*, which brought a load of gold seekers to Lewiston in 1861. Soon the crush of passengers and freight bound for the mines was so great that two additional boats had to be built. In the early years it required three separate steamboats to climb the Columbia and Snake rivers from Portland to Lewiston. Two short railways portaged passengers and freight around rapids and waterfalls, but not until completion of The Dalles–Celilo Canal in 1915 could the river journey from Portland to Lewiston be made without interruption.

During the mining boom in the Boise Basin, the Oregon Steam Navigation

Company of Portland constructed a steamboat at old Fort Boise in the hope of intercepting traffic bound from Portland and Salt Lake City to the Idaho diggings. When the craft took shape during the winter of 1865–66, all of its fittings and hardware had to be hauled overland from the Columbia River.

The 120-foot sternwheeler christened *Shoshone* began service on May 16, 1866, but was immediately beset by lack of cargo and fuel. Unfortunately for the Oregon Steam Navigation Company, the middle Snake River proved navigable only from Olds Ferry to a point near the mouth of the Bruneau River, a distance of about two hundred miles and well short of the main road from Salt Lake City to the Boise Basin. Worse still, there were simply too few trees along the route to fuel the craft.

The landlocked *Shoshone* languished until 1869 when a salvage plan was worked out: a river captain and a skeleton crew would ease the steamboat into the current of the Snake River and make the wild journey through Hells Canyon. But scarcely had they reached the canyon's churning waters before the captain and crew abandoned the project.

Another captain and more boatmen had to be hired to finish the journey the following year. Early in the trip the steamboat hit a rock that tore away its nameplate, which floated downstream; when it washed ashore at Umatilla, it seemed to offer positive evidence that the luckless vessel had been battered to bits. Onlookers were thus quite surprised when the *Shoshone* steamed into Lewiston in "a badly demolished condition" but still serviceable.[2]

A copper-mining boom in the Seven Devils Mountains east of Hells Canyon caused a second steamboat, the *Norma*, to be launched on the middle Snake River in 1891, but after a frustrating four-year attempt to capitalize on the mining trade, it too shot the rapids to pursue a more profitable future elsewhere. No steamboat ever completed the journey upriver through Hells Canyon.

A large fleet of steamboats once operated on Lake Coeur d'Alene and the St. Joe River. The vessels appeared on the lake with the 1884 mining rush and regularly hauled passengers and freight up the Coeur d'Alene River as far as the landing at the old Cataldo mission. From there, freight continued up the river's north fork in dugouts and bateaux. The first steamer on the Kootenai River dates from the 1880s and connected Bonners Ferry with Nelson, British Columbia. A small number of steamboats also operated at intervals on Lake Pend Oreille, beginning with the *Mary Moody* in 1866.[3] Steamboats carried freight and later tourists on Hayden Lake.

The heyday of the steamboat on Idaho waters lasted from the 1880s until the late 1920s, when river traffic declined as a result of rail and highway competition. In the mid-1970s, however, a series of new dams and locks rejuvenated the Snake River as a water highway from Lewiston to the sea.

Empire Builders: The Railroads

In the East, railroad lines connected preexisting population centers and markets, but western lines had to extend across hundreds of miles of rugged and lightly populated country. They had to generate passenger and freight revenue by running from nowhere in particular to nowhere at all. Only by creating new towns and markets and fostering the development of countless acres of farm and timberland could the railroads of the West survive. In this way they also provided the basis for the modern Idaho economy.

The whistle of a railway locomotive first echoed through the canyons of Idaho in 1874. That year the Utah Northern hesitatingly extended a narrow-gauge line north from the transcontinental railroad connection at Ogden across the boundary into Franklin. Then work stopped. After corporate reorganization, the Utah *and* Northern tracks headed north again across the upper Snake River plain to reach the booming mines of Butte, Montana, in 1881.

As important as Idaho's initial railway line was, it had no impact on most of the territory, which remained a remote and sparsely settled hinterland until two new transcontinental railroads finally reached across the Rocky Mountains to tap the riches of the far Northwest. The Northern Pacific inaugurated service from St. Paul to Tacoma in September 1883, but because its tracks traversed only the far northern panhandle, the Northern Pacific (now part of Burlington Northern) affected Idaho much less than the Oregon Short Line, which began running trains across southern Idaho in late 1884.[4]

The Oregon Short Line added hundreds of miles of new track to the expanding network of lines already owned or controlled by the Union Pacific. True to its name, the Oregon Short Line provided a shortcut from Omaha to Portland (by eliminating the need to go by way of San Francisco) and gave the Union Pacific an outlet to the Pacific Ocean. Its tracks stretched across southern Idaho from Montpelier to Weiser and, following acquisition of the Utah and Northern in 1878, reached north into Montana and south into Utah from the new crossroads community of Pocatello. A seventy-mile-long branch line extended north from Shoshone into the booming Wood River mines and not only tapped a new source of revenue but also enabled the railroad baron Jay Gould, head of the Oregon Short Line, and other affluent Americans to spend summer holidays in the Wood River valley. Hailey Hot Springs may well have been Idaho's first real summer resort.

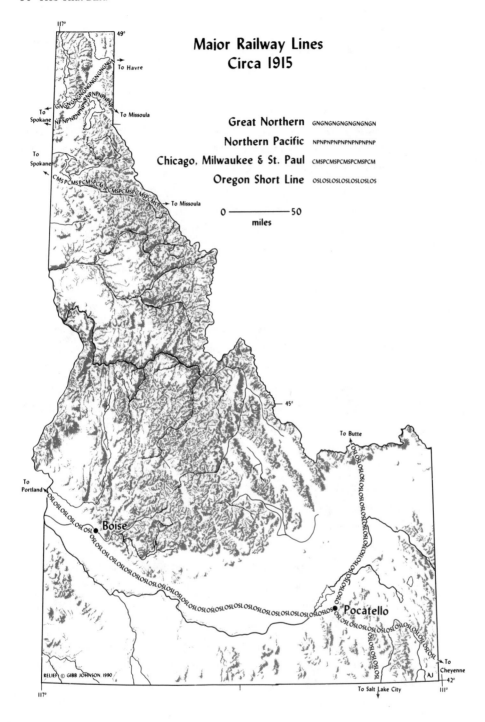

Major Railway Lines
Circa 1915

Great Northern GNGNGNGNGNGNGNGN
Northern Pacific NPNPNPNPNPNPNPNP
Chicago, Milwaukee & St. Paul CMSPCMSPCMSPCMSPCM
Oregon Short Line OSLOSLOSLOSLOSLOSLOS

0 ———————— 50
miles

20. "When you want a Pointer." A turn-of-the-century map advertising the route of the Northern Pacific Railway. Courtesy Spokane Public Library.

The most obvious benefit that railroads conferred was the conquest of distance: a journey from Omaha to Portland that once required six months on the Oregon Trail could now commence on Monday and terminate by Friday, and a passenger with money could even enjoy the luxury of a sleeping car. Within a year of its completion, the Oregon Short Line shipped millions of dollars' worth of gold bullion, livestock, and wool from Idaho to distant markets.

The tracks of two additional transcontinental lines eventually threaded their way through the canyons of northern Idaho—the Great Northern, completed in 1893, and the Chicago, Milwaukee, and St. Paul (or Milwaukee Road, as it was later known), completed in 1909. The Milwaukee Road sent 98 miles of tracks snaking over the Bitterroot Range and down the St. Joe Valley, and for fifty years (1911–61) it operated a luxury passenger train from Seattle to Chicago along this scenic corridor. In 1916 the railroad even electrified its line from Avery, a division point in the Bitterroots, to Harlowton, Montana, a total of 440 miles. Experts considered this state-of-the-art system a model worthy of emulation by railroads in other parts of the world.

In addition to linking the Gem State to the rest of the United States, railroads thrust out a growing number of branch lines to reach remote commu-

The President as Railroad Engineer

President Warren G. Harding took the throttle of the Milwaukee Road's big Baldwin-Westinghouse electric locomotive piloting his special train down the west slopes of the Bitterroots to Avery on July 2, 1923. Although the president died suddenly a few weeks later, he had realized a boyhood dream. Bubbling with enthusiasm, he described the fifteen-mile descent as "the most delightful ride I have ever known in my life."

"He acted just like a kid," reported Asahel Curtis, who was the official photographer for the occasion. The railroad, delighted by the free publicity, printed Harding's remarks in a promotional brochure, one of many that the company issued to advertise the technological and scenic wonders of its electrified line across Montana and Idaho.

For years the Milwaukee Road maintained a commemorative plaque on the side of the Harding locomotive.

nities within Idaho. Most such lines dead-ended at mountain barriers or impassable canyons, and none ever formed a through route from north to south. A hundred-mile gap from New Meadows to Grangeville was never closed. The legislature of 1915 and the Public Utilities Commission recommended closing the section by building a line north from New Meadows by way of the Salmon and Snake rivers to Lewiston, but this was never done.

In 1918, shortly after the mileage of the nation's railway network peaked, there were 2,841 miles of line in Idaho, of which 1,658 belonged to the Oregon Short Line and 231 to the Northern Pacific, which ranked a distant second. In addition to the four transcontinentals, several short lines served Idaho communities. It is difficult to generalize about all these small railroad companies that once linked mining and sawmill towns and farm centers to metropolitan corridors formed by the main lines, but the Pacific and Idaho Northern, which ran from Weiser to New Meadows, was perhaps typical. The Pacific and Idaho Northern, like the Idaho and Washington Northern and a dozen or so similar lines, was eventually acquired by one of the transcontinental giants.

The Gilmore and Pittsburgh Railroad and the Intermountain Railway were two of the lines that simply faded away in the face of motor competition. The trains of the Intermountain quit running in 1934 and those of the Gilmore and Pittsburgh in 1940; some of the abandoned right-of-way of both lines was used for new state highways. Also abandoned was the seventeen-mile line that the United States Reclamation Service once operated from Barber to Arrowrock Dam. The Spokane International, now a part of the Union Pacific system, was unusual among Idaho short lines in that, for a few years prior to the First World War, it participated in the joint operation of a luxury passenger train that ran from St. Paul to Portland by way of Canada and the Idaho panhandle.

Until the dawn of the automobile age and the rise of the big oil companies, few forms of corporate enterprise had more power or influence on political and economic life than railroads had in their heyday. When tracks first reached an Idaho community, it was invariably a time for celebration and predictions of a great future. The *Idaho County Free Press* of Grangeville summed up the prevailing sentiment in 1906 when it predicted that the coming of the Camas Prairie line would "add thousands of people and millions in value to the area and become one of the main factors in its growth and progress." But for towns passed by, the consequences could be fatal.

In almost every county in the state may be found remnants of towns, perhaps but a single ruined shack, about which have centered at one time the business energy and social life of a pioneer community. The railroad eventually came through the country, left the village a few miles to the right or left, the business houses and the homes moved to the railroad, and the shack alone is left as a reminder of the townsite project of the pioneer.[5]

Railroads opened new and distant markets for the products of Idaho's forests, fields, and mines and made the acquisition of modern fashions and technology as easy as thumbing through a catalog and ordering a new dress or buggy or cream separator sent out from Chicago by train. Railroad stations functioned as important community centers. In many a small town, the daily arrival of the train was a time for people to gather at the station, scrutinize the new faces, and pick up mail and packages. Especially in larger cities, the railroad station was a matter of community pride. It functioned as a civic showplace and gateway to the other destinations along the metropolitan corridor.

All four of Idaho's transcontinental railroads were active promoters of the state's resources. Especially after the advent of large-scale irrigation and reclamation on the Snake River plain, the Oregon Short Line encouraged population growth by spawning a network of feeder lines and bringing in trainloads of emigrants. Railroads also stimulated tourism and promoted vacations in national parks and forests. During the mid-1930s the Union Pacific built a new resort complex called Sun Valley in the mountains of southern Idaho, a model for similar winter sports facilities in the West.

For all the benefits they conferred on Idaho, railroads also created new forms of dependency. Their rates often determined which industries or com-

21. When main-line passenger train service finally reached Boise in 1925, it was cause for a community celebration. Courtesy Oregon Historical Society, 32439.

modities would prosper and which would be unable to compete in distant markets. Their timetables fixed the times of the local passenger train, which for most communities was limited to one a day each way. In fact, one reason why the private automobile later became so popular is that it freed travelers from the tyranny of the timetable.

From Telegraph to Telephone

Complementing advances in transportation were innovations in communications. Although a telegraph line was strung across southeastern Idaho from Salt Lake City to Virginia City as early as 1866, the invention had little impact on Idaho until 1869, when the Deseret Telegraph Company linked Franklin with Salt Lake City. A telegraph line reached north from Winnemucca to Silver City in 1874 and to Boise the following year. By linking the territorial capital to a transcontinental line, the telegraph provided the latest news from the East "by lightning." During the next decade telegraph lines, like railroads, connected many of Idaho's scattered communities to large and distant population centers.

Telephone lines appeared in Hailey in September 1883, only seven years after Alexander Graham Bell gave his first public demonstration of the device at the Philadelphia world's fair. Idaho's first phone system served twenty-five subscribers. Its operator was twelve-year-old Nathan Kingsbury, who went on to become a vice-president of the communications giant, American Telephone and Telegraph. In those early days operators often provided weather reports and other personal services for subscribers.

Three months after Hailey, telephone service began in Boise. At the time of statehood approximately five hundred people belonged to telephone systems. The early systems were all local operations, consisting of lines strung to connect the homes of subscribers and often maintained by a farmer or merchant between regular chores. The Gem State's first long-distance line connected Boise and Caldwell, but not until 1915 did a transcontinental link offer Idaho telephone subscribers nationwide service.

With the advent of transcontinental railroads and telegraph and telephone lines, Idaho moved inexorably into the postfrontier world of industrialism and urban growth. From the 1880s until the First World War, two generations of men and women would transform the old frontier by building cities and towns, railroad networks, and irrigation systems.

There is scarcely any reputable vocation wherein the same capital and good management which insures success in Eastern communities will not yield greater returns here. Now, above all other periods, is the time to put money into commercial ventures, real estate, mines or live stock, as the heavy immigration will enhance the value of such property to a degree not now possible to comprehend.—from a Union Pacific Railroad pamphlet titled *Idaho: A Complete and Comprehensive Description* (1891)

Nurturing a New Economy

Well before their first face-to-face contacts with Euro-Americans, the Indians of future Idaho had established elaborate trade networks based on natural resources like fish and roots. With the coming of whites, the fur trade became a global business. Remote Rocky Mountain streams and lakes functioned as part of a complex economic network dominated by large cities in Europe and North America.

Superseding the trade in furs and skins was mining. Unfortunately, the decade-long boom that began on Orofino Creek in 1860 was followed by the dull years of the 1870s when the first wave of gold seekers receded and left behind only a residue of non-Indian settlers. Yet even as mining communities declined or were abandoned, farmers and stock raisers continued their slow but steady advance into Idaho's watered valleys and across its sagebrush-covered plains. Agriculture, however, proved no more immune to boom-and-bust cycles than mining or furs.

During the fur trade era, London, Montreal, and St. Louis supplied much of the capital used to exploit Idaho's natural resources. In later years Portland, San Francisco, and St. Paul played similar roles in developing timber and mineral wealth, although in each instance Idaho itself remained only a colonial hinterland. In fact, for most of its history Idaho supplied raw materials to distant markets that controlled its economic health. Dependency gave life in the Gem State a peculiar characteristic: natural resource–based economies typically ride the roller coaster of boom-and-bust. From early territorial years

22. The once booming mining town of Pierce as it appeared in the late nineteenth century. Courtesy Idaho State Historical Society, 548-B.

to the present, one of Idaho's most intractable problems has been economic instability.

All That Glitters: Mining Booms Again

After the excitement of the 1860s, Idaho's mining industry experienced a long and disappointing slump. The decade of the 1870s passed without any significant new finds. But boom times returned in 1880 with a lead-silver rush to the Wood River valley that was reminiscent of the Boise Basin excitement twenty years earlier. The Wood River boom was only the beginning of a new era of prosperity. When prospectors discovered yet another bonanza on the north fork of the Coeur d'Alene River in 1883, they set off one of the biggest stampedes in all Idaho history.

During the heyday of the Wood River mines, Hailey boasted the finest hotel in Idaho Territory, the most expensive courthouse, three daily and two weekly newspapers, an ironworks, a smelter, several sawmills, and two hospitals (not to mention eighteen licensed saloons). Telegraph service came with the railroad in 1883. That year Hailey acquired Idaho's first electric lights and its first phone service. Then came the bust and a long sleep that

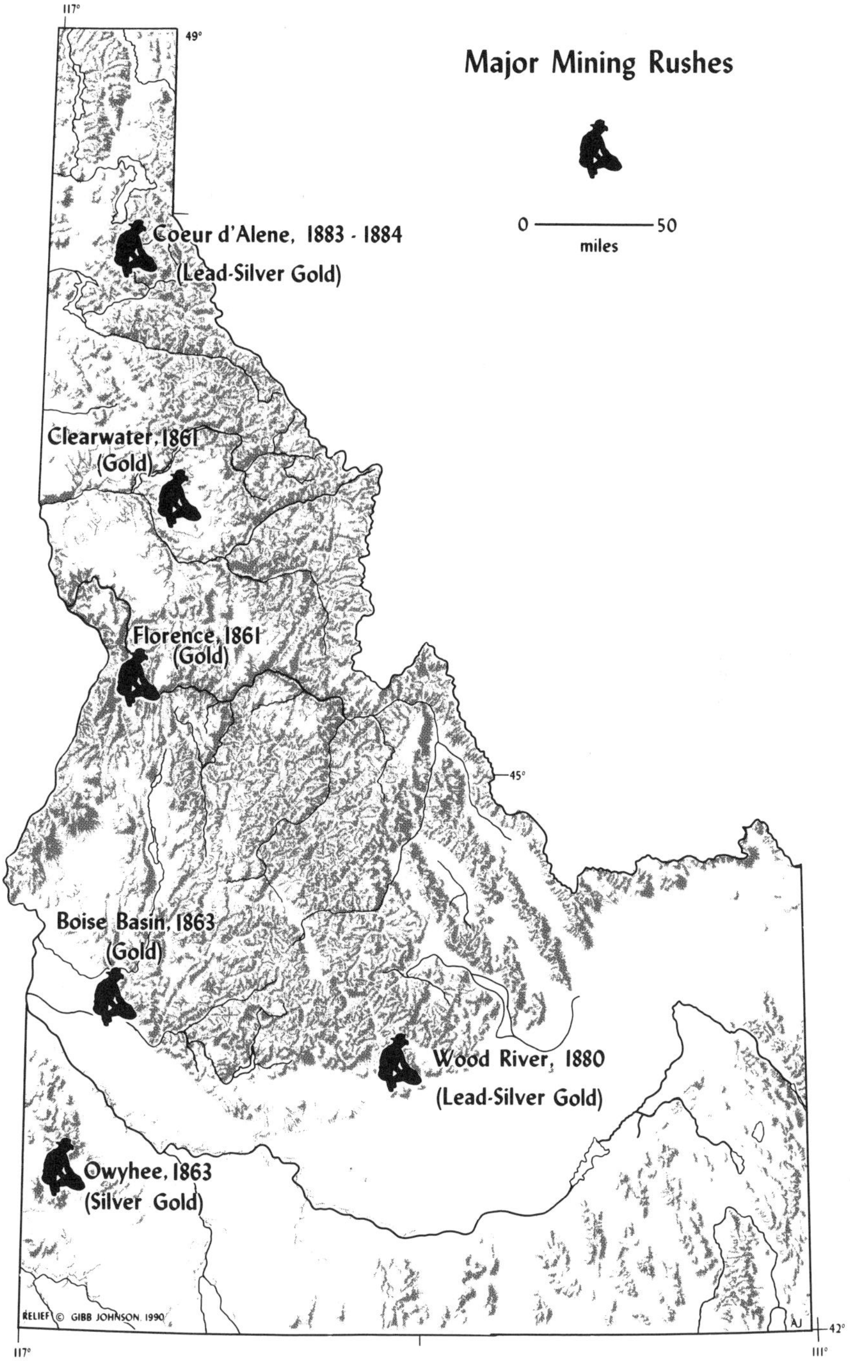

Major Mining Rushes

0 ——————— 50
miles

Coeur d'Alene, 1883 - 1884
(Lead-Silver Gold)

Clearwater, 1861
(Gold)

Florence, 1861
(Gold)

—45°

Boise Basin, 1863
(Gold)

Wood River, 1880
(Lead-Silver Gold)

Owyhee, 1863
(Silver Gold)

RELIEF © GIBB JOHNSON 1990

Gold and Silver Days

Lode mining of silver in Idaho dates
from 1863 with the opening of the country around Silver City. The white metal
was located in formations quite unlike
the placer deposits found in streams and
rivers. In the latter, gold occurred in
pure (native) state and represented
eroded parts of lode or vein deposits.
To find it, the prospector needed only
the simplest of tools: a pick, a pan, and
a shovel. He partially filled his pan
with pay dirt, added water, then shook
the pan with a swirling motion calcu-
lated to separate the heavy gold from the
lighter sand. Panning, however, was
limited to prospecting and clean-up
work; sluices and rockers were used for
production.

More expensive methods of surface
mining required water cannons called
monitors. Another example of advanced
mining technology was the dredge, essentially a floating sluice box equipped
with a digging apparatus. It was first introduced in the late nineteenth century.

More than fifty dredges once operated in
Idaho; only two remain today. The largest and best preserved is now a museum
on the Yankee Fork in the south-central
part of the state.

Although gold often lay underground,
either in its native state or in close association with other elements, in most districts silver occurred only in combination with other elements such as lead
and zinc. Extracting underground deposits was much more difficult than capturing surface metals. Lode or hard-rock
mining, which typically involved tunnel-
ing into the earth and hauling out gold-
or silver-bearing rock by the ton to re-
fine a few ounces of precious metal, required complex technology and large
amounts of capital. Hand drilling and
blasting with black powder was slow, la-
borious, and dangerous. Although innovations like dynamite and the pneumatic
drill made work easier, they also posed
serious health hazards. Early versions of
the pneumatic drill spewed out such
thick clouds of silicosis-causing dust that
they were aptly termed widow-makers.

lasted until the Sun Valley resort with its new bonanza—tourism—came to the Wood River valley in the late 1930s.

The Coeur d'Alene stampede occurred during the winter and spring of 1883–84 when five thousand gold seekers scrambled to reach the diggings. Buoyed by the hope of sudden riches, they braved snowdrifts twenty feet deep in the passes during January, February, and March. They used tobog-gans and snowshoes, the only transportation available until the snow melted in April.

Miners at first used relatively simple and inexpensive placer methods to recover the gold. Many of those who staked claims were Palouse farmers who panned for the yellow metal after the harvest. But by the time Noah Kellogg, an unemployed carpenter, discovered silver on the south fork of the Coeur d'Alene River in 1885, the character of the rush had already begun to change dramatically.

Ownership of Kellogg's Bunker Hill and Sullivan Mine soon passed into the hands of investors from outside Idaho. Simeon G. Reed of Portland, Oregon, purchased the property in 1887, then sold out in 1892 to other investors, notably "the Harvester King," Cyrus McCormick of Chicago. Recovery of silver involved lode or hard-rock mining, a complex and expensive technology. Only large sums of money could develop mines, build milling and smelting facilities, and extend railway lines.

One of Idaho's silver mines, the Sunshine, near Kellogg, would ultimately yield more of the white metal than all the properties in Nevada's famed Comstock Lode.[1] When in 1985 the billionth ounce of silver was mined in the Coeur d'Alenes, the district claimed the largest recorded silver production in the world.

Mining silver required a large labor force that soon made Coeur d'Alene towns look like industrial centers in Pennsylvania and West Virginia. Spokane, the main supply point for the mines, became the district's dominant urban center. Strengthening this relationship was a combination of boat and

23. Excitement gripped the Coeur d'Alene mining district in 1884, and the photographer F. Jay Haynes recorded this view. He posed the gold seekers next to a sluice box. Courtesy Montana Historical Society, H 1387.

24. One of Idaho's once numerous mining dredges was located at Idaho City; this scene probably dates from the early twentieth century. Courtesy Idaho State Historical Society, 1900–23 F752 B62.

railway lines that linked the growing Washington metropolis with the dozen or more mining towns of the Idaho panhandle.

The Growing Importance of Agriculture

Unlike other western territories, Idaho was settled largely by emigrants from other parts of the West, not by people who came straight from the East or Midwest. The typical newcomer was a person who had established a farm or store in Oregon before being lured to the goldfields, or was a Mormon who had emigrated north from the Salt Lake Valley.

Except for the Mormon pioneers, few people were initially drawn to Idaho for its land. A good deal of it, especially on the Snake River plain, appeared sterile and forbidding. Even today, Idaho's agricultural lands are scattered all over the state in islands of various size, a pattern that is quite unlike the vast and contiguous expanse of farmland that stretches from eastern Ohio to western Kansas and is known as America's breadbasket.

Few of the gold seekers of the 1860s expected to remain longer than two or three years. They came only to get rich and then retire to a life of ease elsewhere. Even territorial officers and delegates to Congress made no secret of their intention to quit Idaho as soon as possible. However, among the argonauts were farmers who made money feeding the miners. Agrarians took up land in the Boise, Payette, and Weiser River valleys during the 1860s and there produced fine crops of oats, wheat, and barley. At the same time Mormons learned to farm the Malad, Cache, and Bear Lake valleys, and they too sold some of their surplus to feed the hungry miners.

Eventually someone discovered that the sagebrush-covered land of the Snake River plain would grow fine crops if only it had water. The transforming power of large-scale irrigation made it possible to settle Idaho's last farming frontier during the early years of the twentieth century.

A somewhat similar pattern of development took place in the Palouse country of the panhandle, where some of Idaho's earliest and richest agricultural lands were located. Today the area produces bumper crops of wheat and barley, but at first the rolling bunchgrass-covered hills seemed as unpromising as the sagebrush plains of the Snake River country. Agrarians initially confined their fields to the fertile lowlands and left the hillsides for sheep and cattle to graze. Only gradually did they learn that the slopes could grow crops equal to those of the bottomlands. By the turn of the century, growers had converted the Palouse country into a swelling ocean of wheat and other grain. Only once, in 1893, when drought was followed by unseasonable rains that caused the grain to rot in the fields, did the area suffer general crop failure.

During the 1880s railroads entered Moscow, Genesee, and other Palouse towns and vastly expanded the market for their grain. Agriculture became a big business and the annual harvest in August or September an important and colorful event. An army of itinerant laborers, a parade of reapers and combines drawn by dozens of horses or mules, and smoking and puffing steam-powered threshing machines contributed to the drama. In 1914, seventy-five horses and thirty men were required to harvest 1,000 bushels of wheat a day; now a single operator riding in an air-conditioned and computer-controlled combine and a couple of truck drivers can harvest 2,500 to 3,500 bushels a day.

When nimble fingers had sewn up the last sacks of grain, steamboats hauled the crop down the Snake and Columbia rivers to the docks in Portland, where much of it went by sailing ship to markets as distant as London. It was no small feat to transport wheat from the Palouse plateau down the

---

A Woman's View of the Harvest

There was another side to the harvest, one that Annie Pike Greenwood, a twentieth-century pioneer on the Snake River plain, recalled with obvious distaste:

"There is never a moment of stopping for us two women. We can hear the hum of the machine, and through the living-room window, where the table is set the length of the room, we can see the monster spewing forth the ivory straw, which the sun tips with silver glitterings like Christmas-tree tinsel. A cloud of dust, like smoke, hangs over everything.

"We do not talk, we two women. We must rush, *rush,* RUSH! There is no such pressure on the men out-of-doors as there is on the women in the kitchen.

Everything must be ready on the very dot of time when the threshing-machine stops with a great silence. Probably the earth would change its orbit, and a few planets crash, if it should ever occur that the threshing meal was not exactly ready when the first tableful of men was ready for it. . . .

"The best part of threshing is the very tip of the tail of the last day, when you see the monster and its attendant dragon crawling down the road to another farm. You can never know what it is to be really light-hearted and free until you have endured the galley-slavery of a week or two of cooking for threshers."

—Annie Pike Greenwood, *We Sagebrush Folk* (1934), 177ff.

---

rimrock to the Snake River landings two thousand feet below. The job required aerial trams, incline railways, special pipelines, and a variety of other devices.

Over time an increasing amount of grain went by railway boxcars to ports on Puget Sound. Even so, much of it still traveled to market in sacks until rising prices during World War II encouraged growers to switch from burlap bags to the less expensive bulk-loading methods used today.

Wheat and barley, along with the relative newcomers dried peas and lentils, remain the big money-makers in the Palouse country. Wheat growing now, however, is scattered all over Idaho, both north and south, and as of 1987 accounted for about 10 percent of the revenue from agricultural production. At one time there were thirty-four flour mills in the state, but one by one they shut down, and today wheat must be shipped out of state to be processed. Most of Idaho's wheat now goes to Asian markets, where it is made into flour for noodles and cakes.

Not all agrarians were lured to Idaho to grow grain. Some raised large herds of sheep and cattle on the abundant rangeland. During the twentieth century, Idaho occasionally ranked among the nation's leading producers of lambs and sheep. That was not the case during the territorial years, when cattle dominated the open range.

During the mining boom of the 1860s, cattle raising first emerged as a

25. Harvesting with steam near American Falls in 1914. Courtesy Idaho State Historical Society, 1958.0004.

large-scale enterprise in southern Idaho when the high cost of meat encouraged some disillusioned miners to become stock raisers. In the spring of 1864, William Byron imported five hundred head of cattle from Washington Territory. He butchered these to feed the miners of the Boise Basin.

Byron and others soon discovered that cattle throve on the bunchgrass and edible varieties of sage that covered the Snake River plain. More cattle soon arrived from Texas, Nebraska, and California. With rangeland open to all, it seemed that a profitable business could be launched with just a few cows and a branding iron. Stockmen also raised horses to supply draft animals for the growing number of stage and freight lines.

By the 1870s some herds numbered as many as thirty thousand animals. Cattlemen held roundup twice a year. In the spring they concentrated on branding and marking bull calves, in the fall on sorting out fat beef for market. To help with this arduous work, the largest ranchers employed hundreds of young men as cowboys, about three hands for every thousand animals. Idaho's first cowboys were called vaqueros, and as late as the 1880s, the foremen of large ranches on the Snake River plain were majordomos. A number of early ranching terms and many of Idaho's first cowboys were of

Shearing sheep near Rexburg, Idaho.

Potato Digger and Pickers, J.B. Keeler Ranch, 2 miles E. of Twin Falls, Idaho. 300 Bu. Per Acre. Between Apple Trees. Bisbee Photo. 107.

26. The backbreaking work of shearing sheep was photographed near Rexburg in the early twentieth century. Courtesy Idaho State Historical Society, 78–94.50.

27. A labor-intensive process: potato diggers and pickers near Twin Falls in the pre–World War I era. Courtesy Utah State University Special Collections and Archives, A3463.

Hispanic origin. Both had migrated north from Texas and the American Southwest.

Before railroad lines reached southern Idaho in the 1880s, ranchers drove thousands of cattle each year to railheads such as Cheyenne and Winnemucca. The coming of railroads and the introduction of stockcars and refrigerated cars during the latter decades of the nineteenth century opened up markets as distant as Chicago for Idaho beef.

By that time large cattle outfits were scattered through what are now Owyhee, Twin Falls, and Cassia counties, with sizable operations also located in the Wood River valley. Early cattlemen were an adventuresome lot: they might make huge profits one season and lose everything the next. Especially was that true during the hard winters of the 1880s, which did much to shake the confidence of the cattle industry and open the way for sheepmen to share the open range.

The economic value of cattle lay in beef and leather; that of sheep lay in mutton and wool, the latter finding its way from shipping points like Mountain Home, Ketchum, and Soda Springs to textile mills in the Willamette Valley and elsewhere. Idaho woolgrowers organized in 1893 with the future governor Frank R. Gooding as president. Like the ranchers, the sheepmen developed a distinct style of operation. Generally, a lone herder accompanied only by his dog tended two thousand to three thousand sheep. Because sheep needed to keep moving every few days after they cropped the available forage, the sheepherder's wagon evolved into a comfortable mobile home.

Sheep did best on the grasslands of the interior, but there they met opposition from cattlemen, who considered the open range their own. To cattlemen, the sheepmen were interlopers whose woolly beasts destroyed the range for cattle. Confrontations took place in various legal arenas as well as on remote parts of the range, where scattered incidents of vandalism and violence were meant to discourage sheepmen.

Strife culminated in 1896 with the murder of two sheepherders in an area south of present-day Twin Falls. "Diamondfield" Jack Davis was arrested for the crime. The employee of a large cattle company, he was found guilty on the basis of largely circumstantial evidence and sentenced to hang. The celebrated case aroused intense feeling among the cattlemen who proclaimed his innocence and the sheepmen who favored execution. In 1899 Davis got a dramatic last-minute reprieve from the gallows and was pardoned in 1902.

The free open range ended in 1905 when President Theodore Roosevelt initiated a system of fees and permits on the federal lands that then constituted some 90 percent of Idaho's rangeland. Faced with a diminished resource, cattle and sheep interests generally learned to live in harmony. Today they both make significant contributions to the state's economy.

No Small Potatoes

Famous Potatoes! Because of that slogan on automobile license plates, the potato is as closely identified with the Gem State as dairy products are with Wisconsin. The slogan first appeared briefly on license plates in 1926 but vanished until 1948, when it appeared as World Famous Potatoes. The present slogan dates from 1957. Perhaps as a result of turning every resident's car into a rolling billboard, Idaho is better known for potatoes than for any of its other major crops. It is hard to recall now that until the First World War, potatoes were strictly a small-time enterprise in the Gem State.

Potatoes were grown first by Henry Spalding at his Lapwai mission and later by Mormon pioneers at Franklin. A major breakthrough came with the development of the Russett Burbank variety, which was resistant to blight and found favor as a tasty baking potato. In the days before the Great War, farmers of the newly irrigated lands of the Snake River plain learned that potatoes grew well in the sandy volcanic soil; the crop benefited from fertilizers and from the research of University of Idaho scientists. Russett Burbanks soon found a growing market in Chicago and other distant locales. Production climbed from two-thirds of a million bushels in 1900 to twenty-five million bushels in 1929. Yields per acre increased likewise.

In the 1920s Idaho still ranked far behind Maine as a potato producer. But in the contest for national supremacy, Idaho's big baking spuds eventually stood eye to eye with Maine's, and the easterners blinked first. Idaho became the nation's number one potato producer in the late 1950s. The growing popularity of french fries in fast-food restaurants made the Idaho potato one of the most sought-after food items in America.

Methods of distribution were at first quite primitive. A farmer loaded bags of potatoes into railroad cars, padded and insulated the cargo with straw, and in freezing weather accompanied it and kept a charcoal stove burning in the car to prevent freezing. The railroad provided him a seat in the caboose. Equally crude were the early mechanical diggers that unearthed the tubers and left them exposed so they could be picked up by hand. The potato harvest once required many workers.

Progress was made not only in growing and distributing potatoes but also in marketing them. Joe Marshall crusaded so hard to sell the Idaho potato to the rest of the United States that for years he was known in trade circles as the Idaho Potato King.

Following in the footsteps of botanists and publicists was the businessman John Richard ("Jack") Simplot, whose company developed a hundred or more frozen potato products. In 1940 alone he shipped ten thousand carloads of Idaho potatoes to market. During the Second World War, Simplot developed dehydrated potato products that enabled the military to lighten the load of food it shipped to soldiers around the world. Following the war, Simplot's frozen potato products created an important new domestic market for growers.

As the quality of Idaho potatoes became known, agrarians in other states occasionally succumbed to the temptation to sell their products as Idaho or Idaho-type potatoes. Gem State marketers considered retaliating by stamping each potato with the words "Grown in Idaho" but instead had the phrase registered as a trademark in 1955. The Idaho Potato Commission, which traces its roots back to 1937, not only advertises the state's famous spud but jealously guards its reputation.

Among the numerous other crops that flourished on the Snake River plain were sugar beets. First grown by Mormon pioneers in Utah, they became a big business when the Pacific Northwest's first beet sugar factory opened near Idaho Falls in 1903. This plant subsequently became part of the Utah-Idaho Sugar Company formed in 1907. Unhappily for growers, when soft drink manufacturers increased their use of corn sweeteners during the 1970s, they dealt the beet sugar industry a severe blow.

As of 1987 there were twenty-four thousand operating farms in Idaho, some 85 percent of them individually or family owned. Idaho's diversified farmers grew dozens of different crops, although seven items accounted for 83 percent of the value of all agricultural commodities. These were cattle, milk, potatoes, wheat, barley, sugar beets, and hay. Cattle alone accounted for $569 million of the $2,047 million in agricultural receipts. Ironically, because of transportation difficulties between north and south, supermarkets in the panhandle often cannot supply residents with the state's famous potato.

Tall Timber Country

For most of the twentieth century, the Idaho economy has rested on a three-legged stool: mining, agriculture, and timber. Of these three, the last to play a significant role was timber. Until the Pacific Northwest timber boom of the early 1900s, Idaho mills produced mainly mine timbers, railroad ties, and building materials to supply local needs. It was the combination of expanding markets in the East and in California and dwindling stands of timber on the Great Lakes that created new opportunities in the Gem State.

The Great Lakes invasion of Idaho's extensive stands of ponderosa and white pine began rather quietly about 1890, but the pace picked up dramatically ten years later when the St. Paul timber baron Frederick Weyerhaeuser spent nine days touring the state's timberlands on horseback. He was impressed by what he saw. More than anything else, Weyerhaeuser's willingness to gamble on Pacific Northwest timber sparked the rush by midwestern and eastern capital to acquire Idaho forest land.

Soon Weyerhaeuser and several associates had formed the Clearwater Timber Company in Lewiston, the Rutledge Timber Company in Coeur d'Alene, and the Potlatch Lumber Company, which in 1906 opened what was the largest sawmill in Idaho until 1927. By 1903 most private timberland in northern Idaho had passed into the hands of large companies.

Shortly after Weyerhaeuser became involved in Idaho timber, railroads lowered their rates and thus enabled lumber from the interior Northwest to compete successfully in distant markets. Satisfactory rates played a crucial role in encouraging the industry to expand in landlocked Idaho, where railroads lacked the competitive stimulus that water transportation provided west of the Cascade Range.

The earthquake and fire that meant tragedy for San Francisco in 1906 further stimulated Idaho timber production. Mills added extra shifts to supply the lumber necessary to rebuild the California metropolis. Several dozen mills were constructed in the panhandle, and Lake Coeur d'Alene came to resemble an enormous millpond.

Between 1898 and 1914, Idaho tripled its timber production. Most of it came from the state's ten northern counties. In 1910 there were seventy-two active sawmills in Kootenai, Benewah, and Shoshone counties alone. Production increased from 350 million board feet in 1904 to 1,100 million in 1925, but dropped back during the depression days of 1932 almost to the 1904 level. At the turn of the century, approximately 700 persons were engaged in logging and sawmilling in Idaho. By 1910 that number had jumped to slightly more than 2,500, and it would climb to approximately 5,550 by 1920.

Idaho logging started in the far north and gradually moved south. The Sandpoint mills peaked around 1910, and the industry shifted its attention to the Lake Coeur d'Alene region, then to the St. Joe Valley, and finally to the Clearwater Valley after a big mill opened in Lewiston in 1927.

28. The gigantic planing mill of the B. R. Lewis Lumber Company in Coeur d'Alene. Courtesy Eastern Washington State Historical Society, 4321.

Of the new timber operations, none was more ambitious than the one that took shape on the forested edge of the Palouse country. In 1905 the Potlatch Company commenced building its namesake town in the rolling Palouse country eighteen miles north of Moscow; there it also constructed one of the world's largest mills in order to utilize the western white pine so abundant in the nearby hills.

Alas for Idaho timber producers, the opening of the Panama Canal in 1914 allowed timber from the west side of Oregon and Washington to reach East Coast markets more cheaply than Idaho timber going by rail. By 1928 fully 20 percent of the lumber manufactured in the United States was shipped via the canal—and almost half the production of the Pacific Northwest states. Cheap sea transportation made it impossible for Idaho timber to compete successfully with Washington and Oregon timber for markets east of Cleveland, Ohio.

Not until the Second World War was there full demand for Gem State timber. In fact, as late as 1940 fire still harvested more Idaho timber than the lumber companies. By the time production boomed again during the war,

Idaho's Colorful Log Drives

As demand for Idaho timber rose after the turn of the century, new technologies had to be developed to haul logs out of the rugged mountains. Lumber companies in some places built special railroads; in others, they used splash dams and flumes. One of the most dramatic methods was to float logs downriver to the mill. This technique was used at various times on the Priest, Boise, Payette, and Coeur d'Alene rivers, but the most colorful drives occurred on the north fork of the Clearwater, where an estimated 1.8 billion board feet of timber floated down to the big Potlatch mill in Lewiston.

Almost every spring from 1928 until 1971, when construction of Dworshak Dam blocked the north fork, a year's harvest of logs made the ninety-mile journey down the Clearwater. Most drives lasted two to three weeks, although some were finished in a week, and one required eighty days.

A specially recruited crew of approximately thirty men worked the drive. They used pikes and peaveys and an occasional stick of dynamite to break up jams and herd errant logs off sandbars and back into the current. Men of strength and agility jumped from log to log to keep the mass moving. Their home during the drive was the wanigan, a floating cookshack and bunkhouse. After a day of pitting life against the logs and enduring the cold water and raw winds, the men relaxed with a large evening meal followed by games of checkers and cards and tales of the day's activities.

Over the years the drive changed. In the early days, logs were floated to the North Fork in flumes; later they were decked on the river's banks. In more recent years Caterpillar tractors and jet boats assisted the crews in breaking up jams. Rubber pontoons superseded the log poles under the wanigan, and motors replaced oars. Walt Disney's feature film *Charlie, the Lonesome Cougar* dramatized the Clearwater log drive.

most of the small companies had become part of Potlatch in the north and Boise Payette (Boise Cascade since 1957) in the south.

Integral to the Idaho timber story are the national forests that encompass a larger percentage of land in the state than in any other except Alaska. Federal forest reserves date from 1891, when Congress permitted President Benjamin Harrison to set aside timberland. His successor, Grover Cleveland, added still more land, creating a total of twenty-eight reservations on 41,000,000 acres, but no one equaled Theodore Roosevelt, who vastly enlarged the national forests. In fact, the term *national forest* dates from 1907 and the Roosevelt administration. By 1915 there were twenty-two national forests in Idaho, comprising a total of 19,550,827 acres or about 35 percent of the area of the state. As a result of consolidation, Idaho has twelve national forests today.

Roosevelt's zeal for national forests did not go uncontested. Among his critics was Idaho's Weldon R. Heyburn, who after his election to the United States Senate in 1903 became chief spokesman for opponents of the forest

29. The conflict between Weldon Heyburn and Theodore Roosevelt over the national forests is depicted in a cartoon that presents the Idaho senator as Mother Hubbard who went to get her dog (Timber Syndicates) a bone and found the cupboard bare. Courtesy Spokane Public Library.

"Old Mother Heyburn went to the cupboard
To get her poor dog a bone;
When she got there, the cupboard was bare,
And so the poor dog had none."

reservation system. He considered the reserves a threat to the sovereignty of Idaho and at one point protested to Roosevelt that they paralyzed the state's economic growth. Heyburn headed a successful fight in the Senate in 1908 to forbid any further expansion of national forests in Oregon, Washington, and Idaho. But the wily Roosevelt set aside seventeen million additional acres *before* he signed the measure. Heyburn continued his war on the national forests until his death in 1912.

A State of Dependency

Being forced to grapple year after year with economic instability left its mark on the thinking of Idahoans. As Governor Thomas W. Bennett observed to the seventh legislature in 1872, "The people of this Territory are poor, and 'times' with them are 'hard.' And experience has convinced me that they are a people easily governed, well disposed to obey the laws, and are very much in need of the simplest and cheapest government that can be devised, consistent with sound sense and justice."[2] Much the same thing could have

25.
PAYETTE OIL WELL
BLEW MAR. 30, 1930
PAYETTE, IDAHO

been said during the early 1980s when Idaho once again rode the down slope of the economic roller coaster.

30. Commercial quantities of "black gold" have never been discovered in Idaho, although for a brief time in 1930 this oil well created considerable excitement in the Payette area. Courtesy Oregon Historical Society, 34277.

Today, as in the early years, Idaho's farms, ranches, mines, and mills produce far more than the state's small population can ever hope to consume. Distant markets that played a vital role in the economy since territorial days remain a primary cause of the instability. At the turn of the century, 93 percent of Idahoans employed in stock raising produced for markets outside the state. That figure was 97 percent for the gold and silver industry; 90 percent for lead and zinc; and 67 percent for lumber and logging. In contrast, only 10 percent of Idahoans employed in crop agriculture produced for out-of-state markets. Also in 1900, wage earners in manufacturing comprised less than 1 percent of Idaho's population.

Even as the state's economy evolved during the course of the twentieth century, its nineteenth-century beginnings were very much evident. Especially was that true in the large sector still based on natural resources. The problems of a century ago remain problems today.

1107
MORE
THESE GOODS
INSIDE
House & Lot
FOR SALE
House for Rent

CHAPTER 9

But no matter what the wealth of a mineral
country may be, it is never looked upon with
the same favor by the permanent settler or
home-seeker as the agricultural region, because there is always a looking-forward to
the time when the mines will be worked out,
while to the cultivation of the earth there is no
end.—from Hubert Howe Bancroft, *History of
Washington, Idaho, and Montana* (1890)

Town and Country
Urban Roots of a Rural State

Idaho's Euro-American pioneers established towns and villages before they
settled the surrounding countryside. Miners' crude camps provided the
first markets for the farms and ranches that appeared in nearby valleys.
Towns also were the spearheads of Mormon settlement. Despite the Gem
State's urban beginnings, not one of its communities ranked as a metropolis
when the twentieth century dawned. Even Boise, the most populous town
since 1870, had only 4,026 residents at the time of statehood and only 5,957
in 1900.

The Town Builders

Mormon pioneers established Franklin, Idaho's first town, in 1860. By the end
of the decade, fellow believers had founded Paris, Preston, Malad, and numerous other agricultural towns and villages. The first non-Mormon agrarian
settlements also arose during the 1860s to supply food and draft animals to
Idaho's numerous mining camps. The latter communities date from the
founding of Pierce City only a few months after Franklin.

The contrast between the pietistic agrarian Mormon settlements and the
get-rich-quick mining camps was stark, creating a cultural as well as geographic division that endured for decades. Largest of Idaho's early mining
camps was Idaho City, the dominant community in the Boise Basin. In fact,
with a population of seven thousand residents in 1864, it outranked Portland
for a year or two as the Pacific Northwest's largest urban center. During its

heyday, Idaho City boasted more than two hundred businesses: it had two theaters, Protestant and Catholic churches, lodges, several saloons, a newspaper, and the offices of the Boise County government.

Most early camps owed their existence to the relatively simple and egalitarian work of mining stream beds for gold, but Silver City, founded in the Owyhee Mountains in 1863, was the first of Idaho's many lode-mining centers. Precious metal was the lifeblood of both placer- and lode-mining communities. Bars of silver bullion, sometimes stacked three feet high, stood outside the Wells Fargo office in Silver City awaiting shipment to Portland and San Francisco. Silver City remained a big producer into the 1890s.

One of the most obvious differences between Idaho's agrarian settlements and its numerous mining camps was that the latter were predominantly male. Sometimes there were four males for every female. Perhaps that gender imbalance, along with the lack of family responsibilities, was one reason why the mining camp population was so notoriously restless. In most camps some restaurants never closed and were frequented largely at night when the tinhorn gamblers gathered to ply their trade.

The coming of railroads in the 1870s and 1880s encouraged the rise of numerous small trading centers from which farmers and ranchers shipped their products to markets more distant than nearby mining camps. Many of these communities were spaced along the tracks at regular intervals so that farmers could reach town to transact business and return home the same day.

Railroads also fostered settlement where they located division points and repair shops. Residents of Eagle Rock, now Idaho Falls, believed their future assured when their town became a division point and site of the Utah and Northern's repair shops in 1880. But in 1887 the railroad moved its shops to the budding community of Pocatello. What the railroad gave, it could also take away. When its population suddenly dropped from 1,400 to 250, Eagle Rock had to battle to survive without the benefits a railroad payroll conferred on its workers and merchants.

Pocatello, which was located where the tracks of the Oregon Short Line crossed those of the Utah and Northern, emerged as Idaho's leading railroad center. In 1881 the site was only a sagebrush-covered plain, but the Oregon Short Line reached Pocatello the next year and built the Pacific Hotel to accommodate its passengers. After its shops moved from Eagle Rock, the railroad built "company row" to house its growing number of employees.

Pocatello was incorporated in 1889. By 1900 it had a population of 4,096 and had become a transportation hub—the Gate City, as it liked to style

31. Downtown Pocatello in the mid-1890s. Courtesy Arizona Historical Society, Tucson, 25488.

itself—and an industrial complex of railroad shops and yards. Dependence on the railroad made Pocatello something of an anomaly: its economy was industrially oriented and its work force more heavily unionized than was usual in the Gem State. Its population exhibited greater racial and ethnic diversity than was typical of Idaho communities and was largely non-Mormon in a Mormon-dominated region.

Among Idaho's other railroad towns were Shoshone, Nampa, and Avery, which was named for Avery Rockefeller, whose father was a director of the Chicago, Milwaukee, and St. Paul line. Railroads also played at least an indirect role in the naming of several communities. On the Washington, Idaho, and Montana line in the panhandle are located Princeton, Harvard, Stanford, Yale, Vassar, Cornell, Purdue, and Wellesley. Although some of these places antedated the railroad, most were named by the young college men who surveyed the right-of-way and supervised construction. Despite the impressive names, few of the sites ever amounted to more than lonely railroad sidings.

Idaho's early towns were invariably fashioned from a similar array of businesses: saloons, livery stables, hotels or boardinghouses, and general stores. Banks, however, were often scarce. When a miner wanted to stash his gold, he sometimes turned to a trustworthy storekeeper, who kept it in his safe. In time, some of these merchants became bona fide bankers. Idaho's oldest

32. A secondhand store in Nampa doubled as an employment office in the early 1900s. Courtesy Idaho State Historical Society, 70–187.2.

chartered national bank was the First National Bank of Idaho (now West One Bank), which got its start in Boise in 1867. Any successful town also needed a newspaper to recite its virtues and a hotel to lodge newcomers, business-men, and speculators.

Saloons were numerous in all but the Mormon settlements. Especially popular among males, the saloon functioned as a poor man's club in Idaho's numerous mining camps. Many saloons employed talented musicians at high salaries and engaged "hurdy-gurdy girls" to dance with all comers at fifty cents per dance. With drinks for self and a partner at fifty cents, each dance cost a dollar. Governor William J. McConnell recalled that the hurdy-gurdy girls were "almost invariably German girls" who eventually married Wild Bill, Texas Pete, or some other man they met while dancing. Hurdy-gurdy girls were not necessarily prostitutes. McConnell described them as women who danced only because they were poor: "They proved themselves loyal wives and tender, affectionate mothers."[1]

The general store, filled to the ceiling with all manner of hardware and food, and redolent with the pungent odors of everything from turpentine to cinnamon, was another popular gathering place, more so when it also housed

33. The interior of the Boise Basin Mercantile, Idaho City, was typical of general stores around the state in the early twentieth century. Courtesy Idaho State Historical Society, 78–65.28.

the local post office. Storefront advertising typically included the barber's red-and-white pole, the jeweler's oversize watch, and the tobacconist's wooden Indian. The various businesses lined a main street and together with churches and schools formed the heart of a community. Until the advent of large national enterprises like James Cash Penny's Golden Rule Stores, all of these businesses were locally owned.

Larger communities had department stores, like those in Boise, lined from floor to ceiling with wood-and-glass cases displaying everything from hats and corsets to dresses and gloves. One of the lures of the "big city" was the large emporium of merchandise that dazzled the eyes of country folk.

Capitol Controversies: Lewiston and Boise

When Congress created Idaho in 1863, it authorized governor William H. Wallace to designate a temporary capital. He picked Lewiston. Since it was the major supply center for the northern mines and had stage connections to Walla Walla and steamboat service to Portland, Lewiston seemed a logical choice.

Idaho's first two legislatures met there in a small false-fronted frame structure located across the street from the Luna House Hotel. But because the building was not large enough to accommodate the entire assembly, the House of Representatives convened in a small building opposite.

Governing the oversize territory from a site on its extreme western border was no easy feat, especially when 16,000 of Idaho's 40,000 residents lived in the Boise Basin, and more moved in daily. The second legislature recognized the population shift when, on December 7, 1864, it voted to move the seat of government to Boise City. Little more than a year old, Boise already had a population of 1,658; that of Lewiston had dropped from more than 2,000 in 1862 to fewer than 400. Nonetheless, citizens of Lewiston protested that the relocation was illegal.

Ironically, because the act creating Idaho confirmed the right of the Nez Perce Indians to their reservation, early Lewiston was technically not even part of the territory. A new treaty was negotiated in 1863, but the United States Senate did not ratify it until April 20, 1867, at which time Lewiston legally became part of Idaho. By then it had already lost the capital fight.

Boise was platted in 1863 following the discovery of gold in nearby mountains. That year the United States Army ordered Major Pinckney Lugenbeel to select a site for a fort where wood, water, grass, and fertile land could be found. From here the army would also protect travelers on the Oregon Trail. On July 4, 1863, Lugenbeel found his site some forty miles up the Boise River from the old Hudson's Bay Company post of Fort Boise.

Three days later eight men met in a cabin to lay out a settlement between the fort and the river. Besides the military post and the mining boom in its hinterland, Boise City's chief assets were an abundance of fertile land and a milder climate than that of the mining towns of the Boise Basin. The name Boise was apparently derived from a French word for wooded land and probably came into use early in the nineteenth century among French-Canadian fur hunters to identify the Boise River.

The army barracks was the first building erected in Boise City. It was followed by a store, several saloons, a livery stable, and a couple of hotels. Many of the first structures were tents and brush shanties. Boise soon became a trade and transportation hub. By 1867 six lines of stages on four different routes arrived and departed each day. In 1869 the federal government authorized construction of the Boise Assay Office, and soon millions of dollars in gold passed though the settlement en route to the mint.

Although mining activity declined in the late 1860s, Boise gained a look of permanence as trees grew from what had been sagebrush plains. Soon the settlement became known as the City of Trees. It profited from the growing number of farms and orchards that lined the Boise River. In 1870, when there were only 414 farms in all of Idaho Territory, 65 percent of them were located in the Boise area. The population of the city increased to 2,311 by early 1890, and that number would more than double by 1900, largely as a result of a boom in irrigated farmland in the Boise Valley. Thus Boise was also a city of families, unlike the typical mining camp.

Officers from Fort Boise contributed greatly to the new town's social life by hosting dances and music or minstrel shows. Masquerade balls were in vogue in the 1870s. Horse racing was a favorite sport in early Boise. Among the entrants at one race in 1871 were "Crooked Back Bill," "Gambler's Ghost," and "John the Baptist." Then as now, camping was popular with Boise families, who headed into the nearby mountains for two or three days of hunting, fishing, and hiking.

As the city grew, its residents took pride in the "fireproof" brick and adobe buildings that replaced rough cabins along its wide streets. A favored type of business structure was built of brick and featured three arch open-

34. A map of Boise City in 1885 depicts the growth of the community west of the military reservation that had given rise to it twenty-two years earlier. Courtesy Idaho State Historical Society, Map Collection, Ada County.

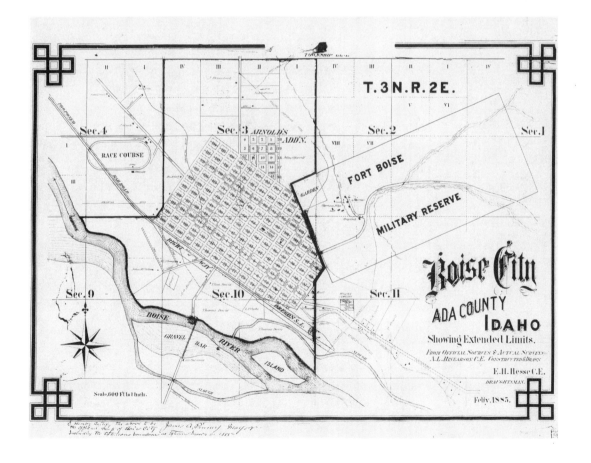

ings, a style popular in mining camps in southern Oregon and California. By the end of the 1860s, Boise had more than four hundred buildings, mostly wood, but twenty-four were of brick and eight of stone. Not among these, however, was a territorial capitol building.

The territory's third legislature met in Boise in 1865, but twenty years passed before lawmakers provided for a permanent capitol building. Even then, Hailey residents who wanted their booming community to be the site obtained a temporary injunction to block construction. Until the five-story red brick capitol was completed in 1886, there had been no permanent depository for territorial records. In fact, for twenty years the legislature and various government offices moved from one building to another as quarters could be rented. Territorial business was conducted at such places as the Good Templar's Hall and Crawford and Slocum's Store.

When the state outgrew its first capitol building, planning for the present structure commenced in 1905. The new building was completed in sections as funds became available—the central portion in 1912 and the final wing in 1920. The outside walls were faced with sandstone that came from state-owned Table Rock east of Boise. Convict labor quarried and delivered the stone.

Townscapes and Living Spaces

Idaho's first Euro-American settlers lived in a variety of simple but adequate structures that ranged from tepees, willow huts, and tents to log cabins and adobe buildings. When lumber was sawed by hand at the rate of eight to twelve dollars a day, it made frame buildings of any type a luxury. Many pioneers simply fashioned their dwellings from logs hand-hewn on two sides and chinked with mud or moss. The floor was of earth, and because glass was so scarce, stretched cotton cloth or deerskins served for windows. A large iron stove often provided warmth.

Early mining towns frequently amounted to nothing more than tent cities. One popular type of building was made by erecting poles upon which rafters were set. The sides, ends, and roof were covered with brown muslin. There were no windows, and the doors were frames of small poles covered with the same type of cloth.

More than 120 fabric structures lined the streets of Lewiston during the early mining excitement. Because they quickly became frayed and weather-beaten, people called the place rag town. Sunlight brightened the interior during the day, and candles and lamps illuminated both the interior and the street at night. Residents needed no streetlights. "Such buildings, obviously,

35. An early-day settler's cabin near Riggins, in the Salmon River valley. Courtesy Idaho State Historical Society, 1275.

presented slight opposition to burglars, and as a protection against stray bullets they were a failure," recalled Governor William J. McConnell. "To provide against the last it was customary to pile sacks of flour or sand around the beds of those who slept." [2]

Occasionally an early settler simply dug a home in a dry hillside and hastily roofed it over with pine boughs, which he then covered with dirt. It was not uncommon for several families to live together in one rude shelter. Miners' dugouts and log cabins lined every gulch and ravine in the Boise Basin in 1863. But as the number of sawmills increased, buildings of sawed lumber became more common.

Boardinghouses and company-owned bunkhouses provided temporary homes for countless men who worked in Idaho's mining and timber camps. Hotels, some of them large and elegant, appeared in every town worthy of the name, not just to cater to travelers and tourists but also to provide rooms for young families and others who had not yet settled permanently in the community.

Because the pioneers' chief building material was wood, it was used for everything from sidewalks and bridges to log cabins, false-fronted stores, and barns. Most early government buildings were also fashioned from wood. Un-

Economic Families in the West, 1900

	Total Population (in thousands)	Economic Families (Percent)
Wyoming	93	15.6
Montana	243	15.3
Washington	518	13.8
Nevada	42	11.6
Arizona	123	11.2
California	1,485	11.1
Oregon	414	10.1
Colorado	540	8.0
Idaho	162	7.4
Utah	277	3.4
New Mexico	195	3.1
United States	75,994	3.4

Note: The 1900 Census recognized two types of families: natural and economic. The latter included dwellers in hotels, boardinghouses, institutions, and construction, timber, mining, and military camps. Thus, "economic family" defined people who lodged together but had no natural or private family relationship.

fortunately, wooden structures illuminated by candles or oil lamps were highly vulnerable to fire. Almost every Idaho community recorded a major fire that ravaged its business section.

As society became more stable, and crude settlements achieved the patina that comes with age and affluence, wealthy Idahoans built and furnished opulent Victorian mansions that were as elegant as anything found in the East. A parlor crammed with all kinds of ornaments became a symbol of prosperity and refinement. By the 1890s large and elegant residences heated by geothermal energy lined fashionable thoroughfares like Boise's Warm Springs Avenue. People with money also built vacation homes on the state's mountain lakes. Even workers found enough time and money to erect simple cottages.

Around the turn of the century, affluent Idahoans increasingly hired professional architects to design their residences and public structures. One popular architect in the panhandle was Kirtland Cutter of Spokane, a self-trained artist who favored a Swiss-style chalet design to create rustic but elegant buildings well suited for northern Idaho's mountain and lake environment. Cutter also designed the Idaho building for the 1893 Chicago world's fair and homes for the department store magnates C. C. Anderson and Leo Falk in Boise.

The Boise architect John Tourtellotte designed the state's Roman Revival capitol, many other public buildings, and numerous private dwellings in the opening years of the twentieth century. When the University of Idaho rebuilt after the fire that destroyed its administration building in March 1906, President James Alexander MacLean turned to Tourtellotte, who designed the Tudor-style structure that still forms the centerpiece of the campus.

Idaho's built environment included not only edifices—business blocks, railroad stations, courthouses, and residences—but also landscape. To design a campus that complemented the new Administration Building, the University of Idaho's President MacLean turned to John C. Olmsted, a member of the nation's most prestigious landscape architecture firm, the Olmsted Brothers of Brookline, Massachusetts. The firm, whose founding father, Frederick Law Olmsted, had earlier designed New York's Central Park, now turned its considerable talents to an elaborate plan that gave the campus a central mall or commons that remains a distinctive feature to this day.

36. The Oregon Short Line built the Idanha Hotel in Soda Springs in 1887 as a dining stop for its passengers. The building burned in 1921. Courtesy Church Archives, Church of Jesus Christ of Latter-day Saints.

NO66 THE CAMPUS U.OF.I. MOSCOW IDAHO.

37. The University of Idaho's new Tudor-style Administration Building fronted a campus not yet made over by the landscaping talents of the Olmsted Brothers. Courtesy Latah County Historical Society, 17–3–53.

Four other Olmsted sites in Idaho were the Coeur d'Alene Country Club, the C. C. Anderson home on Boise's Warm Springs Avenue, the Boise Board of Education, and the property that is now the Hayden Lake Golf and Country Club. John Olmsted also designed the 158-acre grounds for Kirtland Cutter's chalet-style Bozanta Tavern that was the showpiece of the Hayden Lake resort.

Idaho's architectural gems ranged from the Mission-style Union Pacific station in Boise to the ornate Eastlake-style McConnell Mansion in Moscow. Few if any structures, however, were more elaborate than Boise's Moorish-revival Natatorium, which opened to the public in 1892. The Nat, as it was commonly called, housed a 125-foot-long pool, dining room, club room, tearoom, and bath. Until 1933 it was a center of social and recreational activity.

It has often been said of the United States that the nation was born in the country and moved to the city. Idaho, by contrast, moved from its mining camps and agricultural villages into the country and seemed reluctant to return to an urban environment. In 1900 the state had only two communities of 2,500 or more residents. Boise at that time topped the list with 5,957 residents.[3] Well into the twentieth century, Idaho managed to keep one foot firmly planted in the country while sliding the other ever so tentatively toward the city.

CHAPTER 10

For twenty-seven years, 1863–1890, Idaho was a territorial ward of the federal government. The census of 1890 claimed there was no longer a defined frontier line, and Idaho's admission to statehood that year is symbolic of the passing frontier.—from F. Ross Peterson, *Idaho, a Bicentennial History* (1976)

Passages
From Territory to State

The 1880s were critical years for Idaho. The decade opened with the renewed optimism generated by the Wood River mining boom; it closed with statehood almost within reach. In 1883 and 1884 Idaho at last achieved railroad connections to the outside world. Hand in hand came two other new technologies—telephone and electric lights—that seemed beyond the wildest dreams of the pioneers.

Yet during the 1880s the territory also came within a few presidential pen strokes of losing the panhandle to Washington and thereby setting the stage for the probable absorption of the rest of Idaho by Nevada. These were years of renewed assault on Indian lands, a rising tide of violence against the Chinese, and increased hostility toward Mormons. In short, the 1880s represented a decade of technological and economic progress, continued political strife, and unsettling new manifestations of social backwardness. This was Idaho's time of passage from a troubled childhood to an uncertain adolescence.

Anti-Mormonism: Here and Hereafter

In addition to a variety of economic problems, Idahoans grappled with the consequences of a largely secular population of gold seekers confronting Mormon agrarians. Nowhere else in the United States did the Mormon and non-Mormon populations divide as sharply as they did in Idaho, and therein lay the seeds of an anti-Mormon crusade.

38. An anti-Mormon cartoon caricatured the supposed squabbles of a polygamous family. Courtesy Church Archives, Church of Jesus Christ of Latter-day Saints, P1300, Cartoon 39.

The Mormon sense of group solidarity and Mormon religious and dietary customs caused outsiders, or "Gentiles," to regard them with suspicion. Being a "peculiar people," a Biblical term the Latter-day Saints applied to themselves, inevitably seemed to breed persecution. Some Gentiles considered Mormon devotion to church to be un-American; others undoubtedly coveted the fertile Mormon farmsteads.

As they grew in population and influence in southeastern Idaho, Mormons became caught up in the sectional political rivalries that wracked the territory. Their growing numbers gave Mormons power at the polls, especially when they tended to vote as a bloc for Democratic candidates, who were nearly always victorious in Idaho elections before the 1880s. Because of this voting pattern, losers charged that Mormons took orders from their church headquarters in Salt Lake City and had no real interest in Idaho matters.

Above all, however, it was the belief that males had the right to have more than one wife, a practice referred to as polygamy, that made Mormons convenient targets for hostile non-Mormons. In fact, probably no more than 3 percent of Idaho's Mormons actually engaged in plural marriage.

More than anyone else it was Fred T. Dubois who shaped vague anti-Mormon resentments into a powerful political movement. After attending Yale College, Dubois moved to Idaho where he eventually became a United

States marshal. When Congress passed the Edmunds Act in 1882, which barred polygamists from voting, holding office, or serving as jurors in cases involving plural marriage, it handed Dubois a powerful weapon to use against Mormons.

In May 1886, in a typical scenario, Dubois went armed with 140 warrants to arrest suspected polygamists but was able to apprehend only 20. Mormons had developed an effective early-warning system that permitted most polygamous men to avoid arrest. Few successful raids could be made in Paris, for example, because the marshals who got off the train at Montpelier were invariably conspicuous as they hired transportation for the last ten miles to Paris. And even if lawmen managed to elude spotters in Montpelier, two watchmen stationed at each end of Paris formed a second line of defense. They sounded an alarm on tin horns, enabling polygamists to hide in secret passages in their homes or escape to nearby fields where the ground cover was deliberately kept high.

Marshal Dubois was interested in more than simply harassing polygamists. He sought to undermine the Idaho Democratic party by associating it with Mormons and thereby to elevate himself among Republicans, whose party had denounced Mormons since it was formed in the territory. From 1872 through the early 1880s, a practically unanimous Mormon vote had helped to maintain Democrats in office.

Dubois was successful in his quest: anti-Mormons in the legislature created the Idaho Test Oath, a stringent measure that could be used to force a person to testify under oath whether he belonged to the Mormon church or believed in its doctrines. A person did not have to be a practicing polygamist but only belong to an organization that sanctioned polygamy in order to be denied the right to vote, hold public office, or serve on a jury.

After the Test Oath Act became law in 1885, Mormons fought it all the way to the United States Supreme Court and lost in the case of *Davis* v. *Beason*, a decision announced on February 3, 1890. As Republicans grew in power, Dubois rode the wave of anti-Mormon sentiment to Capitol Hill, where as territorial delegate he worked to get Idaho admitted as a state. Framers added provisions of the Test Oath Act to the Idaho constitution, and voters overwhelmingly ratified it.

In September 1890 the church's president, Wilford Woodruff, urged all Latter-day Saints to comply with civil laws regarding marriage, but this did not prevent Idaho's first state legislature from barring Mormons from the polls. The 1893 legislature, however, removed most of the anti-Mormon restrictions. As for Dubois, he became one of Idaho's United States senators

Laying Steel Mile 20   #53.

16   Sheepshearers Band

before taking himself and the anti-Mormon cause into the Democratic party in 1900. From that camp he enlivened Idaho politics during the early years of the twentieth century. By that time the state legislature had restored the franchise to Mormons, some of whom now voted against their old tormentor, while others, in an ironic twist, became his political associates.

Some Idahoans still wanted to disenfranchise Mormons because they continued to sanction plural marriage in heaven, but the state's judiciary ruled that so long as Mormons complied with civil law, Idaho could not extend its jurisdiction into the hereafter. In 1982 Idaho voters finally removed the anti-Mormon provision from their constitution.

Must the Chinese Go? Patterns of Race and Ethnicity

Over the years several distinct racial and ethnic groups called Idaho home. Patterns of immigration and settlement were not random. New arrivals were often attracted by climate, topography, and job opportunities similar to those they left behind. Letters from first arrivals helped attract fellow nationals to a particular location, and so did the old ties of family and neighborhood. The foreign-language press played a similar role.

For reasons such as these, Basques clustered in Boise, Greeks emigrated to Pocatello where they formed a predominantly male subcommunity employed by the Oregon Short Line, Cornishmen ("Cousin Jacks") went to mining areas to apply skills they had developed back home, and Swedes were attracted to logging and agriculture in the panhandle. Enough Irish and Germans migrated to Idaho to form their own cultural organizations.

European emigrants often came to Idaho only after living first in another part of the United States. After all, until the completion of the transcontinental railroads in the 1880s, Idaho remained isolated from America's main population centers. Even with improved transportation, getting to Idaho still meant a long and expensive journey. Distance and cost proved an impediment both to impoverished arrivals from southern and eastern Europe and to blacks from the rural South.

Among Idaho's largest and most enduring ethnic groups were the Basques, who emigrated to the West from a homeland they called Euzkadi (which straddled the Spanish-French border). Thousands of Basques found their way into southern Idaho communities. Some of them arrived via California and Nevada, but most came directly from Spain shortly after 1900.

Contrary to popular impression, not all Basques were sheepherders. In fact, many had little or no experience working with sheep prior to their arrival. Herding was often only a stepping-stone to other occupations. Some

Basques did save up a little money to acquire herds of their own, though fewer than 5 percent of the second generation actually herded sheep.

The first Basques typically arrived as single males and congregated in Boise, which became the nation's leading Basque center, and from there they ventured into mining or hired themselves out to construct irrigation canals and dams. Many eventually sent home for their wives and sweethearts. The years from 1900 to 1920 saw the greatest influx of Basques into Idaho, but when Congress imposed an immigration quota system in the mid-1920s, it contributed to a rapid decline in new arrivals. One observer estimated that 2,500 to 3,000 Basques lived in Idaho in 1922, most of them in Boise.

There, as was the case wherever members of one nationality collected, the Basque community developed its own hotels and boardinghouses. It established a mutual aid society in 1908 to assist people out of work, sick, or temporarily in need of money. Boise also had a Basque Roman Catholic Church. Basques, like other ethnic groups, shared their language, foods, and customs, and in that way they found shelter from the nativist prejudice all too common at the time.

Another large immigrant group drawn to Idaho was the Chinese. Among the territory's early Asian residents, the Chinese were by far the most numerous. They began arriving as individuals or in groups shortly after 1860, and although they could be found in various occupations, mining and railroad construction attracted the greatest numbers.

By 1870 more than 4,000 Chinese lived in Idaho, and they constituted one-quarter of the territory's population. At that time more than half of Idaho's 6,579 miners were Chinese; approximately 700 Chinese lived in Silver City in 1874 at the peak of mining activity. There they maintained a Masonic lodge, two temples (commonly called Joss Houses), four stores, three or four restaurants, two laundries, and five gambling establishments.

Idaho's Chinese came from many different backgrounds, but to most whites they were all alike and thus were the victims of prejudice, violence, and various special taxes and property-holding restrictions. The territorial legislature in 1866 levied a tax of five dollars per month on foreign miners. Lawmakers defined all Chinese—from gardeners to laundrymen—as miners and permitted the local sheriff to seize property if the tax were not promptly paid and sell it at auction on three hours' notice.

The common expression "Why, he hasn't a Chinaman's chance" summed up well the prevailing prejudice. James O'Meara, editor of the *Idaho World* of Idaho City, reflected popular hostility when he warned in 1865: "The

41. Chinese engaged in hydraulic mining in the Rocky Bar region around 1900. Courtesy Idaho State Historical Society, 76–119.2/a.

Chinamen are coming. Lord deliver us from the locusts of Egypt, they devour all men before them."[1]

Because Chinese miners were willing to work claims with great patience and accept a small return for their efforts, whites universally regarded their presence in the diggings as a sure sign that a mining region had passed its peak. The belief that Chinese had accumulated great quantities of gold through their hard work and frugality led to one of the most vicious massacres in Pacific Northwest history. In that incident a gang of "cowboys" shot or hacked to death thirty-one Chinese miners.

The site was north of Hells Canyon, the year was 1887, and robbery was the probable motive. The murderers tortured their victims in an apparent attempt to learn where they had hidden their supposed cache of gold. Only the death count in the slaughter of forty to sixty Chinese miners by Paiute Indians in 1866 exceeded this toll.

When hard times hit the Pacific Northwest in the mid-1880s, unemployed white workers participated in several crusades to drive the Chinese from the region. The agitation against "cheap labor" led to anti-Chinese violence in

42. At Fort Sherman's main gate, a black soldier stands at parade rest in the 1890s. Courtesy Museum of North Idaho, FiSh-1–57.

Tacoma and Seattle, martial law, and the dispatching of federal troops to quell the disorders. ''The Chinese Must Go!'' was the rallying cry.

Trouble also occurred at Pierce City, Idaho, in 1885, when vigilantes lynched five Chinese who they believed were responsible for the brutal murder of a white merchant. Miners in the newly organized Coeur d'Alene mining district in 1886 passed a formal resolution that the first Chinese who came to camp would be hanged.

The number of Chinese in Idaho declined from 4,274 in 1870 to 1,971 in 1890. In fact, throughout the Pacific Northwest in the 1890s, the Chinese population decreased while the Japanese increased dramatically. The exit of the Chinese from mining, railroad construction, and timber opened a door for Japanese immigrants, typically young males who arrived without families. The first Japanese who came to Idaho endured many of the same forms of discrimination that afflicted the Chinese.

Japanese laborers were employed on the Oregon Short Line in southern Idaho as early as 1892, and by the end of the decade they had become a

Non-Caucasians in Idaho, 1900–1980

	1900	1920	1940	1960	1980
American Indians	4,226	3,098	3,537	5,231	10,418
Blacks	293	920	595	1,502	2,716
Chinese	1,467	585	208	311	905
Japanese	1,291	1,569	1,191	2,254	2,585

common sight all along the line from Nampa to Pocatello. In the first decade of the twentieth century, many Japanese men found work in the expanding sugar beet industry. Menial jobs typically served as way stations to entrepreneurship. Some Japanese became successful truck gardeners, and others prosperous merchants in the region's larger cities. By 1940 Idaho had twelve hundred residents of Japanese ancestry, some 60 percent of them native-born Americans. A large portion earned a living in agriculture.

As early as the summer of 1919, several thousand of the sugar beet workers in southeastern Idaho were Hispanic Mexican or Mexican Americans who emigrated from the Southwest. During World War II, many Mexican laborers came to Idaho as part of the federal government's "Bracero program." Idaho received 2,410 braceros (strong-armed workers) in 1944 to harvest sugar beets and other crops during a time of acute labor shortage caused by the war. Until then, white itinerant farm workers had been the rule at harvest time.

Idaho has never had a large black population. Of the 595 blacks who lived in the state on the eve of the Second World War, most clustered in the railroad center of Pocatello. The 1940 census also reveals that of the Chinese once so numerous in Idaho, only 208 remained. Of Idaho's 3,537 Indians, only a few lived off the reservations. Nowhere in the state in 1940 was there a large foreign-born population.

Land Grab: The Fate of Indian Lands

As for Idaho's original inhabitants, during the late nineteenth century they became a colonized and beleaguered people, confined to shrinking and increasingly undesirable lands. After first promoting the reservation system in an effort to keep Indians and whites separate and thus minimize conflict, Congress changed its mind and passed the General Allotment Act (or Dawes Severalty Act) in 1887. The new measure threatened traditional tribal customs by encouraging Indians to become agrarians and assimilate into

43. Between two worlds in 1908: A Nez Perce woman who had attended the Carlisle Indian Industrial School in Pennsylvania works as a typist in Lewiston. Courtesy Idaho State Historical Society, 77–60.4.

white society in defiance of a Native American tradition of collective property relations. Indians, of course, were not consulted before the proposal became law.

Although the Dawes Act was intended as a reform measure, in practice it proved just the opposite. It diminished reservation lands across the United States by nearly two-thirds between 1887 and 1934 by periodically opening major portions of the natives' land base to white settlement. Each of the 638 remaining Coeur d'Alene Indians of northern Idaho, for instance, received 160 acres under the Dawes Act. At the same time, however, three-fourths of their former reservation was opened to white homesteaders. The state of Idaho purchased some Coeur d'Alene lands from the federal government in 1911, and the tract surrounding scenic Lake Chatcolet became Heyburn State Park, the Pacific Northwest's first major state park.

There were also periodic land rushes: a pistol shot at high noon on November 18, 1895, opened the Nez Perce reservation to white homesteaders, who scrambled to claim three thousand pieces of real estate. The tribe received a cash settlement of $1.6 million divided into five installments for their alienated land. Today the Nez Perces retain only a fraction of the acreage that made up their reservation in 1863. The basic flaw of the Dawes Act, apart from its failing to recognize the value of Indian culture, was that it did not set aside land to take care of the needs of the young people born to Indians. Framers of the act apparently assumed that Indians would only decline in number.

The Bumpy Road to Statehood

With all the troubles it experienced during the 1880s, it is a wonder that Idaho Territory survived intact until statehood. No fewer than four sessions of its legislature petitioned Congress to annex the panhandle to either Washington or Montana. Northern Idaho was represented in a constitutional convention in Walla Walla in 1878 and included in Washington's statehood plans for more than a decade.

Dismemberment seemed imminent in the mid-1880s when the Nevada politician William M. Stewart successfully urged Congress to attach northern Idaho to Washington. This step was but a prelude, many believed, to giving the remainder of Idaho to Nevada, a state with serious economic problems because of the moribund condition of its all-important mining industry. Both houses of Congress approved the detachment of northern Idaho in early 1887.

When news reached Lewiston that the panhandle was to be annexed to Washington, townsfolk responded with brass bands and a community celebration. But their revelry was cut short when four days later they learned that President Grover Cleveland had vetoed the bill because of protests by the territorial governor, Edward A. Stevenson.

Losing the panhandle was one thing, but for Idaho to be swallowed up by a "rotten borough" like Nevada was apparently quite another. To placate the angry and frustrated northerners, the 1889 legislature voted to place Idaho's new university in the panhandle town of Moscow.

In the end, statehood for Idaho was delayed not so much by local matters as by a political impasse on Capitol Hill. Congress blocked statehood for territories of the far Northwest because the Democrats who at various times controlled either the Senate or the House did not want to admit states that appeared likely to vote Republican.

The Capitol Hill logjam remained unbroken until Republicans captured the White House and both houses of Congress in 1888. In the lame-duck session of 1889, outgoing Democrats dropped their delaying tactics, apparently in the hope of reaping some last-minute favor for supporting statehood.

President Cleveland signed the Omnibus bill and thus set in motion the admission process for Washington, Montana, and the two Dakotas. This measure, however, conspicuously slighted Idaho and Wyoming, although powerful senators urged both territories to prepare for statehood anyway. Thus in 1889, Idaho proceeded without formal congressional approval to hold a special convention and draft a constitution. In that way, it came to be classified with the Omnibus States.

On July 4 seventy men gathered in Boise to write a state constitution. They had come in response to a proclamation issued by Governor Stevenson (and reaffirmed by his successor, George L. Shoup of Salmon). Everything about the Idaho convention represented an act of faith: the Boise citizens who underwrote its expenses hoped to be reimbursed by the first state legislature.

Idaho's constitution was submitted to the voters on November 5, 1889, who ratified it by 12,398 to 1,775. Congress narrowly approved the document despite its anti-Mormon provision. Idaho became the nation's forty-third state on July 3, 1890. George L. Shoup, who served as the last territorial governor, was elected the new state's first chief executive.

As a result of intricate maneuvering dictated by state sectionalism, Idaho's first legislative session had the dubious distinction of needing to select *four* United States senators during its brief term (three of whom were actually seated).[2] In yet another concession to sectionalism, the constitution confirmed that Boise would keep the capitol and Moscow the state university, and it required the Idaho Supreme Court to hold sessions in Lewiston as well as Boise in order to diminish geographic obstacles to litigation.

Among the important issues repeatedly raised at the Constitutional convention was whether the women of Idaho should have the right to vote. The matter was not finally settled until the fall of 1896, when, after a quiet campaign to amend the constitution, all counties except Custer (which the leading Northwest suffragist Abigail Scott Duniway called home for several years) approved the measure.

Idaho was now cited as a good example in suffrage campaigns in other parts of the United States. Only four states allowed women to vote in 1896: Wyoming, Colorado, Utah, and Idaho. Idaho's neighbors Washington and Oregon extended the franchise to women only in 1910 and 1912.[3] That was a curious departure from the usual pattern in which Idaho lagged behind the two other Pacific Northwest states in enacting reform legislation.

The amazing thing about the vote to enfranchise Idaho's women in 1896 was that it stirred so little controversy. Since the 1860s, Idahoans had been a contentious lot. In fact, every decade had seen the rise of at least one

44. Idaho's new Capitol
Building decorated for
the inauguration of Gov-
ernor John M. Haines,
January 1913. Courtesy
Idaho State Historical
Society, 70–1.16.

wrenching controversy. Many of these disputes simply faded away or were defused in the political arena, but others culminated in violence.

There was conflict between Yankees and Rebels in the 1860s, whites and Indians in the 1860s and 1870s, Mormons and non-Mormons in the 1880s. The 1890s saw the rise of so many disputes that to Idaho's all-male electorate woman suffrage may have seemed innocuous by comparison.

CHAPTER 11

Idaho is still a very young state. Because its
social development remains largely in the future, it has little to boast of in the arts, in education, and in names of men who have made
history.—from Vardis Fisher's *Idaho: A Guide
in Word and Picture* (1937)

The Quality of Life

During the years 1863 to 1917, two generations of Idahoans learned not only
how to wrest a living from a harsh and unforgiving land but also how to
create a livable society. They ordained governments, built schools to educate
a growing number of young people, cultivated the mind by establishing libraries, literary associations, and newspapers, and provided for necessary
social contacts through a variety of church and fraternal organizations.

Education for Life

Schooling was a matter of slight importance in the boom-and-bust mining
communities that typified early Idaho. After all, the camps were populated
largely by single males who likely balked at being taxed to pay for a school
when in all probability they would live somewhere else next season. In the
more stable agrarian settlements populated by families, education was
viewed in a different light. Schools were required for the future well-being of
the community: they fostered learning, culture, and patriotism and were
widely considered necessary to attract additional settlers.

The Mormons of Franklin established Idaho's first non-Indian school in
1860. The teacher taught the pupils in her home, although townsfolk soon
built a schoolhouse. It was a one-room structure heated by a huge sandstone fireplace. They constructed benches of wooden slabs and writing
slates of rock from the nearby mountains. The entire class shared a single
reading book.

45. Roosevelt School west of Meridian during the 1905–1906 term was probably a typical example of Idaho's elementary school facilities at that time. Courtesy Idaho State Historical Society, 60–156.2.

Idaho's first public school opened in Florence with six pupils in 1864. When the second legislature met in Lewiston that year, it provided for the territory's first public school system. The next year, according to Idaho's first official report on education, there were 1,239 children in three public and four private schools.

The term was irregular and rarely lasted longer than three months. It was arranged to free students to help around the farm or ranch at critical times. Most of Idaho's first teachers were women. They commonly received forty to eighty dollars per term. County superintendents initially issued all teaching certificates. Seldom did they require any education beyond the elementary level. The legislature in 1911 raised the requirements to six weeks of normal or teacher training for certification to teach third grade, twelve weeks for second grade, and eighteen weeks for first grade. Subsequent legislatures gradually tightened the requirements.

The number of schools in Idaho grew slowly during the nineteenth century. The typical elementary school remained a one-room structure, meagerly furnished with learning materials and presided over by a teacher who taught the rudiments of education to all six grades. Boise's public school was at one time housed in an old brick building so crowded that students attended only half-day sessions. The common subjects taught in the elementary grades were reading, writing, arithmetic, spelling, history, geography, language, grammar, and, later, physiology.

Schools, no matter how crude by today's standards, were sources of public pride and centers of community social life. They hosted dances and box suppers, literary societies, picnics, and debates. In early Franklin, when dances were held in the schoolhouse, water was sprinkled on the dirt floor to pack it firmly, and couples danced in their bare feet.

Although most Idahoans came to accept the idea of tax-supported elementary schools, public high schools were another matter. Only slowly did the idea win popular support. This pattern of resistance was typical of western states and territories in the late nineteenth century.

Idaho's first high school was established in Boise in 1881, but during the next several years, the number of secondary facilities increased only gradually. In fact, when the new state university opened its doors in Moscow in October 1892, Idaho had so few high schools that some 30 of the 133 students in attendance that first year could barely write their names, and only 6 seemed of college caliber.

From the beginning, Idaho's public colleges and universities were shaped more by political realities than by academic concerns. When the last territorial legislature created a land-grant university and placed it in the panhandle town of Moscow, it did so mainly to make a political statement: the new University of Idaho was intended as an olive branch to calm the panhandle's many secession-minded residents.

During the twentieth century the state legislature created a second university in Pocatello and a third in Boise. In the fall of 1988, students attending the state's universities numbered 9,444 at the University of Idaho, 7,616 at Idaho State University, 11,400 at Boise State University. Another four-year institution is Lewis-Clark State College located in Lewiston.

Lewis-Clark, which today emphasizes "hands-on" learning, was one of two state educational institutions that originated as normal or teacher-training colleges. The other, the Southern Idaho College of Education, was located in Albion, but it closed in 1951 when it failed to receive state funding. The same fate also befell Lewis-Clark (then called North Idaho College of Education), but unlike the Albion school, it reopened its doors in 1955. In addition to the four-year schools, the state partially funds two-year colleges in Coeur d'Alene and Twin Falls.

When Vardis Fisher compiled the *Idaho Encyclopedia* in the late 1930s, he believed that the state's distinctive contribution to the history of American education was a board of education that coordinated all levels of public schooling. The "Idaho Plan" originated in 1913 when the legislature replaced six boards with one to oversee education from the primary grades through the university. In reality, though, each of the state's universities developed its own legislative constituency, and each seeks a large slice of an educational pie that is not very big even in the best of times.

It might be worth noting, however, that although public funding at all levels of education has been meager throughout Idaho's history, education still accounted for a whopping three-quarters of the state's general budget in the mid-1980s. In addition, Idaho's literacy rate remains one of the highest in the nation.

Coexisting with institutions of public higher education are three private colleges. Ricks College in Rexburg is a two-year Mormon facility that dates its founding a year earlier than that of the University of Idaho and currently boasts an enrollment only slightly smaller than that of the state's oldest university, some seventy-seven hundred students in the fall of 1988. Idaho's other colleges are Northwest Nazarene, founded in Nampa in 1913, and the College of Idaho, which originated in 1891 as a Presbyterian school in Caldwell.

Idaho's early private and public colleges and universities bore many resemblances. All passed through what could be labeled a heroic phase of development, a time of low enrollments and meager and uncertain funding that required extraordinary dedication by faculty and administrators. On all campuses, public and private, the morals and deportment of students and faculty were once a matter of close administrative concern and scrutiny. During those strenuous years, college and university educators were expected to teach a variety of academic disciplines.

In addition to the schools, Idaho's newspapers, theaters, lyceums, churches, and libraries functioned as sources of education, especially for adults. As early as the 1880s it was common for fraternal organizations and union halls to maintain reading rooms stocked with newspapers, magazines, and books. Public libraries date from 1891 with the establishment of a facility in Lewiston. Another appeared the following year in Boise, and a third in Coeur d'Alene three years later. The public library was aptly described as the people's university.

Especially during the 1880s and 1890s, reform clubs proliferated to debate temperance, government ownership, and other controversial ideas. About fifteen such clubs existed in 1900. These promoted a variety of progressive laws, from the abolition of child labor and pure food measures to anti-gambling statutes and laws affecting the status of women. In several cities and towns, women's clubs also spearheaded the formation of libraries and reading rooms, parks, and art exhibitions. The women who belonged to Boise's Columbian Club in the 1890s established the first traveling library in the West. They crated up books and sent them around the state to isolated mining camps and sparsely settled farm areas. The traveling library was so popular that the state took over the program. This process of removing the rough edges from frontier society was not lost on promoters, who lured a new generation of settlers to Idaho by advertising its cultural and social amenities alongside its economic opportunities.

In an age largely informed and entertained by television, radio, and the movies, it might be difficult to understand how vital newspapers and periodicals were as social and educational institutions in pioneer societies. It was a poor community, indeed, that could not claim at least one newspaper, and over the years the number in Idaho certainly totaled in the hundreds.

The press, in fact, formed the most broadly based educational influence in the community. It both mirrored and shaped local society, and it played a vital role in town building and adult education. Letters and newspapers were the two chief agencies that connected early Idaho mining communities with the outside world. Pony express riders brought letters and newspapers to the miners at a premium price. In their eagerness for news, miners sometimes paid as much as $2.50 for a single newspaper from California.

From the rush of miners into the Clearwater region came subscribers for the first newspaper published within the present boundary of Idaho, the *Golden Age* of Lewiston, which appeared August 2, 1862. The oldest Idaho newspaper still published is the *Idaho Statesman* of Boise, which dates from July 26, 1864. The mortality rate among pioneer papers was extremely high. Operating on high hopes and a shoestring budget, few survived longer than a year or two.

Anyone with either a modest amount of cash or a patron, a modicum of education and technical know-how, and a passion to say something could start a newspaper. A pioneer paper was an intensely partisan and personal operation. Editors advocated controversial and unpopular causes and published embarrassing news about individual citizens' manners and morals, items almost certainly libelous today. They blasted rival editors with all the invective at their command. In Idaho City an attack on a rival editor was titled, "A Dirty Dog's Vomit." Such verbal excesses were not unusual and came to be known throughout the Pacific Northwest as the Oregon Style of journalism.[1]

Personal threats from irate readers, some of whom were not satisfied merely with words, occasionally enlivened the work of a frontier editor. During the Civil War, Southern sympathizers in Lewiston took such violent exception to the views expressed by the Republican editor of the *Golden Age* that on several occasions they fired bullets through the Union flag flying above his office. Readers expected a newspaper editor above all else to function as a community booster who promoted its attractions and damned all rivals. The worst thing an editor could do was to transfer his press and allegiance to a rival community.

Cultures Popular and Unpopular

Popular culture took many forms. It was a remarkable assembly of people who gathered on the shore of Spirit Lake each summer before the First World War. They came to this idyllic setting from all parts of northern Idaho and eastern Washington to hear lectures and participate in discussions of current social problems and world affairs. The Spirit Lake Chautauqua was hailed as an important step toward the social and educational advancement of the Inland Empire. Behind the movement were prominent regional businessmen, but the speakers included nationally famous labor and religious leaders.

The chautauqua, a leading purveyor of popular culture in turn-of-the-century America, appeared at several Idaho locations besides Spirit Lake. The largest of these gatherings resembled a combination of college classroom and camp-meeting revival service. Not all chautauquas, however, took the form of mass assemblies. Little Kendrick boasted a chautauqua circle as early as 1892; its membership consisted of five women and the local minister.

The chautauqua movement, perhaps the most highly organized form of popular culture, belies the notion that Idahoans were too busy making a living to have much time for the life of the mind. In fact, a noteworthy mix of cultural activities existed in Idaho from the early days of the mining frontier. These ranged from string quartets and choirs to brass bands and drama clubs. Lantern picture travelogues were popular. Church organizations along with schools and newspapers fostered community cultural development.

Professional and amateur theater companies of varying quality brought entertainment to remote parts of Idaho. In 1864, the play *William Tell* was produced in Charles C. Rich's log cabin in Paris. An amateur drama company organized in Malad in 1871, and by 1892 another was well established in

46. The Red Men of America lodge of St. Maries. Ironically, although Benewah County contained a large portion of the Coeur d'Alene Reservation, bona fide Native Americans were not admitted to membership in this national fraternal organization until the latter part of the twentieth century. Courtesy Idaho State Historical Society, 77–125.2.

Preston. Local actors made the scenery and carried it with them as they toured the small towns of southeastern Idaho.

One of the most controversial purveyors of popular culture was the concert hall or opera house, a name applied to a variety of forums that offered public entertainment. Some opera houses were home to productions staged by itinerant Shakespearean companies; others featured balalaika players, dancing dogs, and a mixed assortment of melodramatic offerings, although lewd ones such as the popular and scandalous *Black Crook*, in which actresses wore tights and exposed their legs, were apparently not performed in Idaho.

Cultural life also encompassed Idaho artists and writers who achieved national reputations. Mary Hallock Foote (1847–1938) was the first prominent writer to use Idaho as a setting, although she was often critical of what she observed. She moved to the West with her husband, a civil engineer, and resided in Idaho from 1884 to 1893, years when she penned some of her best fiction.

Beginning with *The Chosen Valley* (1892), Foote wrote and illustrated a series of highly autobiographical novels and short stories about the mining and irrigation frontiers, though most of them were superficial and over-romantic by today's standards. Her *Coeur d'Alene* (1894) viciously attacked the hard-rock miners who participated in a celebrated strike in 1892; the book was filled with heroes and villains but showed no real understanding of the conflict.

Another writer of note was Vardis Fisher (1895–1968), who published thirty-six books beginning with *Toilers of the Hills* (1928), a novel that vividly portrayed the trials of pioneers in the dry and lonesome sagebrush country of his native state. Born of an impoverished pioneer family in a rural part of southern Idaho, Fisher could never be accused of unduly romanticizing the frontier.

His largely autobiographical *In Tragic Life* (1932) was a brooding account of the underside of frontier life. When several eastern publishers rejected the manuscript, J. H. Gipson of Caxton Printers of Caldwell announced that he would publish the work even "if I have to walk barefooted down the streets." Despite forebodings of financial disaster, *In Tragic Life* was well received by critics and established Fisher as an important novelist in the 1930s.[2]

Fisher, who graduated magna cum laude with a doctorate in English literature from the University of Chicago in 1925, taught at various universities and wrote history as well as fiction. Perhaps he is best known today for his work in the 1930s as director of a New Deal project that compiled a detailed guide to the state of Idaho. For twelve hours a day, seven days a week, he traveled Idaho's roads collecting data. He and his researchers amassed so much material that he produced two companion volumes—the *Idaho Encyclopedia* (1938) and *Idaho Lore* (1939), which continue to reflect Fisher's skills as a writer.

The Spirit of Community

Idahoans are for the most part cooperative individualists. That is, they prize the spirit of independence but often work together voluntarily for a variety of purposes. Some of their associational activities have centered on religion. The Mormon church typically formed the heart of community life in south-eastern Idaho, where cooperative activity among believers existed from the time Franklin was founded. Mormons have often accounted for about half of Idaho's churchgoers, the other half being Catholics, Presbyterians, Methodists, and a variety of smaller denominations.

Lodges and fraternal organizations prominent in Idaho ranged from various Masonic orders to the Red Men of America and the Grange. Men who

47. An outing on Payette Lake near McCall in the late 1920s or early 1930s. Courtesy Oregon Historical Society, 33874.

joined secret societies before coming to Idaho sought out their "brothers" in the mining camps and in this way organized some early lodges. Such social groups provided a sense of instant community in newly formed towns populated by strangers.

Fraternity was a very important element in early-day labor unions. Miners' unions often fielded tug-of-war teams, and men and women gathered in union halls to hear debates and lectures. Occasionally the hall was the setting for a prize fight. There were also civic clubs and chambers of commerce. Shortly after the turn of the century, at least one hundred commercial clubs existed in Idaho. Territorial pioneers established a historical association in Boise in 1881 that evolved into the Idaho State Historical Society of today.

The spirit of association took a less formal shape when citizens gathered to celebrate a national holiday, cheer their favorite baseball team, or join a lawn social. Major holidays were scrupulously observed, notably the Fourth of July. In Challis, on July 4, 1878, the predominantly male population observed the day with a dance, although only three women were present to provide partners for one hundred men.

48. Lava Hot Springs as it appeared in its primitive days in the early twentieth century. The facility today features a modern outdoor swimming pool in a scenic mountain setting. Courtesy Idaho State Historical Society, 79–25.65.

Life on the Idaho frontier was synonymous with egalitarianism, or so it may now seem, yet in most settlements some form of social distinction quickly appeared. Carrie Strahorn, an early-day commentator on Idaho life, recalled that in Hailey,

after the first year or two of joining hands with everybody in a social way there was a secret meeting of some of the elite to separate the gambling and saloon element from social functions. Every circular sent out, and invitations also, were signed "By Order of the Committee," so no one knew who was at the bottom of the movement, but from that time on, parties were as select as anywhere in the United States, and no gentleman appeared at a dinner or other social affair except in the conventional dress suit.[3]

Outdoor Life

Blessed with an attractive and varied natural setting and an enormous amount of public land close at hand, Idahoans have over the years enjoyed a variety of outdoor-oriented activities. The list today includes backpacking, fishing, hunting, white-water rafting, downhill and cross-country skiing, golf, and swimming. This indulgence in the great outdoors is the basis of a moneymaking industry that continues to grow. White-water rafting alone adds millions of dollars each year to the state's economy.

Resort hotels, dude ranches, and hot springs have been popular almost from the day the Oregon Short Line first made the Wood River valley accessible to large numbers of tourists.[4] All three types of facilities continue to attract visitors. Of the state's more than one hundred major mineral springs, perhaps the most famous today is Lava Hot Springs, which the federal government deeded to the state in 1902 to provide health and recreation opportunities for all in an attractive natural setting. A nonprofit foundation still manages the popular facility, located on U.S. 30 between Montpelier and Pocatello.

Early on, Idahoans bragged about the juxtaposition of Hayden Lake's charming country club, with its tennis courts and golf course, and pristine mountain lakes and trout streams. From the time the facility opened in 1907 until the mid-1920s, an electric interurban railroad whisked excursionists from Spokane to the lakeside retreat in elegant parlor cars; the trip took less than two hours. The Campers' Limited was scheduled to leave Spokane so that businessmen would arrive at the Bozanta Tavern in time for dinner with their vacationing families.

Another popular summer destination was Coeur d'Alene, where the electric cars from Spokane connected with steamboats for a trip across the lake and up the "shadowy" St. Joe River, an excursion of some two hundred miles. Occasionally a small party of campers would be put ashore for an extended stay. A reporter in the 1890s observed that one such group brought, along with all sorts of gear, a cow, which greatly amused passengers when it was pushed into the lake to swim ashore.

Idaho boosters were quick to sell the state's outdoor wonders. Even the arid Snake River plain evolved into a tourist attraction by the late nineteenth century, with perhaps the most notable site being Shoshone Falls. None of the perceived drawbacks of outdoor life daunted promoters: "To some the thought of camp life brings visions of insect pests to be endured. Not so at the majority of northern Idaho lakes, for their elevation, from two thousand to two thousand five hundred feet above sea level, is such that nights are always too cool for insects to live or be active, thus affording campers the most refreshing and restful sleep." Or so one booster claimed in the early twentieth century.[5]

Curiously, when Father Nicholas Point visited the same area in the 1840s, he observed, "Fish are abundant in lakes, rivers, and small streams. I will

49. "Successful Hunters," reads the original caption for this photograph taken in Coeur d'Alene in 1937. Today, some Idahoans might have a different response to the killing of these animals. Courtesy Museum of North Idaho, Rear, 3–11.

not speak here of the mosquito or of the other insects harmful to man. One is devoured by them in certain seasons. Nor will I speak of the serpents which are present in large numbers. In a single day I chased two out of my bed. Fortunately, rattlesnakes are rare there."[6] The way people described Idaho's out-of-doors obviously changed with the rise of tourism as a paying proposition.

Idahoans retain a high regard for the quality of life, especially when it is measured not just in terms of per capita income (where Idaho has never ranked high) but also in terms of room to roam, clear skies, mountain grandeur, and solid, if not always spectacular, educational and cultural opportunities. Although "you can't eat the scenery" is a truism, the quality of life in Idaho cannot be treated as a matter merely of dollars and cents.

Ten years ago the entire country was complaining of hard times, and Latah county was about as hard hit as any other section that found itself hard up and with no apparent way of getting out of the difficulty. The people had little or no money, their farms were mortgaged, back interest was due, small debts had accumulated, their products found poor markets, and it was an unusually sanguine man who could see daylight ahead.—from *An Illustrated History of North Idaho* (1903)

Decade of Turmoil
1892–1902

The first decade of statehood was a time of trouble. That, of course, was nothing new to Idaho. For most of its brief existence, trouble had seemed a fact of life. Vigilantism, Indian wars, economic instability, political factionalism, and racial and religious animosity had punctuated the territorial years. What was new about the troubles of the 1890s was the severity of the economic downturn, the rise of a new party of political protest, and the emergence of organized labor to demand a better life for workers.

Populist Protests: Silver to the Rescue

In response to a variety of grievances, Idaho's most important third party organized in 1892 as the People's or Populist party, a branch of a nationwide insurgency that swept the South and West in the 1890s. The party's chief demands were for a graduated income tax, a postal savings bank, government ownership of railroads and of telegraph and telephone lines, and the free and unlimited coinage of silver by the federal treasury. The latter was an inflationary measure favored by both mineowners and workers, who believed it would bolster their depressed industry. Agrarian debtors prominent in newly developed parts of Idaho also supported the cause of free silver, as the panacea came to be known.

Opposing them were creditors, chiefly eastern-based bankers and insurance executives, who favored the gold standard and loathed the inflationary silver standard as a dishonest way to pay off debts. The battle of the standards was a very complex matter, but in Idaho it translated into the simple belief that what was good for the silver industry was good for Idaho. Thus although Idaho's Populist party originated in the southern part of the state, it soon attracted a mass following in the Coeur d'Alene mining district as a result of the free silver issue.

An indication of the almost universal appeal of the silver issue was the fact that in the 1892 election Idaho Democrats rejected their party's presidential nominee, Grover Cleveland, and endorsed the Populist candidate, James Weaver, and silver.[1] Adding stature and legitimacy to the Populist cause was the conversion of William H. Clagett, a northern Idaho lawyer who had chaired the state constitutional convention in 1889.

Further bolstering the fortunes of the Populists was the crash of 1893, a terrible depression that began on Wall Street in early summer and within days washed across the country like a devastating tidal wave. In its wake numerous workers lost their jobs or had their wages slashed, farmers were driven from their land when commodity prices collapsed, banks and businesses closed, and several of the nation's largest railroads went bankrupt, including both the Union Pacific and Northern Pacific lines that served Idaho.

One spectacular bankruptcy was that of the McConnell-Maguire Company of Moscow, the state's largest mercantile firm. The principal stockholder at the time of the crash was Idaho's governor, William J. McConnell. In Boise the situation grew truly dark when the mayor turned off all but eight of the streetlights as an economy measure. Residents complained that thieves took advantage of the darkness.

Thievery and insolvency were not all that worried Idahoans. In the cities of the West Coast, unemployed workers banded together in industrial armies and attempted to take their grievances en masse to Capitol Hill. One army of approximately two hundred jobless men made its way east from Portland. Its ranks included unemployed railroaders, desperate men who stole a train in Montpelier and were steaming furiously toward Rock Springs, Wyoming, when the United States Army overtook them.

Troops brought the prisoners back to Boise for trial. Most of them ended up spending a few months in a makeshift prison erected along the Snake River where the tracks of the Oregon Short Line entered the state from the west. Following on the heels of the industrial army (or Coxey movement) was the Pullman strike, the first nationwide railroad walkout, which disrupted rail service in much of Idaho.

A coalition of Populists, silver Republicans, and Democrats (whose party platform now embraced free silver) dominated the state after the 1896 elec-

50. Harvest workers sew up sacks of grain in the Palouse country around the time of World War I. Courtesy Idaho State Historical Society, 60.62.813.

tion. That year Idaho voters defied the national majority and supported William Jennings Bryan, the presidential candidate of both the Democratic and Populist parties, and Frank Steunenberg, a Populist-Democrat whom they sent to the governor's office. Not until 1902 would a majority of Idahoans quit clamoring for free silver and follow the rest of America in voting for either Republican or Democratic candidates.

Human Machines: Labor in the New Economy

Intimately associated with the Populist insurgency and strongly supported by it was organized labor, which for the first time emerged as an influence in Idaho political and economic life. The rise of organized labor was a product of the growing number of wageworkers in Idaho—and one more manifestation of a nationwide response to industrialism. In the days of the wageworkers' frontier, which lasted from the 1870s until the 1920s and encompassed much of the West, a large population of laborers supplied the muscle needed to harvest Idaho's timber and grain, mine its precious and base metals, and construct its railroad lines and irrigation dams and canals. Before the First World War, the wheat harvest alone required hundreds, even thousands, of itinerant workers each season.

Such laborers were typically young, single, and mobile. They worked in all-male gangs and supplied strong arms and backs. They were "human machines" who exchanged physical labor for a daily wage. The work they did was invariably heavy, dangerous, and dirty. Although some might remain in a single industry and gain considerable proficiency as miners or loggers, often the work was not steady. The most mobile hands became known as floating workers and bindle stiffs, and a common saying in timber and railroad construction camps was that there were three crews connected with any job: "one coming, one going, and one working."

Logging camps flourished in the early 1900s, most of them located either on riverbanks or along the tracks of special railroads built by the lumber companies. These camps traditionally closed in winter—about November or December—and reopened in April or May. As the forest was cut, the camps moved. Loggers worked six days a week and ten hours a day. They typically wore two-piece woolen long underwear both winter and summer. Unfortunately, early-day camps rarely provided bathing facilities or laundry tubs.

Idaho was never a strong state for organized labor, but pioneer unions developed among railroad workers and hard-rock miners. One of the first

51. The 1906 Labor Day parade in Twin Falls, a town barely two years old. Courtesy Idaho State Historical Society, 73–221.799.

Percentage of Persons Employed, 1910, by Occupation

	Idaho	Oregon	Utah	Washington
Agriculture	44	29	28	25
Mining	6	2	8	3
Manufacturing	17	27	23	27
Transportation	8	11	10	10
Trade	10	10	10	12
Public Service	<1	1	2	3
Professional	5	6	6	5
Domestic Service	7	9	8	10
Clerical Service	3	5	5	5

labor organizations was the Owyhee Miners' League, organized in October 1867. Another early union appeared among miners in the Wood River valley in the early 1880s. Unions also formed among Coeur d'Alene miners in the late 1880s, and by 1891 they had grown strong enough to establish the Miners' Union Hospital in Wallace, the first such institution among hard-rock miners of the West.

Not much is known about the early labor movement in Idaho, but an official state survey taken in 1907—a time when organized labor was receiving considerable publicity across America—revealed that the state's forty-five local unions enrolled a total of 2,240 members. Of these, half were single. The largest lodge was the Mullan local of the Western Federation of Miners, which numbered 375 members, of whom 36 were married and 339 single. Ten of the Mullan miners were homeowners and 365 were renters.[2]

On the wageworkers' frontier, the employment relationship that some laborers disparaged as wage slavery coexisted with the enduring western ideal of individual freedom and advancement. Perhaps it was not good for workers to learn they could not make their dreams come true, for time and again the clash between dreams and reality gave rise to radical crusades and militant unions like the Industrial Workers of the World, famed for its colorful and unorthodox attempts to organize the Pacific Northwest's many wageworkers in the years before World War I. Most workers were not revolutionaries, however; they wanted only a fair return on their labor.

In the end, changing technology did most to close the wageworkers' frontier. During the years between the two world wars, mechanical harvesters and the shipment of wheat to market in bulk rather than in burlap sacks

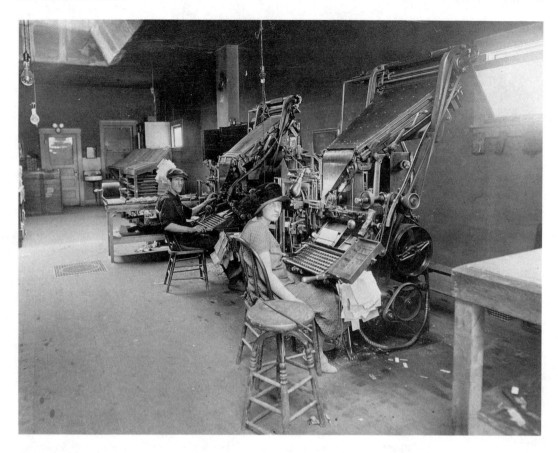

52. A woman operator of a Linotype machine in Burley in 1926. Courtesy Idaho State Historical Society, 79–375.

dramatically reduced the need for harvest hands. Steam shovels displaced many of the common laborers who constructed and maintained railway lines and irrigation ditches. Improved living conditions in the logging industry made it possible for the lumberjack to get married and settle down outside the camps. In a number of cases, a logger was able to drive to work in his own automobile. For many workers, "automobility" was the equivalent of upward social mobility.

Few Idaho women worked for wages prior to the Second World War. Because so much of the state's economic activity centered on natural resource industries dominated by males, it was a rare woman who found a job in mining or timber except as a clerk, cook, or laundress. An unknown number of women worked as prostitutes, especially in the predominantly male-oriented world of the wageworkers' frontier. Across Idaho a few women found jobs in skilled trades, such as operating a Linotype machine, and many more became telephone operators. By far, the largest number of wage-earning women held jobs as schoolteachers and nurses.

Women could be found in any mining camp, though not at first in large numbers. A few arrived as wives; others, to manage rooming houses and eating places. The Bannock (Idaho City) mining district in 1862–63, for example, recorded a population of 59 women out of 670 people. The women enjoyed great prestige, and if a mining camp survived to become a town or village, the ratio of males to females tended to normalize as miners got married and raised families. In the logging camps, however, which were essentially makeshift work sites in the woods, there were few females. Some loggers, in fact, regarded a woman in camp as bad luck.

War in the Coeur d'Alenes: Industrial Violence

During the troubled 1890s, two major episodes of industrial violence wracked the new state of Idaho, one in 1892 and another in 1899. Labor-related violence occurred in many parts of the United States during the 1880s and 1890s, years of unsettling economic change. Unemployed workers could expect no help from government, and no legal authority governed labor-management relations. Employers and workers were forced to grope their way along unfamiliar terrain toward the resolution of conflicts, and their search for common ground was not always successful.

Idaho's worst industrial violence centered in the Coeur d'Alene mining district, where newly organized mineowners confronted newly unionized miners. A variety of problems beset the owners, chiefly the falling price of silver and rising railroad rates, but their greatest concern was the growing power of union labor. Mineowners formed a protective association in 1889 and responded to organized workers with a variety of antiunion weapons: they cut wages, hired spies and armed guards when workers struck, fired union members, and imported nonunion or scab labor. By mid-1892 the owners had employed more than eight hundred strikebreakers from outside the region and protected them with armed guards.

Months of escalating tension culminated on July 11, 1892, when guards barricaded in the Frisco mine's ore-processing mill in Gem exchanged gunshots with union members. Sporadic shooting continued for hours, then suddenly a roar shook the valley. Dynamiters had launched a bundle of explosives down a pipe that carried water into the Frisco mill.

The blast demolished the structure, and falling timbers killed one worker and injured several others. The guards and scabs promptly surrendered, as did those at other mines and mills farther down the canyon. Miners disarmed the scabs and marched them to trains to ship them out of the valley. In the

Coeur d'Alene Mining Region, (Silver Valley) Idaho, 1910

wake of the violence, six men were dead (three on each side) and about twenty-five injured. As strikebreakers hastily departed the district, someone tacked a broom onto the last boxcar to signify a clean sweep.

With the scabs gone, union miners celebrated their victory. But their jubilation was premature. Because of the violence, Governor Norman Willey declared martial law. State and federal troops arrived to put down the insurrection and protect the scab workers as they returned. Union men, who had hoped never to see the strikebreakers again, were crestfallen and sullen.

Soldiers rounded up hundreds of people. One witness predicted that in two days the Coeur d'Alenes would be a huge military prison for the miners union. That prophecy came true when authorities collected three hundred men in a vast dragnet—and not just union workers but justices of the peace, lawyers, merchants, and saloonkeepers who happened to be in the wrong place when the troops swept through.

Military personnel herded prisoners into two makeshift prison camps known as bull pens at Wallace and Wardner, where many of them were confined for nearly two months awaiting a hearing. At first most of the men considered their arrest a joke; they laughed and sang and enjoyed supper prepared by the ladies. But as the weeks passed, they complained loudly, and tempers grew short. Sanitary conditions became unbearable in the summer heat, and even those outside the Wallace stockade complained of noxious odors pervading the town. The state finally transported twenty-five union leaders to Boise for trial. Several of the accused used their time in the Ada County jail to create a new and more powerful union, the Western Federation of Miners.

Trouble erupted again in 1899 when miners commandeered a train near Wallace and headed for Wardner to teach a lesson to the mighty Bunker Hill and Sullivan Company, the most important single enterprise in the mining district and widely regarded as setting the tone for labor relations. Following the violence of 1892, the Western Federation of Miners had successfully persuaded most of the large mines in the Coeur d'Alenes to pay union-scale wages, but not the Bunker Hill and Sullivan. Its managers claimed that low profits forced them to cut costs and use only nonunion labor. Union members attempted to infiltrate the company's work force, but the Bunker Hill and Sullivan invariably identified and discharged them.

The armed men who commandeered a train at Gem loaded several tons of explosives aboard. When the "Dynamite Express" approached the Bunker Hill and Sullivan complex, company guards fled along with the superintendent and manager—a wise move considering that two thousand men were

54. The former governor Frank Steunenberg, assassinated at his home in Caldwell on December 30, 1905. Courtesy Idaho State Historical Society, 13.

nearly upon them. The workers burned the company's office and boarding-house and placed three thousand pounds of dynamite around the concentrator's support pilings. At 2:26 that afternoon, someone—probably several miners—lit the fuses. Three explosions reduced the half-million-dollar structure to matchsticks.

Miners rejoiced and congratulated themselves on their victory in the "Second Battle of Bunker Hill," a reference to the Revolutionary War battle. Next morning, most of them reported for work as usual. But one young miner prophesied correctly, "You can't steal railroad trains, dynamite mines, and burn villages without some reaction." [3]

Telegraph lines sped news of the violence to Governor Steunenberg. A man who emphasized the common touch—he refused to wear a necktie to any state function—Frank Steunenberg had once been a member of a printers union. With the backing of labor he was elected governor in 1896 and again in 1898. But he could not condone what had happened in the Coeur d'Alenes. The governor promised to punish those who he believed had openly violated the law to commit murder and other crimes.

Because in 1899 the Idaho militia was stationed in the Philippines in the aftermath of the Spanish-American War, Steunenberg wired for federal troops and declared the Coeur d'Alene region to be in a state of insurrection. Brigadier General Henry Clay Merriam and almost eight hundred bluejacketed soldiers arrived by special train on May 3, and the general promptly ordered every miner herded into the bull pen—a total of between six hundred and seven hundred people. In the end, this combination of state and federal power fatally weakened the union. Mineowners instituted a permit system to screen former union members from the work force. It lasted until 1901.

In late 1905 Harry Orchard wrote a bloody postscript to the Coeur d'Alene mining wars when he planted a bomb that killed Steunenberg at his home in Caldwell. For that crime, the state convicted and sentenced Orchard to spend the rest of his life in prison. He cheated the gallows only by claiming that top officials of the Western Federation of Miners had actually hired him to assassinate the former governor in revenge for his actions in the Coeur d'Alene dispute six years earlier.

Armed with Orchard's long and sordid confession, Idaho officials quietly pursued William D. ("Big Bill") Haywood, the union's secretary-treasurer; Charles Moyer, its president; and George Pettibone, a blacklisted Coeur d'Alene miner and now a hardware merchant. With the full support of the governor of Colorado, Idaho lawmen kidnapped the three suspects in Denver and rushed them to Boise on a special train. Idaho's high-handed extradition by abduction outraged organized labor and civil libertarians and thrust the case into the national spotlight. The United States Supreme Court ruled that although the seizure had been illegal, the three men were now in Idaho's custody and had no legal remedy.

The most sensational trial in Pacific Northwest history opened in Boise in 1907, almost eighteen months after Orchard was arrested. It pitted Idaho's special prosecutor and newly elected United States senator, William E. Borah, against the famed Chicago attorney Clarence Darrow for the defense. For almost two months, local and national attention focused on the proceedings. In the end the jury deliberated twenty hours before acquitting Haywood.

Idaho law required a witness to corroborate Orchard's claim of a union

55. A scene from the most famous trial in Idaho history. Harry Orchard (number 1, seated at the extreme left) testifies against William D. Haywood, identified as number 11 in the photograph. Courtesy Idaho State Historical Society, 2005.

conspiracy, and Stephen M. Adams, the only person who might have done so, retracted a confession he claimed was coerced by a Pinkerton detective, James McParland. Many people found it difficult to believe Orchard's many sensational claims to bigamy, arson, assassination, and mass murder. After eighteen months in the Ada County jail, Haywood was again a free man.[4]

After Haywood's acquittal, Idahoans seemed eager to forget the years of trouble. The opening years of the twentieth century had brought the Gem State newfound prosperity and a confidence it had seldom experienced before.

CHAPTER 13

Confident Years

America's bout of hard times lasted from 1893 until 1897. When prosperity finally returned, Idahoans seemed to possess unprecedented confidence in their state and its future. Among the tangible measures of confidence were a new skyline for Boise and the thousands of acres of irrigated farmland reclaimed from the once sagebrush-covered Snake River plain. Other measures of confidence were rapid population growth between 1900 and 1920 and a proliferation of new counties, mainly in the southern part of the state. Every legislature established new counties, and in fact, nearly half of Idaho's forty-four counties were created during the boom years from 1900 to 1919.

Adjustments: From Populism to Progressivism

If the turn-of-the-century years gave rise to a generation of builders, it also called forth adjusters, the reform-minded men and women who would shape laws and inherited patterns of thought to fit a complex new postfrontier world of urbanization, organized labor, nationwide transportation and communication networks, and expanded governmental responsibilities for the welfare of citizens. Their adjustments included giving Idaho women the right to vote in 1896 and urging the state to take the first steps toward making the workplace safer for everyone.

In the 1890s America's reformers were often called Populists; in the early twentieth century, Progressives. Regardless of the label, they wrestled with the consequences of a village-based economy that had evolved into a nationwide one dominated by large and distant manufacturing establishments. Across the nation, reformers sought to curb the abuse of power in high places by enacting direct legislation measures that gave average citizens a say in government matters. The Idaho legislature passed a direct primary measure in 1909, initiative, referendum, and recall measures in 1911, and a workmen's compensation law in 1917.

The Progressives also brought prohibition to Idaho in 1916 in an effort to eliminate the social and political ills associated with alcohol. Reformers responded to dirty and dangerous foods processed in distant cities by enacting pure food and drug laws on the national level and by funding a bacteriologist and a scaler of weights and measures on the state level.

Although the Populist party disintegrated shortly after the turn of the century, it left an unfinished agenda that attracted the interest and support of the next generation of insurgents. Some of them were Democrats, but most were men and women active in the Republican party's Progressive wing.

Idaho, which clung tenaciously to the cause of free silver for a decade, turned overwhelmingly Republican in the 1902 election. Of the 120 contests for statewide offices held between 1902 and 1930, the Republicans won all but 9. Only during the interval 1917–18 did Democrats control the legislature, and only two men succeeded in breaking the Republican hammerlock on the governor's office. They were James H. Hawley (1911–13) and Moses Alexander (1915–19). During these years, no single Democratic or Republican politician emerged to lead the Progressive crusade as Robert M. La Follette did in Wisconsin, Hiram Johnson in California, and George Norris in Nebraska, and perhaps as a consequence, progressivism was far less influential in Idaho politics than it was in neighboring Oregon and Washington.

Idaho's William E. Borah was squarely in the Progressive tradition of his Senate colleagues La Follette, Johnson, and Norris, but he did not identify with progressivism at the state level. He helped sponsor such Progressive measures as the income tax and direct election of senators.

Also in the Progressive tradition was Fred T. Dubois, Borah's immediate predecessor. Dubois had once been bold enough to defend Theodore Roosevelt on conservation matters, but when he resurrected the old anti-Mormon issue in 1908, he divided and practically destroyed the Idaho Democratic party. Both Borah and Dubois considered issues more important than party lines. As for Weldon B. Heyburn, who served in the Senate from 1903 to 1912: he was a conservative Republican with few Progressive inclinations. He nonetheless sponsored the Pure Food and Drug Law in a reluctant Senate.

Progressivism's high-water mark probably occurred in 1912 when Theo-

56. Three famous men in Idaho history rest on the steps of Ira B. Perrine's home on the Snake River near Twin Falls. From left to right they are Senator Fred T. Dubois, the three-time Democratic presidential candidate William Jennings Bryan, and Perrine, who was best known for his promotion of the Twin Falls project. Courtesy University of Idaho Library, Historical Photograph Collection, 6–57–3.

dore Roosevelt broke ranks with his fellow Republicans and formed the new Progressive or Bull Moose party with Hiram Johnson as his running mate. In the end Woodrow Wilson, the Democratic standard-bearer and only real beneficiary of the Republican split, carried Idaho.

The Canal Never Fails? Irrigation and Reclamation

In a sense the Progressives were social engineers, seeking to make society better by means of thought and planning. They had many counterparts outside the political arena who believed that to make the state's harsh natural environment more livable required no small measure of engineering know-how.

In fact, the settled parts of Idaho today represent to a large degree the triumph of engineering. Such skills made it possible to develop mineral and timber resources as well as to build railroads, hydroelectric plants, and cities. Complex feats of engineering were required to complete Idaho's North and South Highway in 1919, to make Lewiston a seaport in 1975, and to develop the facility that became the Idaho National Engineering Laboratory in 1974.

57. The Perrine Memorial Bridge under construction across the 1,400-foot-wide Snake River canyon at Twin Falls. Work on the cantilevered network of steel some 200 feet above the river began in the fall of 1926, and the bridge was opened to traffic in 1927. Courtesy Idaho State Historical Society, 73–221.5.

58. Mary Hallock Foote's romantic view of the new Eden created by irrigation reached a national audience through the pages of the *Century* magazine in 1889. Courtesy Idaho State Historical Society, 76.2.67.

In all of this there were trade-offs, of course, although opponents of some of the technologies employed are far more numerous today than they were even twenty years ago.

Of all of Idaho's engineering achievements, perhaps none was more impressive than the irrigation and reclamation that made large-scale settlement of the Snake River plain possible. Populating the irrigated lands marked the final phase of the settlement process that began when emigrants first plodded west along the trail to Oregon.

Construction of irrigation systems in Idaho proceeded slowly in the 1860s and 1870s, then picked up speed in the 1880s, and accelerated dramatically in the late 1890s. Early methods of irrigation varied greatly, from simply diverting water onto an open field to building extensive networks of ditches and canals. Utah's Latter-day Saints first solved many of the thorny problems involving engineering and water law and then exported their expertise to Mormon settlements in southeastern Idaho.

Early irrigation involved a certain amount of trial and error that occasion-

ally left a ditch unable to meet the water needs of people living along its banks. Often lacking survey instruments, early canal builders sometimes used a frying pan or gun barrel to determine the necessary fall. Following the survey work they excavated the land with plows, scrapers, and shovels. In this manner small-scale irrigation projects went forward, though not always successfully.

Irrigation in Idaho passed through four somewhat overlapping stages as it matured: first was individual effort, then corporate enterprise, then government aid to private enterprise, and finally large-scale federal reclamation. Following the farmers—often Mormon—who individually or cooperatively built simple ditches to serve local and limited needs came private canal companies promising to irrigate substantially larger tracts. Some of the companies were headquartered as far away as New York.

Frequently, however, private funds alone were inadequate to do a proper job. Thus in order to stimulate state and private cooperation, Congress passed the Carey Act in 1894; eight years later it created the Reclamation Bureau and offered western agrarians a generous program of federal assistance.

The Carey Act encouraged reclamation by giving each western state a million acres of land if it found a way to irrigate them, with either private or public money. As a result of this stimulus, Idaho by the turn of the century ranked first in irrigated land in the Pacific Northwest. In fact, Idaho ultimately contained three-fifths of all land irrigated under the Carey Act and became a national showcase.

A prime example of what the Carey Act might accomplish was the Twin Falls project headed by Ira B. Perrine. The largest private irrigation project in America gave birth to the agricultural boomtown of Twin Falls in 1904. As impressive as such accomplishments were, the total amount of western land irrigated under the Carey Act actually equaled only two average-size agricultural counties in Illinois.

The Carey Act sought to keep federal participation to a minimum. That policy changed with passage of the Newlands Act of 1902, which created the United States Reclamation Service (Bureau of Reclamation after 1923) to supervise construction of a number of new dams and canals and complete defunct older ones like the New York Canal near Boise. The Minidoka project, which first received water in 1909, was one of two large federal reclamation undertakings in Idaho that reclaimed thousands of acres of farmland and created a host of new agricultural communities.

59. On an isolated stretch of the Snake River plain in 1899, a construction crew working on the Last Chance Ditch pitched its camp. Courtesy Idaho State Historical Society, 79–95.37.

Arrowrock Dam supplied the Boise Valley with a surplus of water for the first time and made possible 1,167 irrigated farms totaling 67,454 acres. Standing 348 feet high, Arrowrock was the world's tallest dam until 1932 and a special source of pride for Idahoans.

Today approximately three million acres are under cultivation on the Snake River plain—where roughly two-thirds of Idaho's irrigated lands are located—the massive circular sprinkler systems developed after World War II being used to supplement older canal methods. By 1960 the Bureau of Reclamation had sunk 170 wells to tap the waters of the vast Snake River aquifer, and private individuals sank hundreds more.

Reclamation was never simply a matter of engineering, economics, or law, just as irrigation canals were never merely sources of water. Canals and their life-giving water fostered the growth of special kinds of oasis communities that combined the complexity and dependency of urban life with a rural agricultural environment.

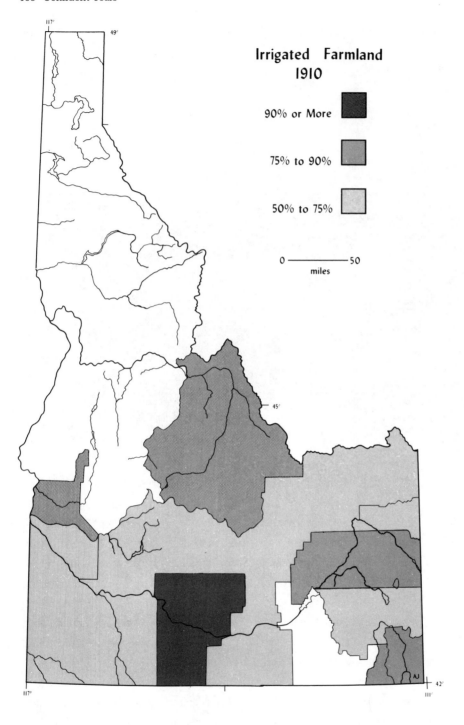

Irrigated Farmland
1910

90% or More

75% to 90%

50% to 75%

0 ——————— 50
miles

60. A Twin Falls photographer, Clarence Bisbee, strikes the expansive pose of a booster surrounded by a field of wheat. Courtesy Idaho State Historical Society, 73–221.1708.

Promoters often described such communities as perfect gardens of Eden, but they were also highly vulnerable: one booster claimed that although clouds might fail to bring rain "the canal never fails," yet reality was never so uncomplicated. The social and economic well-being of dwellers on reclaimed lands depended to a large degree on federal money, power, bureaucracy, the technological expertise of the few, and occasionally the caprice of nature. Moreover, there was never enough water even in the wet years to satisfy every need and demand. In 1919, when the Twin Falls Canal Company could furnish only 30 percent of the water in a normal year, desperate farmers in the upper Snake River valley made illegal use of water at night and broke the locks on headgates.

Irrigation as a Way of Life

Annie Pike Greenwood reflected on the vulnerability of an irrigation community well as the potential for conflict there when she wrote, "Water among us sage-brush folks was money. When a man stole your water, he committed grand larceny, no matter how much he himself might feel his crime mitigated by the hymns he sang to Jesus a-Sunday. Water in the sagebrush country is not free, as the rain from heaven. Both the just and the unjust have to pay for it, or it is shut off, though the Water Company is not hard-boiled about it, so far as I know. If your head-gate, is stuffed with weeds or gunnysacks, it may mean the loss of all the money you can make that year, for your crop will die. There is dry farming in Idaho, but our farms were not operated in that manner."—Annie Pike Greenwood, *We Sagebrush Folk* (1934), 380.

The Selling of Idaho

The growing number of irrigated acres gave increased impetus to an long-standing campaign to promote Idaho both as a good home and a profitable field for investment. The process of "selling Idaho," in fact, probably reached its fullest flower during the confident years of the early twentieth century. The work had begun when the first transcontinental railroads reached the territory in the 1880s and forced it to compete for national attention with other western states and territories.

In 1885, for example, Moscow citizens suggested printing pamphlets to extoll the town's virtues and hiring a person to go east to distribute them. At that time a single agent in Omaha stocked ten thousand pamphlets and a hundred thousand flyers about Idaho to distribute throughout the East. In a similar effort, the businessmen of Eagle Rock created a promotion sheet called "The Resources of Idaho" to be issued monthly at ten cents a copy. Community leaders sought to attract prospective settlers and entrepreneurs in order to promote growth and a prosperous future. Individual publicists and chambers of commerce joined with railroads in this informal crusade to sell Idaho.

Transcontinental railroads spent millions of dollars to advertise their vast western land-grant holdings and were among the most prominent boosters of Idaho. The Union Pacific Railroad in the mid-1880s hired an immigration agent to provide prospective settlers with sample potatoes and apples grown along its right-of-way. The Northern Pacific launched numerous campaigns to advertise the new Northwest's farms, mineral wealth, and trade connections to the Orient. Both railroads distributed pamphlets all over the United States and Europe and established free information bureaus.

Railroads paid professional promoters to collect statistics and weave them into compelling pamphlets. Carrie Strahorn, who accompanied her husband, Robert, on many of his fact-gathering trips for the Union Pacific, described the process: "We spent some weeks on Wood River gathering statistics which [Robert] wove into entertaining narrative, clothing it in attractive garb that it might coquette with restless spirits in the far East who were waiting for an enchantress to lure them to the great mysterious West."[1]

Publicists were people of vision, imagination, and boundless optimism. A typical product of their vision of the future was an 1889 pamphlet that said of Idaho's sagebrush plains: "Districts which five years ago were sagebrush districts, have bloomed into rich farming lands, where grains, vegetables and fruit grow in profusion. There are thousands and thousands of acres of fine lands only awaiting settlement and irrigating ditches to furnish pleasant homes for settlers."[2]

The territory itself joined the promotional effort when the 1889 legislature established the Idaho Board of Immigration to encourage settlers: "It is a well-known fact," observed the report of the committee that recommended passage of the bill, "that the advantages and resources of Idaho are the least known of all the territories."[3]

Many of the early advertisements amounted to little more than drab, crudely printed tracts. Their often shrill rhetoric was exemplified by an early-day booster organization in Buhl that had as its motto: "Pull for Buhl or Pull Out." But with the coming of large-scale irrigation to the Snake River plain in the early twentieth century, the process of promoting Idaho as a promised land achieved considerable sophistication. Pamphlets became works of art designed to appeal to prospective settlers from a variety of backgrounds.

In the fall of 1911, the former Idaho governor James H. Brady conceived the idea of running a special train to exhibit the resources of the western states. Called the Western Governors' Special, the train toured the Midwest and East. Wherever it stopped, crowds gathered to view the wonders of the West. Promoters hoped that the exhibits would lure newcomers to settle the region. As the easterners passed through the cars, exhibitors were pleased to overhear remarks such as, "Why, I thought the West was nothing but a desert." The turnstile on the Idaho car indicated that ninety-two thousand people visited the touring exhibit.[4]

Among individual boosters of Idaho few if any exceeded Robert W. Limbert in zeal. A taxidermist and furrier in Boise, he used photographic essays to publicize the state's diverse geography as a tourist attraction. At the Panama-Pacific International Exposition in San Francisco in 1915, he crowned a display of Idaho's increasingly famous potatoes with an eleven-foot model

See Idaho First: The Beginnings of Tourism

Transcontinental railroad companies were probably the first organizations to advertise Idaho as a tourist destination. Although it had no Yosemite or Yellowstone parks to use as lures, its fishing, hunting, and other outdoor opportunities were nonetheless attractive. Idaho was promoted as a sportsman's paradise filled with elk, deer, antelope, mountain sheep, and many other forms of wildlife.

Such relatively low-budget attractions as excursion boats on Lake Coeur d'Alene appealed to urbanites from Spokane bent on escaping the summer's heat. Rustic dude ranches appealed to city folk eager to "rough it" in comfort.

Promoters of tourism also sought to woo those who customarily vacationed in Europe: "To the tourist who travels for pleasure, the slogan 'See America First' applies with unusual force to the whole Rocky Mountain region, and more especially to Idaho. To the invalid seeking to restore his health, the healing properties of Idaho's hot and mineral springs offer as many inducements as the famous waters of Carlsbad or Baden, to which may be added the pure, mountain air and the scent of pine forests, things not to be found in any European watering place."
—Quoted in James H. Hawley, *History of Idaho: The Gem of the Mountains* (Chicago: S. J. Clarke, 1920), 1:814.

of the Russett Burbank variety. To the popular phrase See America First, Limbert added the corollary Begin with Idaho.

In the 1920s Limbert came to believe that tourism would ultimately supplant logging and mining as Idaho's leading industry. To lure sightseers he wrote and illustrated articles that appeared in mass-circulation journals, including *National Geographic*. In the process he did much to publicize the area that President Calvin Coolidge proclaimed the Craters of the Moon National Monument in 1924. Limbert also turned his attention to the Sawtooth Mountains, which resulted in a fifty-four-page promotional pamphlet for the Union Pacific in 1927. The railroad distributed one hundred thousand copies of the publication.

How many settlers and tourists the pamphlets and exhibits actually attracted to Idaho is not known. Undoubtedly the publicists influenced many people. Inevitably some would-be residents were disappointed to learn that publicists occasionally stretched the truth. Other people, however, accepted the challenge of starting life in the new settlements and relished their role as twentieth-century pioneers. When, for example, the name Magic Valley came into general use in the late 1930s in south-central Idaho, it was an apt description of the transformation wrought both by irrigation and by promotional pamphlets.

The Transforming Power of Fire

Even as water transformed the arid lands, the great forest fire of 1910 swept across the panhandle to leave an indelible impression on a generation of Idahoans and scars on the land that are still visible today. There were few lookouts in 1910, and detection of forest fires depended on intermittent patrols. In that year alone several thousand fires blackened 3.3 million acres of woodland in four Northwest states, most of it during a two-day conflagration that began on August 20, 1910. Idaho with 744 blazes suffered 1.7 million scorched acres and the destruction of several communities.

61. The great forest fire of 1910 reduced a third of Wallace to smoldering ruins. Courtesy University of Idaho Library, Barnard-Stockbridge Collection, 8-X90.

Driven by hurricane-force winds, the fires brought heavy smoke and darkness at noon. For a time it seemed as if spontaneous combustion would consume the tinder-dry woods where only a quarter of an inch of rain had fallen since early June. Women and children were hastily evacuated from Wallace before the flames roared in and burned out one-third of the town. The 1910 blaze also consumed homesteads and mining and railroad structures.

NAMPA'S BIG FIRE   JULY 8 09   LEE JELLUM   PHOTO

Smoke from Idaho and Montana drifted as far east as Boston. To help man
the fire lines, President William Howard Taft sent in an all-black regiment of
army regulars, some of whom had earlier participated in the 1899 Coeur
d'Alene troubles. Fire fighters in 1910 hiked twenty-five to thirty miles a day
to do battle mainly with shovels and axes. Seventy-two fire fighters died in
the 1910 blaze. Salvage from the burn took years. In fact, some of the cedar
charred in 1910 was still being sold in the late 1970s. One result of the 1910
blaze was that fire protection became a major function of the United States
Forest Service.

Fire was a menace not only in the woods but also in towns built largely of
wood and illuminated by candles and coal-oil lamps. Idaho City suffered four
disastrous fires between 1865 and 1871. The first left an estimated seven
thousand people homeless. In May 1867 a fire burned 440 buildings there.
Some nineteenth-century communities responded to fire danger by placing
barrels of water at intervals along the main streets; others installed hydrants
and water mains. Volunteer fire companies offered both protection and a
popular social outlet.

Following a devastating fire, many a town replaced wood with brick and
stone in an effort to fireproof the community and give it the appearance of a
prosperous modern city. But a few communities, such as Grand Forks, destroyed by the great forest fire of 1910, never rebuilt.

Urban Growth: Mill Town and City Beautiful

After its urban beginnings, Idaho quickly moved to the country and returned
only gradually to the city. In 1900 a mere 6.2 percent of all Idahoans lived in
urban areas. In 1980 some 54 percent did. What is remarkable about this shift
is that only in 1970 did Idaho become more urban than rural. The nation as a
whole crossed that statistical divide fifty years earlier.

In fact, urban areas never had quite the magnetic attraction for twentieth-
century Idahoans that they had for residents of many other states. It is true
that almost 25 percent of all Idahoans now live in the Boise metropolitan area,
but that is not so impressive a figure when compared with the 75 percent of
all Arizonans who live in the Phoenix and Tucson metropolitan areas.

By census definition, Idaho today ranks as one of America's most rural
states, but that statistic must be used with caution. The federal government
defines communities of twenty-five hundred or more residents as urban.
Many Idahoans, though not living on farms and ranches, are residents of
towns too small for the federal bureaucracy to classify as urban. In fact, one-

Urban Population in the West, 1900

	Total Population (in thousands)	Urban (percent)
California	1,485	52
Colorado	540	48
Washington	518	41
Utah	277	38
Montana	243	35
Oregon	414	32
Wyoming	93	29
Nevada	42	17
Arizona	123	15
New Mexico	195	14
Idaho	162	6
United States	75,994	40

Note: According to the Census, an urban population is one numbering 2,500 or more residents.

third of Idaho's forty-four county seats in the mid-1980s had fewer than twenty-five hundred residents and thus did not qualify as urban. Yet it was to those towns and villages that nearby residents went to transact legal business, take care of banking needs, purchase groceries and other supplies, and catch up on local news.

No settlement founded more recently than Twin Falls (1904) has become one of Idaho's larger cities. By the First World War, most of the state's urban centers had assumed the roles they would play until the 1980s. Shoshone was synonymous with railroading; Lewiston, Sandpoint, and Coeur d'Alene with forest products; Wallace and Kellogg with metal mining; and Moscow with education and agriculture.

For eighty years Potlatch was a company town, and timber was the lifeblood of the community. Beginning in 1905 the Potlatch Lumber Company constructed more than 250 buildings on hills that overlooked the largest white pine sawmill in the world. At one time, two thousand people lived in the bustling community that could boast an opera house, paved streets, and wooden sidewalks.

MAIN ST., HOLLISTER, IDAHO.
OCT. 2ND, 09.
210
BISBEE PHOTO.

63. Town builders on the irrigation frontier. City fathers of Hollister, near Twin Falls, lay out Main Street on October 2, 1909. Courtesy Idaho State Historical Society, 73–221.790./b.

But the mill closed in 1981, and many sawmill workers left. A way of life ended. The millsite is today a concrete slab in a grassy field. The community survived, however, by serving as a bedroom community for the university towns of Moscow and Pullman, just across the border in Washington. A similar slump affected Elk River when its mill closed in the early 1930s, but it was too far from other centers of population to function as a satellite suburb. Elk River barely hangs on today.

The irrigation colony of New Plymouth was one of Idaho's few non-Mormon planned communities. Launched in 1895 by the Payette Valley Irrigation and Water Power company, it was intended, in the words of its cofounder William E. Smythe, "to represent a high social and industrial ideal."[5]

Many New Plymouth colonists were professionals from Chicago and the urban Midwest. Their dream was to make the town self-sufficient through the development and operation of small diversified farm plots that produced for local and the eastern markets. In this way the founders of New Plymouth hoped to give agrarians the advantages of town life while preventing the isolation all too common in a rural environment.

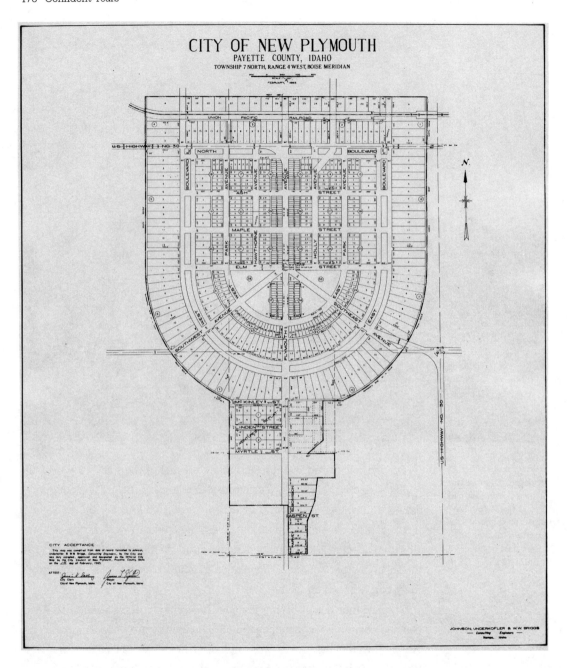

64. The unusual city plan of New Plymouth recalls the town's origin as a planned community and irrigation utopia. Courtesy Oregon Historical Society, 83081.

The confidence that gave rise to New Plymouth also transformed older, more established communities. After the turn of the century, cities in the Pacific Northwest got new skylines, and Boise was no exception. The Idanha Hotel, an elegant and expensive French chateau structure six stories high, was completed in 1900 and inaugurated the skyscraper era that gave Boise the appearance of a modern metropolis. Four more six-story buildings were

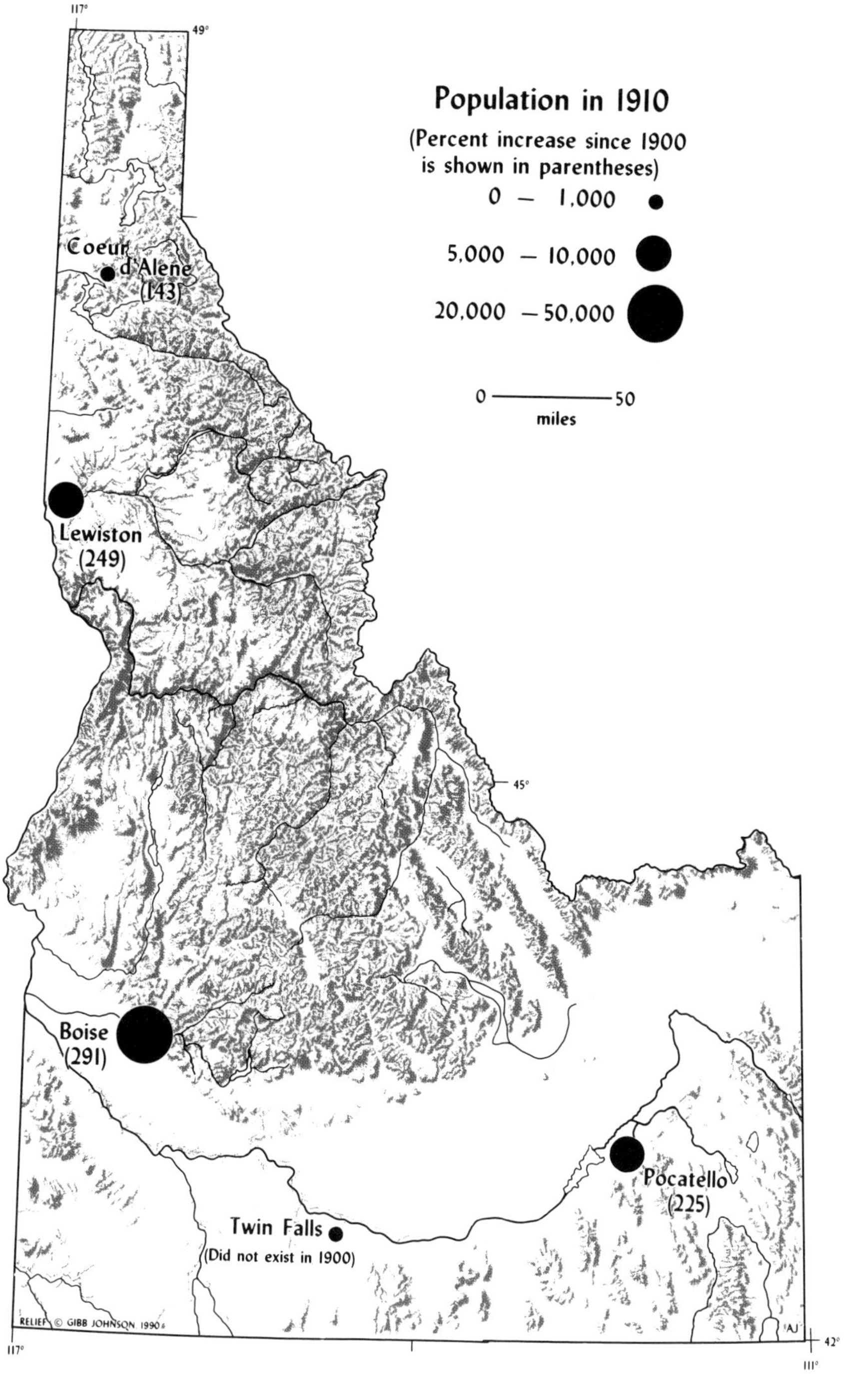
Population in 1910
(Percent increase since 1900
is shown in parentheses)
0 – 1,000
5,000 – 10,000
20,000 – 50,000
0 50
miles
Coeur d'Alene
(143)
Lewiston
(249)
Boise
(291)
Pocatello
(225)
Twin Falls
(Did not exist in 1900)
117°
49°
45°
42°
111°
RELIEF © GIBB JOHNSON 1990
AJ

65. The new Idanha Hotel dominates downtown Boise in this undated view of Main Street. The landmark building still stands. Courtesy Idaho State Historical Society, 73–11.3.

constructed there between 1906 and 1913, along with a capitol dome that towered over them all.

The City Beautiful movement, which swept the nation after the Chicago's 1893 world's fair, also left its mark on Boise in the form of classical-style public buildings, bridges, and parks. Boise liked to promote itself as the Athens of the sagebrush, a phrase first used by Clarence Darrow in 1906. From 1914 to 1930, however, no new tall buildings were built in Boise, and the emphasis shifted from the city's skyline to its homes. A network of streetcar and electric interurban lines made it possible for Boise to expand outward as new neighborhoods and suburban communities were built.

By a quirk of geography, when the Oregon Short Line laid its tracks across the Snake River plain, it bypassed Idaho's largest community. The railroad preferred to follow a more level route south of the city and shunt passengers into the capital from Nampa. Boiseans resented this arrangement, but not until 1925 did they gain a through passenger line. The Union Pacific's new Mission-style station on the benchland south of downtown and the arrival of the first through train occasioned a major celebration. Capitol Boulevard, an

Largest Communities in Idaho, 1890, 1990 (By Population)

	1890		1990
Boise	2,311	Boise	125,738
Montpelier	1,174	Pocatello	46,080
Weiser	901	Idaho Falls	43,929
Paris	893	Nampa	28,365
Bellevue	892	Lewiston	28,082

impressive thoroughfare through the heart of Boise, linked the station to the capitol.

The advent of motorized transportation in the 1920s had a major impact on urban Idaho. All-weather roads and automobiles greatly extended the reach of medium- and large-size trading centers, and motorized buses enabled schools to consolidate, diminishing the number of one-room rural facilities. Thus the county seats and trade centers prospered at the expense of remote villages, many of which simply disappeared.

Urban Idaho would experience another major transition during the 1980s when several natural resource–oriented communities turned to tourism as their mills and mines shut down. Coeur d'Alene, Wallace, McCall, and Riggins are all examples of timber or mining towns that became tourist centers.

As a new year dawned in 1917—even as the United States pondered its future in a world wracked by war—most Idahoans had reason to congratulate themselves on how much their young state had changed since the beginning of the century. There were now twice as many people as in 1900. Idaho had suffered some setbacks, like the great fire of 1910 and the adverse publicity surrounding the abduction and trial of Big Bill Haywood, and there were differences of opinion over such matters as national forest land. But at least the old racial and religious animosities of the past seemed to have eased.

The rise of the timber industry brought new prosperity to the panhandle, and the magic of irrigation transformed the Snake River plain. These were exciting times and, for the most part, good years, especially when viewed from the vantage point of the era that was to include the Great War, economic depression, and new forms of conflict.

THE WAR! THE WAR! Down at the school-house was a constant boiling, like a great kettle, patriotic city steam scalding the quiet rural air—speeches, speeches, speeches, to pry loose the few coppers still clinging to the interiors of overall pockets; to make farm women cook such penurious concoctions as city women would scorn to attempt.—from Annie Pike Greenwood, *We Sagebrush Folks* (1934)

War and a Troubled Peace
1917–1929

The year 1917 saw Idahoans coping with the demands that World War I created. They responded to the crusade to "make the world safe for democracy" with patriotic fervor. For almost two years they supplied raw materials, labor, and military personnel to the Allied cause. But hardly had the Gem State celebrated the nation's victory over Germany and the Central Powers in November 1918 before economic problems contributed to a troubled postwar decade.

Military Idaho before 1917

Idahoans served in the armed forces at a rate higher than the national average in the Spanish-American War of 1898 and in the two world wars. Young volunteers were fired by patriotism and a positive image of military service.

Beginning with the first contact between Indians and Lewis and Clark's Corps of Discovery in 1805, military personnel played a variety of roles in Idaho history. During the Great Reconnaissance of the 1840s and 1850s, members of the army's Corps of Topographical Engineers mapped Idaho's mountain passes and provided geographical information to aid Oregon-bound travelers.

The United States Army first stationed units in the Pacific Northwest in 1849 to protect the Oregon argonauts and later to enforce treaties with the Indians. It was a combination of rising Indian hostility to Oregon-bound emigrants and Civil War tensions between Republicans and pro-Southern Democrats that prompted the federal government to establish a series of new army posts, notably Fort Boise in 1863.

For several seasons, army escorts traveled out from Fort Boise to meet the emigrant trains and escort them safely through the Snake River country. During the Indian wars of the late 1870s, Fort Boise served as a base of operations. The post also saw use in 1916 when Idaho soldiers prepared for duty on the Mexican border and again during World War II from 1942 through 1944.

Another army base was located at Fort Hall, about twenty-five miles northeast of the old fur-trading post of the same name. Its purpose was to protect stage and freight routes in the 1870s. In the Clearwater Valley, Fort Lapwai served from 1862 until 1884 when a quieting of tensions between whites and Indians diminished its value as a military base.

Fort Sherman, which was established on the north shore of Lake Coeur d'Alene in 1878 (and later named for the famed Civil War general William T. Sherman) had as its mission to keep the peace in northern Idaho, watch the Canadian border for invasion, and protect railroad and telegraph crews from Indian attack. Never regularly garrisoned after the troops left for the Spanish-American War, the post was abandoned in 1901, and today its grounds are the site of North Idaho College.

Federal troops were used in the 1870s in the famous war with Chief Joseph and the Nez Perces and to quell Indian troubles in southern Idaho. They were also called out during the industrial disputes that convulsed the Coeur d'Alene mining district in the 1890s. After the Spanish-American War ended in 1898, Idaho troops traveled to the Philippines to quell the insurrection led by Emilio Aguinaldo. Idaho National Guard units were mobilized and sent to Nogales, Arizona, where for five months in 1916 they patrolled the border with General John Pershing during the Mexican revolution.

The Great War at Home, 1917–1918

Unlike the neighboring states of Oregon and Washington, Idaho did not develop large-scale industries as a result of World War I. Instead, the Gem State contributed mainly the traditional products of its fields, forests, and mines and some twenty thousand of its young people for military duty.

Not long after the Second Regiment of Infantry, Idaho National Guard, returned from service on the Mexican border, it was drafted into national service. Eventually the "Second Idaho" was merged with two other Gem State battalions into the United States National Guard Army and lost its separate identity. In the nation at large, one in every twenty-two persons was in military service; in Idaho, where patriotic fervor ran especially high, the ratio was one in eighteen.

On the home front, Idaho's farms produced food needed to feed the troops and the wool needed to clothe them. Its forests supplied white pine for aircraft construction, and its mines provided lead and other vital minerals. Idahoans purchased millions of dollars' worth of war bonds and savings stamps to help finance the war. To Madison County belonged the honor of being the first 100 percent thrift-and-war-savings county in the United States. That is, every one of the children in its public schools bought thrift or war savings stamps. In 1917 a volunteer force of schoolchildren was organized to help in the fields during a time of labor shortage.

The middle-class clubwomen of Pocatello rallied to the Allied cause when they undertook a variety of charitable efforts, chiefly sewing and knitting garments for the Red Cross to distribute to the needy. Like their sisters across the state and nation, they also engaged in fund raising and aided in the conservation of meat, wheat flour, and sugar. One hundred fifty Pocatello women found employment in the Oregon Short Line shops cleaning cars and running lathes, drill presses, and other machines, but no real breakdown of the distinction between ''men's work'' and ''women's work'' occurred. Work in railroad shops was not typical of middle-class women.

Idahoans, like most Americans, viewed the First World War in idealistic terms as a great crusade that would put an end to war itself and make the world safe for democracy. Ironically, a strange thing happened to democracy at home, where Americans came to view any type of nonconformity as a threat to the war effort.

In 1917 Idaho's State Council of Defense, a quasi-governmental body, inaugurated a county-by-county card index to flush out slackers, a derogatory term applied to anyone who contributed less than was expected of him to the war effort. Special distrust focused on Idaho's twenty-six thousand German- and Austro-Hungarian-born residents, and self-appointed patriots closely monitored their activities. Germans had to prove their patriotism by abandoning their native language and culture and by buying Liberty bonds. Some communities eliminated German from the school curriculum. Some of the self-appointed patriotic organizations voiced the dark foreboding that German groups would form a secret alliance with the hated and feared Industrial Workers of the World (Wobblies) to undermine the nation's war effort.

Few if any groups suffered more harassment during the war than the Wobblies, feared because of their self-proclaimed willingness to use sabotage, sitdown strikes, slow-ups, and passive resistance to accomplish a revolutionary restructuring of society and economy. Most of their threats amounted to nothing more than bluster, yet ever since Wobblies formed the Lumber Workers' Industrial Union Number 500 in Spokane in March 1917, organizers had been extremely active in the forests of northern Idaho where they demanded an eight-hour day, higher wages, and improvement in camp living conditions. Operators rejected all such proposals.

By the time America entered the war, a series of Wobbly-led strikes completely halted timber production in the white pine region from the Clearwater River north to the Canadian border. Government officials estimated that 80 to 95 percent of all loggers in Benewah County were somehow connected to the Industrial Workers of the World, and it became a common practice to attribute forest fires to Wobbly sabotage.

The union was similarly active among itinerant harvest workers. Organizers moved from field to field to promote the idea of "Six Dollars a Day or No Work." The Industrial Workers of the World had only a small impact on rural Idaho, yet the mere mention of Wobbly agitation could paralyze farmers with fear and anger.

Alarmist reports flooded the office of Governor Moses Alexander, and after the United States declared war on Germany, an increasing number of people issued patriotic appeals to drive out the Wobblies, whom they considered secret agents of the kaiser. Alexander was wary of industry's alarmist rhetoric, but he nonetheless requested that companies of federal troops be sent to Wallace and Lewiston as a precautionary move. More zealous officials constructed makeshift prison camps called bull pens in St. Maries, Coeur d'Alene, and Moscow to confine alleged Wobbly troublemakers.[1]

In its effort to harass and destroy the Industrial Workers of the World, Idaho also passed the first criminal syndicalism law in the United States in early 1917. This statute, which made it illegal for anyone to advocate the overthrow of the American government, was a model for similar legislation in other states. Some citizens would have taken even more extreme measures but for Governor Alexander, who resisted the near hysteria voiced in parts of the state.

This required more than the usual amount of political courage: Idaho's wartime chief executive was not only the nation's first elected Jewish governor but also a native of Germany. Born there in 1853, Moses Alexander had immigrated to the United States at the age of fourteen. He cast his future with Boise in 1891 when he opened a clothing store. At the time of his election in 1914, he owned a chain of stores in southern Idaho and eastern Ore-

No time to pussyfoot.

66. A Spokane newspaper cartoon accurately portrayed the popular pressure on Governor Moses Alexander to use force to suppress the Industrial Workers of the World. Courtesy Museum of North Idaho.

67. Displaying intense feelings on the day the Germans surrendered, November 11, 1918, citizens of Challis burned the kaiser in effigy. Courtesy Idaho State Historical Society, 63–132.1.

gon. He was reelected in 1916 and would be fated to serve as governor during the frenzy of hatred directed against Germany.

When Alexander resisted hasty action on the numerous requests that urged him to short-circuit civil liberties, some people accused him of overt disloyalty, and at least one individual demanded an investigation into how much the German kaiser influenced the Idaho governor. Some vigilante groups were organized, and tensions increased, but Idaho did not suffer the extreme violence that occurred in other states during the First World War.

When the Great War finally ended on November 11, 1918, spontaneous celebrations greeted the news. "EXTRA! WAR'S OVER. CITY WILD WITH JOY," screamed the banner headlines that covered half the front page of the *Twin Falls Daily Post*. Some five thousand men, women, and children paraded behind a band through the city's streets. But even as Idahoans celebrated victory, a troubling new killer cast a lengthening shadow across the Gem State. Tanks and bullets had no effect on the Spanish influenza. In fact, no one was certain how to combat the new scourge that appeared shortly before the Armistice.

Some Idaho communities required people to wear gauze masks in public; others deferred public meetings and closed theaters. Kimberly, a town located just east of Twin Falls, established a self-imposed quarantine, although no case of flu had yet been reported there. It prohibited passengers from leaving the train that passed through town and barred out-of-town motorists from stopping. In Twin Falls, however, the flu claimed several victims. The epidemic subsided in December, then made a brief comeback in early 1919. There are no statewide statistics of influenza deaths in Idaho, but an estimated half a million Americans died of the flu, a figure ten times higher than the nation's fifty thousand combat deaths.

The Troubled Twenties

When the Great War ended, Idaho's farmers found themselves not only fighting influenza but also mired in a financial mess that originated during the boom years when patriotic appeals to grow more food caused them to buy land on credit and expand their capacity to produce far beyond what a peacetime world could consume. Farm prices peaked in 1920, then began a rapid slide. Bankruptcies piled up alongside unsold stores of wheat and other commodities.

A bitter Annie Pike Greenwood, who attempted to farm the Snake River plain, recalled Idaho's postwar years:

> After the Armistice there was the terrible let-down of realizing that our land was worth less than it had been before the war, that there was nothing to do but to worry over the mortgages. The price of wheat had been arbitrarily fixed, but not the price of labor or of anything else that the farmer used. We could have paid off our mortgages and kept even with our expenses had the law of supply and demand been allowed to operate, as in every other field of business. Millionaires were made by the war, and the American farmer was impoverished.[2]

The brief but severe agricultural depression of 1921 jolted the United States. Although prosperity returned to enrich the lives of many Americans, who fondly recalled the 1920s as the Jazz Age or the Prosperity Decade, the pall of hard times never really lifted from Idaho's timber and farm areas. Twenty-seven of the state's banks failed during the 1920s. Farm commodity prices had only begun to recover in 1929 when the onset of the Great Depression caused them to drop again.

The prolonged agricultural depression of the 1920s accounted for the fact that Idaho was second only to Montana among the forty-eight states in the number of residents who moved out during the decade. In fact, it seemed that Idaho's chief export during those years was the bright young men and women who sought jobs elsewhere.

Don't Get a Horse: Innovations in Transportation and Communication

Life in Idaho during the 1920s and 1930s was not all economic gloom and doom. The state got its first federal airmail route on April 6, 1926, when the mail was flown 550 miles from Pasco, Washington, to Boise, and on to a railroad connection at Elko, Nevada. A second mail route opened across southern Idaho in 1929. From this inauspicious beginning, Idahoans increasingly took to the air. Some people viewed the airplane as inaugurating a new era, especially for the state's scattered and hitherto isolated mining camps.

Closer to the ground, Idahoans took to the road in growing numbers in the 1920s, and not until 1935 did the state require a driver's license. During the interwar years Idaho completed the basic network of highways that still exists today—except for the four-lane interstate system first funded by Congress in 1956 and the Lewis and Clark Highway (now U.S. 12) completed over Lolo Pass in 1962.

The motor age was synonymous with the twentieth-century transportation revolution. When the century dawned, Idahoans were still utilizing railroads, steamboats, and stagecoaches as their primary forms of public transportation. The most innovative developments up until then were the new trolleys and interurban railroads that had arrived with the advent of electricity during the 1880s and 1890s.

By promising cheap and convenient transportation, the electric lines gained in popularity during the first two decades of the twentieth century. The trolley was not merely a public conveyance but also a source of community pride, a symbol of modernity. Boise, Twin Falls, Caldwell, and Lewiston—all had electric railroads.

Boise's first electric street railway was chartered in 1890. Two years later its tracks extended out Warm Springs Avenue to the Natatorium, for three decades a popular recreation center. In the early 1900s the electric lines reached west to Eagle, Star, Caldwell, Nampa, and Meridian, and eventually formed a large loop in 1912. A popular Sunday ride was to take "the loop." Boise Valley Traction, as an Idaho Power property in 1916, owned thirteen miles of track in Boise, seventy miles in the valley, and thirty-nine passenger and service cars. Its business peaked in 1920, then dropped dramatically in the face of automobile competition before passenger service ended eight years later.

68. Twilight of the trolley. Automobiles bring an increasing number of visitors to the old fairgrounds in Boise in the 1920s. Courtesy Idaho State Historical Society, 78–39.3.

Because of its low population density and difficult terrain, Idaho never had an extensive network of electric interurban tracks. The various scattered segments totaled only 133 miles of line. In addition to the Boise Valley loop, electric interurbans linked Preston and Franklin to Logan, Ogden, Salt Lake City, and Provo. A five-mile interurban line linked Sandpoint and Kootenai for eight years beginning in 1909. The lines of the Spokane and Inland Empire Railroad extended out from Spokane to reach Coeur d'Alene (in 1903) and Moscow (in 1908).

Trolley companies developed parks and other recreation facilities to increase their excursion business, especially on the weekends. One of the most elegant retreats was the Bozanta Tavern located at the Hayden Lake country club, which the Spokane and Inland Empire Railroad created as a destination for affluent passengers seeking to escape the summer heat of Spokane. Its electric cars also linked up with Red Collar steamboats at Coeur d'Alene to offer a popular cruise on the lake.

In 1909, as crowded special trains sped toward Coeur d'Alene from Spo-

kane carrying excited bidders for Indian reservation land, they collided. The crash killed fifteen passengers, injured seventy-five, and plunged the Spokane and Inland Empire into serious financial problems from which it never recovered. In the late 1920s the Great Northern Railway acquired the ailing company as a feeder line. Some trolley and interurban lines survived into the 1930s—the Utah-Idaho Central hauled passengers to Preston until 1947—but most of the electric lines succumbed to the competition of private automobiles during the 1920s.

Idahoans were slow to embrace the automobile. This was not a matter of innate conservatism or continuing love for horses or trolleys. The state simply lacked good roads and a climate suitable for year-round operation of automobiles before the advent of antifreeze and other technological innovations. When in 1910 there was an average of one automobile for every 197 Americans, Idaho lagged far behind with only one automobile for every seven hundred residents. But by 1920, Idahoans had moved well ahead of the national average. By 1980 only two states had more motor vehicles per thousand population than Idaho.

By the mid-1920s the automobile was no longer popularly regarded as a toy for the idle rich—a useless go-devil, as some farmers had called it. It was now a necessity. Citizens demanded and got more and better roads and highways. Life in Idaho's isolated towns and villages no longer centered on the arrival and departure of the train or stagecoach. Now citizens came and went as they pleased in their own automobiles. The road map, not the railroad timetable, became their window to the larger world.

Passenger trains became less frequent or stopped running altogether, and railroad stations ceased to serve as community gathering places. Many were torn down. Moscow's fine brick union station, for example, was eventually razed and a tavern built in its place.

Idaho's pioneer motorists were an intrepid lot. Among the difficulties they faced were locating fuel, which was initially available only at auto dealers and hardware stores, rough roads that caused many flat tires, and lack of directional signs. The state contained only five miles of oiled or semipaved highway in 1918.

Even in 1930, when Idaho could boast of 1,640 miles of paved roads, the motorist who made the 30-mile trip from Moscow to Lewiston without a flat still had something to brag about. Today the many people who commute back and forth between the two communities scarcely give a thought to how difficult the journey once was.

More than anything else it was the expanding network of roads that encouraged automobile ownership. Until 1919 not even a wagon road connected the northern and southern portions of the state. The sole intra-Idaho link between north and south was an Indian trail so rough that for six months of the year only an expert snowshoer could traverse it.

The dream of uniting Idaho caused the seventh territorial legislature to petition Congress in 1872 to build a military road from Fort Lapwai to Fort Boise. At a time of rising tension between Indians and white settlers, the road could be justified as an aid to the rapid movement of troops, but nothing came of the proposal.

Serious planning for a highway to run the length of Idaho dates from 1913. The name North and South Highway was adopted two years later. Construction commenced in 1916, and after three years of work, it was at last possible for a determined motorist to drive the entire distance on the steep, winding, narrow, unsurfaced path that some dignified as a highway.

Unlike U.S. 95 today, the North and South Highway veered east to St. Maries just before reaching Lake Coeur d'Alene and then proceeded north along the lake's serpentine east shore. There are other places, too, where the modern highway significantly improves on the original route. Yet even in its primitive state, the 525-mile-long highway was widely hailed as launching a new era in Idaho history: "North Idaho and South Idaho are destined to join the ranks of obsolete terms," a Coeur d'Alene writer optimistically predicted.[3]

Idaho first levied a tax on gasoline in 1923 to finance its roads and, armed with this new source of revenue, launched a highway construction boom that rivaled mining days in excitement. Although by the end of the 1920s the state had completed a basic network of roads, during the depression years that followed, it continued to build and improve its roads as a way of putting unemployed men to work. The extension of all-weather highways also encouraged the rapid expansion of Idaho's intercity truck and bus lines. Highway construction and the burgeoning of automobile travel made possible a host of new roadside businesses that catered to motorists.

Most significant, the transportation revolution of the 1920s changed the face of the city by encouraging urban dwellers to move to suburban neighborhoods and by ending the isolation of rural dwellers. Motorized transportation encouraged school consolidations and extended the influence of regional trading centers at the expense of smaller villages. In short, the motor age transformed Idaho during the 1920s and 1930s much as the railway age had during the 1880s and 1890s.

Perhaps second only to the automobile in its impact on Idaho society in

71. Coeur d'Alene's newly motorized fire department in 1925. Courtesy Museum of North Idaho, CDA-6–33.

the 1920s was commercial radio, which brought a whole new world of news and entertainment to the state's widely scattered communities. Even the lonely sheepherder on some remote part of the range could now tune into events halfway around the globe. The state's first licensed radio station was 7YA, started in late 1921 by Harry Redeker, a science teacher at Boise High School. Two or three nights a week it broadcast speech and music. The station acquired the call letters KIDO when it was sold in 1928.

As radio entered its golden age, a fifteen-year-old lad from Rigby, Idaho, designed an electronic device that would alter popular forms of entertainment even more dramatically than radio had. He was Philo T. Farnsworth, who in 1922 showed his high school chemistry teacher his design for a system to transmit pictures electronically. Here was the key to the television age. In 1930 Farnsworth patented the picture-tube electronics he later leased to the Radio Corporation of America, but not until after the communications giant mounted quite a fight. RCA, which initially experimented with an inferior mechanical system, attempted to patent a competing design, but late in the 1930s a court ruled in Farnsworth's favor.

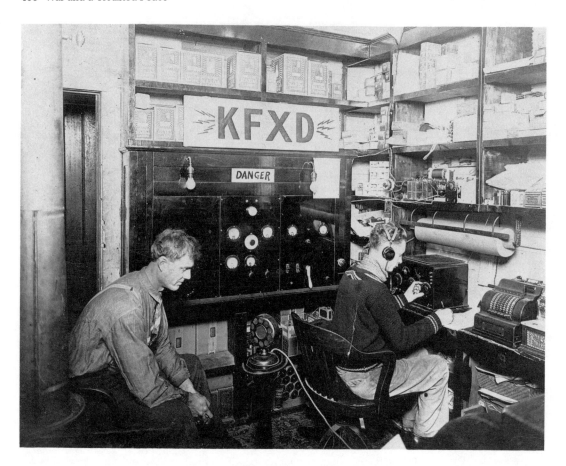

72. Station KFXD of Nampa, Idaho's second commercial radio station, as it appeared in the late 1920s. Courtesy Idaho State Historical Society, 79–45.13.

The Republican Era: Agrarian Protest and Borah

The hard times that followed the Great War, together with the accumulated grievances of farmers on irrigated lands of the Snake River plain, gave rise to a full-scale farmers' revolt in southern Idaho that boosted the fortunes of two insurgent groups, the Nonpartisan League and its successor, the Progressive party.

The Nonpartisan League, which originated among the disgruntled farmers of North Dakota in 1915, reached Idaho two years later. Its socialistic program attracted such phenomenal support that by 1919 it claimed twelve thousand members in the Gem State alone. The league's goal was to retire old-guard politicians by electing reformers regardless of party labels.

In the 1918 primary election the Nonpartisan League alarmed both major parties, especially when its favored farmer-labor candidates scored numerous successes in the Democratic primary. But then the Nonpartisan cause seemed to lose momentum, and its candidates fared poorly in the fall election. Frightened by the insurgency, the Republican-dominated legislature of 1919 repealed the direct primary law that had muddled Idaho politics and served the league's cause so well. The repeal left protesters no alternative but to enter third-party politics.

The agricultural depression of 1921 aided the rise of Idaho's new Progressive party, which like the Nonpartisan League called for a variety of reform measures including government ownership of railroads, direct legislation, and a one-year moratorium on farm mortgage foreclosures. In 1922 the Progressive party elected several candidates to both houses of the state legislature. One defeated Republican from Canyon County lamented that he was "beaten by a socialist." Progressives also captured control of the governments of Jerome, Minidoka, and Canyon counties.

In 1924 the Progressive party promoted the La Follette–Wheeler third-party ticket. Again the Progressives finished well ahead of Democrats in many races. But 1924 was the high point of the new Progressive protest. Four years later the party was gone.

Despite the Progressive insurgency, Republicans still dominated Idaho government during the 1920s. The Republican Charles C. Moore, the first real dirt farmer to run for governor, remained in office from 1923 to 1927. The party also elected three presidents—Harding, Coolidge, and Hoover—and controlled Congress. During these years one of the most prominent Republicans both on Capitol Hill and abroad was Idaho's Senator William Edgar Borah.

Borah was an orator without peer and perhaps the best debater in the Senate. He could draw a crowd to the galleries simply by giving notice of his intention to speak. Even more important, as chairman of the Senate's prestigious Committee on Foreign Relations from 1924 to 1933, Borah played an influential role in national and international affairs, becoming better known abroad than almost any Northwest political figure before or since. In some countries he became the most famous living American. Once a European press agency cabled its Washington correspondent: "Never mind Hoover statement, rush comment from Borah."[4] People of the Gem State took an uncommon pride in Borah, who was popularly referred to as the Lion of Idaho.

During the interwar years, few public figures better exemplified the Pacific Northwest's tradition of political independence than the man who represented Idaho in the United States Senate from 1907 to 1940. Borah, who was born in southern Illinois in 1865 and moved west to Boise in 1890, re-

73. Senator William Edgar
Borah in 1915. Courtesy
Library of Congress,
US262.

The Larger-than-Life Borah

The story is told that in the 1930s a farm boy went to Boise. When he returned home he told his father that he had seen the internationally famous Senator William E. Borah shaking hands with people in the Owyhee Hotel. "Don't be ridiculous," his father scolded. "What would a big man like Borah be doing way out here in Boise, Idaho?"—Frank Church, "Borah the Statesman," *Idaho Yesterdays* 9 (Summer 1965):3.

mained a Republican all his life, yet the dictates of conscience always took precedence over party platforms or labels. Neither an organization man nor an ideologue, he saw himself as a moral force in politics.

Borah gained fame for his role as a prosecutor in the celebrated trial of "Diamondfield" Jack Davis and especially in the case of William D. Haywood, who allegedly plotted the assassination of Governor Frank Steunenberg. Despite his role in the Haywood trial and the probusiness inclination of his party, Borah was not antilabor. In the Senate he demonstrated his independence by representing the cause of labor and vigorously opposing corporate monopoly.

During the First World War, Borah defended civil liberties at a time when the Bill of Rights if put to a popular vote would almost certainly have lost. He supported President Woodrow Wilson's conduct of the war, and that was one reason why the Democratic chief executive privately endorsed the Republican senator's bid for reelection in 1918. But a year later, Borah joined in opposing Senate ratification of the Treaty of Versailles and American participation in Wilson's beloved League of Nations.

The Idaho senator continued his independent ways during the 1920s by championing diplomatic recognition of the Soviet Union, a then unpopular step that President Franklin D. Roosevelt took only in 1933. As chairman of the Senate Committee on Foreign Relations, Borah maintained the belief that the United States must follow an independent course in world affairs.

In domestic politics, he worked for measures to aid farmers impoverished by low commodity prices and thus time and again placed himself out of step with Republican party officials on both national and state levels. Because Herbert Hoover had opposed direct relief to the needy, Borah declined to support the president's reelection in 1932—and thereby earned the title William the Silent. With characteristic independence, Borah supported some of Roosevelt's New Deal reforms while adamantly opposing others. During the

New Deal years he maintained a closer relationship with FDR than perhaps any other Republican senator.

Whatever his apparent inconsistencies and mistakes, Idaho voters remained loyal to Borah, and he to them. A man of amazing energy and drive, he returned to Boise every summer, rented a car, and drove around the state to visit his constituents, loggers and university professors alike. Critics charged that Borah was in fact a "spearless leader," a do-nothing type of statesman who substituted oratory for solid accomplishments. Whatever the merit of that argument, Borah "represented a public asset through which Idahoans could be assured that the rest of the nation knew they existed."[5] As senator he often functioned as Idaho's ambassador to the outside world.

Borah's stature as an international celebrity brought to Idaho more attention than it would have received otherwise, and his lofty profile in the nation's capital helped Borah secure an ample share of New Deal money for his state. Such federal aid was especially welcomed during the lean years of the Great Depression.

NOTICE: No Relief Funds Available in Idaho to Non-Residents.—from a sign posted at the state border in the 1930s by the Department of Public Assistance

Depression Daze and a New Deal

The Great Depression that began on the heels of the stock market crash of late 1929 dealt Idahoans a severe economic blow. The trouble was mitigated only slightly by the fact that Idaho, unlike a good many other states, had never really prospered during the 1920s and thus most of its residents had not indulged in the "two cars in every garage" kind of optimism common in more affluent states.

Hard Times

Of the Pacific Northwest states Idaho was hardest hit by the Great Depression. Even in 1929 wheat brought only $1.30 a bushel. The state's important potato crop, which sold for $1.51 a bushel in 1919, sank to a low of $0.31 in 1922 and rose only gradually during the rest of the decade, nearly reaching the 1919 price in 1929 before plummeting to $0.10 a bushel for run-of-the-field spuds three years later. By, 1930 Idaho farm prices had fallen to 44 percent of their 1929 level; the average farm income dropped from $686 a year in 1929 to $250 in 1932.

The state adopted an income tax in 1931 to help fund extra government programs during a time of financial crisis. But because the farm crisis was both national and international in scope, Idahoans were quite helpless to do anything about it on the local level.

Whereas during the 1920s Idaho had experienced a loss of population, that trend seemed likely to be reversed during the 1930s when refugees from

the Dust Bowl of the Great Plains—commonly called Okies and Arkies—relocated in Idaho, mistakenly hoping to find some relief there. "Drive out on any of the main highways of our State," observed Senator Borah, "and you will see cars, sometimes almost caravans, fleeing from the devastations of the drouth." [1]

Some of the newcomers tried to farm inexpensive cut-over timberland in the panhandle. Most failed because they had neither the knowledge nor the skill to farm the poor soil. They came to realize that ground that grew tall trees was not necessarily suited for crops. Some people earned less than seventy dollars a year on their stump farms. In many cases one migratory farmer gave up the unproductive land to another, who repeated the cycle with the same meager results.

Idaho's Snake River plain experienced a severe drought of its own in the early 1930s. The driest year in southern Idaho since record keeping began twenty-five years earlier was 1934. This spelled heavy losses of potatoes, beets, beans, peas, and hay, not to mention diminished income for the government of a state where half the residents now depended on agriculture for a living.

From 1929 to 1932, the income of the average Idahoan dropped by 49.3 percent compared to 30.5 percent for residents of more affluent Massachusetts. There was virtually no demand for lumber, and the price of Idaho silver fell to twenty-four cents an ounce in 1933. These were years of foreclosures, delinquent taxes, and sharply rising unemployment.

Things got so bad in 1932 that arsonists ignited forest fires and then sought to earn money putting them out. The incendiary epidemic grew so widespread that Governor C. Ben Ross declared the timber country to be in a state of insurrection, proclaimed martial law, and used National Guard troops to bar public access to the forests.

In the 1930 election, when the depression had already begun to play havoc with the Idaho economy, the Democrats elected their first governor since 1917. He was Charles Benjamin ("Cowboy Ben") Ross, a reformer in the Populist tradition and a master entertainer. Two years later, a discontented electorate chose its first Democratic United States senator in fourteen years, James P. Pope, and toppled the state's two veteran Republican congressmen, Burton French and Addison Smith, who between them had forty-six years of service on Capitol Hill. The sole surviving Republican officeholder of consequence was Senator Borah, and he now remained more aloof than ever from the partisan struggle.

In the same election, Franklin D. Roosevelt carried every Idaho county but

75. Rural poverty in the 1930s: a Farm Security Administration photograph taken in Oneida County. The pamphlet in the man's hand is titled "Better Land for Better Living." Courtesy Library of Congress, 15760.

Bear Lake to defeat his Republican opponent and the incumbent president, Herbert Hoover, by winning 59 percent of the popular vote. Just four years earlier, in the election of 1928, Hoover had carried every county except sparsely settled Fremont on the state's eastern edge and won 64 percent of the popular vote.

A New Deal

During the Roosevelt years, Idaho and the nation witnessed the unfolding of a myriad of federal initiatives known as the New Deal. Except for the period of the First World War, Uncle Sam had never before loomed so large in Idaho life. In 1933 Idaho paid $904,000 in internal revenue to the federal government and received back $39.9 million in emergency relief. Only South Dakota paid a smaller percentage in taxes in relation to what it received from the national government. Idaho, in fact, ranked fifth in the nation in per capita New Deal expenditures from 1933 to 1939.

Various New Deal programs built courthouses, parks, and picnic shelters. Others helped to electrify the countryside and to build new roads and streets.

Of all the federal programs, perhaps none loomed so large as the Civilian Conservation Corps, which maintained 163 camps scattered throughout Idaho, more than in any state except California.

In Idaho alone, the CCC provided outdoor relief for almost twenty thousand sons of poor families. One of its major tasks was to eradicate the white pine blister rust fungus that was plaguing the state's forests. Idaho ranked first among the forty-eight states in Forest Service expenditures during the New Deal years.

The National Youth Administration provided parttime employment for five thousand high school and college students. The Reconstruction Finance Corporation and various relief agencies aided some twenty thousand Idaho families. The Agricultural Adjustment Administration helped farmers. Works Progress Administration projects employed twenty-two thousand people building dozens of schools and other community facilities in 1935 and 1936. The Resettlement Administration purchased 140,000 acres of land in Oneida County to give a new start to seventy-five families living on arid rangeland.

One of the largest of New Deal agencies was the Works Progress Administration. Among its programs was the Federal Writers' Project, which put unemployed talent to work preparing special guides to each state. Heading the Idaho project was the state's best-known novelist, Vardis Fisher, who crisscrossed the state and wrote most of the book himself. He endured the bureaucratic ignorance of Washington-based editors who on one occasion told him that the Grand Teton National Park was located in Idaho and that a natural bridge near Arco did not exist because they had never heard of it. To the consternation of federal officials in Washington who hoped that a "more important" state would lead the way, Fisher's *Idaho: A Guide in Word and Picture* was the first of the state guides to appear (in early 1937), and it served as a model for others to emulate.

Although Democrats dominated both the state and federal governments during these years, harmony did not exist between the two groups. Governor Ross had self-help ideas that clashed with the public welfare plans endorsed by federal New Dealers. Programs of benefit to and popular in Idaho, Ross accepted; those of little use to the state, he rejected. Roosevelt and Ross came close to open conflict during the summer of 1933. Cowboy Ben particularly opposed the repeal of prohibition, which his party favored. A popular leader, Ross nonetheless made a big mistake in 1936 when he ran for the Senate against Borah and was crushed in a landslide.

Idaho's other senator, James P. Pope, was a staunch supporter of the New Deal. He distinguished himself as a champion of the Columbia Valley Au-

Family Ties

During the 1930s and 1940s, the brothers Chase and Barzilla Clark and their nephew D. Worth Clark became Democratic candidates to reckon with at election time. Barzilla was elected governor in 1936, and Chase in 1940. The Clark family was the most successful in the history of Idaho politics: it produced two governors, two mayors, a United States representative, and, counting a son-in-law, Frank Church, two United States senators.

thority, a comprehensive agency modeled after the Tennessee Valley Authority. Though the Columbia Valley Authority never won congressional approval, Pope also sponsored legislation that created the Bonneville Power Administration in 1937.

By the late 1930s, Idahoans had clearly become uneasy about the enlarged federal presence. A good many feared the federal bureaucracy that would be needed if the Columbia Valley Authority came to fruition. Politics in 1938 reflected these feelings. Pope expected to win the Democratic primary by cloaking himself in the mantle of Franklin D. Roosevelt, but he was defeated by a conservative Democrat, D. Worth Clark, who went on to victory in the general election.

Power Plays: The Electrification of Idaho

Idaho today consumes far more electric power per capita than any other state. Part of that is because electricity drives the giant pumps and sprinklers that water crops on the Snake River plain, but even as individuals, Idahoans are heavy electric users. A primary reason is that hydroelectric power is abundant in all parts of the state and costs far less than electricity in most other places.

Idaho's first electric generating facility was installed in a Ketchum smelter in late 1882, about the same time that Thomas Edison opened his municipal lighting system in New York City. The Wood River valley was also the site of the territory's first hydroelectric operation, a small generator that powered lights in Hailey. The rate for operating the town's first 214 lights was ten cents a day for each all-night lamp and eight cents for lamps that went off at midnight.

In 1887 Boise became the second Idaho community to have electric lights when an inventive entrepreneur harnessed the flow of an irrigation canal to produce power. A generator connected to a flour mill and powered by an irrigation canal provided electricity to run Boise's first streetcars in 1891.

76. Main Street in Lewiston during the depression decade. Courtesy Oregon Historical Society: 33823.

Early electric systems were community-based operations. Most used gas or steam generators; some used surplus power from flour and lumber mills. In Moscow, electric power dates from 1888 and was a by-product of a steam engine at a local lumber company. These early generating systems powered lights, streetcars, printing presses, and a host of other machines. Hydroelectric dams, transmission lines, and the multistoried structures made possible by electric elevators soon transformed the Idaho landscape both physically and socially.

Martha Spangler, editor of the *Idaho Clubwoman*, commented in 1910 on electrification's social impact on Idaho: "With the household appliances of modern time, woman is fast coming into her own. She has more time for study and recreation, she is brighter, happier, more intelligent, and let us add, a more 'chummy' companion for her husband and children."[2]

Although urban dwellers were first to reap the benefits of electricity, some of Idaho's rural residents were not far behind. Passage of the Reclamation Act of 1902 led to construction of Minidoka Dam, the first federal hydroelectric facility in the Pacific Northwest, between 1907 and 1910. Its power pumped Snake River water to transform fifty thousand acres of arid land, and

77. A crew from the Washington Water Power Company strings its first electric line into Moscow after it acquired a local generating system. The Spokane-based utility began long-distance transmission with construction of a line into the Coeur d'Alene mining district in 1903. Courtesy Washington Water Power Company.

it electrified nearby towns and farms some thirty years before the electrification of most of rural Idaho. The town of Rupert boasted in 1914 that it had the first electrically heated high school in the United States.

Electric equipment was initially crude and not very reliable. But the technology soon improved, and so did the ability to transport power from central generating stations over long distances, a development that made large-scale electric systems possible. One of the first of these was the Washington Water Power Company of Spokane, which in the opening years of the twentieth century built a long-distance transmission line to electrify the Coeur d'Alene mines. The company subsequently expanded into the Palouse with the purchase of many small-town systems and gave local operations a degree of reliability they never had before.

About fifty electric enterprises were originally located in the area now served by Idaho Power of Boise. When Idaho Power commenced operation in 1916, it was owned by the Electric Bond and Share Company of New York. The main investor-owned electric companies operating in Idaho—Idaho Power and Washington Water Power—were early acquired by giant holding companies headquartered in the East and Midwest. Absentee owners retained control until the 1940s when the federal government broke up the holding companies.

During the years before the First World War, Idaho boosters pointed with pride to the growing availability of hydroelectric power ("white coal"). In the Bitterroot Mountains the Milwaukee Road became a world pioneer in the use of electricity to power railway locomotives. Although most of the state's electricity still comes from water power, Idaho also claims the distinction of having the world's first community lighted by nuclear-generated electricity: Arco in 1955.

When the New Deal's Rural Electrification Administration was established in 1936 to encourage the wiring of the countryside, 70 percent of Idaho farms were without electric power. By 1954 fewer than 3 percent of them still lacked electricity. Among the real beneficiaries of this program were the farmers' wives, who before electrification cooked on woodburning stoves, washed clothes by hand, heated irons on the stove to press clothes, and stored food in cellars or cisterns to keep it cool. Some farmwives recall the arrival of electricity with comments like "All I wanted in the world was an electric iron" and "We thought we were in heaven."

Perhaps because of the importance of electric power in the lives of Idahoans, electricity has often been at the center of considerable controversy. At first citizens worried about the monopolistic power of the big systems, then about the absentee owners. In more recent times questions of dams versus free-flowing rivers and nuclear versus conventional power have caused protracted controversy.

During the 1930s the big debate was over public versus private power. Oregon and Washington voters favored public power, but in Idaho, those who denounced it as creeping socialism were far more influential than its advocates. In 1937 the legislature rejected a proposal that would have allowed the creation of public utility districts throughout the state.

The issue of public versus private power also surfaced when lawmakers considered how to market electricity generated by the new Bonneville and Grand Coulee dams. In 1935, Senator Pope of Idaho and Congressman Knute Hill of Washington, two public-power Democrats, first introduced legislation that would have created the Columbia Valley Authority modeled after the massive federal reconstruction of the Tennessee River Valley. It was the first of five unsuccessful attempts to pass such a measure.

Meanwhile, the Bonneville Power Administration was created in 1937 as a stopgap measure. Today it is more than fifty years old and exercises enormous influence as a federal agency that markets electric power throughout the West.

Sun Valley: Tourism Takes on the Great Depression

During the early years of the depression, W. Averill Harriman, the youthful chairman of the board of the Union Pacific Railroad, undertook to develop a ski resort in the western United States. He desired a facility that would rival the best Europe had to offer and would also provide a destination to enhance his railroad's lagging passenger revenues.

The Union Pacific hired Count Felix Schaffgotsch, an Austrian ski enthusiast, to search for the prime location. After a visit to numerous western sites that he dismissed as too high, too windy, or too remote, Schaffgotsch finally located his ideal place on the slopes above the old mining town of Ketchum. It had dry powder snow, spectacular vistas, and all-weather access from the Union Pacific main line at Shoshone.

On Schaffgotsch's recommendation, the Union Pacific purchased a 3,888-acre ranch for thirty-nine thousand dollars. Soon a world-class resort took shape. A massive 220-room lodge was constructed. An unusually high proportion of the lower floors were made of dense concrete because of the company's fear of fires. So cleverly was the concrete etched and stained to resemble wood that few guests realized the difference. The lodge opened on December 31, 1936, although the first snow did not fall until more than a week later. *Life* magazine depicted the resort as a new playground for the rich.

For the less affluent, the company built the Challenger Inn, named after the Union Pacific's economy version of luxury trains. In 1941 Twentieth-Century Fox featured the resort in a feature-length film called *Sun Valley Serenade*.

Since the 1930s Sun Valley has undergone several transformations. From 1943 to 1946, it served as a navy convalescent center. After the return of more normal times, it regained its status as a pleasure ground for the rich and famous. But in 1964, following estimated half-million-dollar losses for several seasons and faced with the cost of major restoration, the Union Pacific sold the complex. Having passed through other hands and undergone several renovations, Sun Valley finally recaptured the luster of earlier years.

Although today Idaho has nineteen downhill ski resorts, snow skiing was not much business before Sun Valley opened. Since the early days of the resort, tourism has emerged as one of the state's largest and fastest-growing industries and is among its biggest employers. Idaho offers posh resorts that match the best in Europe, and it offers 3.8 million acres of wilderness land as well. Mixing refinement and down-home country simplicity, tourism is a mainstay of the state's economy. Tourist facilities attract some four million visitors a year and generate more than a billion dollars in income in the state.

Events of the 1930s gave new life and direction to Idaho's tourist industry. They also dramatically increased the impact of the federal government on the lives of Gem State residents, though not nearly so much as the Second World War.

CHAPTER 16

Winter in Minidoka was as intense an experience as summer had been. In preparation for the paralyzing cold, a crew of men raced from room to room, pounding slabs of white fiberboard to the walls. The fresh white walls gave us a finished decorator's touch, for until then our four walls had looked like skeletons with their ribs of two by fours bare and exposed. We gave a lusty cheer for the government when we were told that they would provide winter clothing for those who needed it.—from Monica Sone, *Nisei Daughter* (1953)

From World War to Cold War

During the 1930s the Gem State witnessed the inauguration of a host of new federal programs. Many of these involved make-work projects designed to help the unemployed. Despite all the federal dollars spent to cope with the Great Depression, the economy remained weak until stimulated by the massive spending that followed Japan's attack on the American naval base at Pearl Harbor, Hawaii, on December 7, 1941.

The Second World War brought social dislocation, privation, and death. It also created unprecedented prosperity and a rare sense of common national purpose. Not since that time have Americans been so united in the conviction that they were fighting a "good war" to defeat unmitigated evil. Such a belief, reinforced in countless ways by patriotic exhortations and demonstrations, helped Idahoans adjust to rationing, high prices, overcrowded trains, and news of destruction and death.

Production for War

Because the Japanese surprised America at Pearl Harbor and because Hitler seemed so clear a menace to the nation's interests, the Second World War, unlike the First, seemed less a crusade than a grim but necessary response to an obvious threat.

On the home front, blackouts of lights and radio stations were common in the early days of the war. Meat, milk, and clothing were all in short supply; the rationing of tires and gasoline and overcrowded passenger trains dis-

78. Russell Lee photographed the Camas Prairie town of Nez Perce and its effort to collect scrap aluminum for defense on the eve of Pearl Harbor, 1941. Courtesy Library of Congress.

couraged vacation travel or even short pleasure trips. People coped with shortages by forgoing vacation trips, by returning to horses and other forms of nonmotorized transport in the case of Idaho fish and game officials, and by such simple expedients as substituting honey for sugar in dessert recipes. Sun Valley closed as a resort late in 1942 only to reopen the following summer as a navy convalescent center.

Idaho's contribution to winning the Second World War was similar to its contribution to victory in the First: it supplied vital raw materials—food, timber, and metals—and military personnel. More than sixty thousand Idaho men and women served in various branches of the armed services. The number of uniformed Idahoans in service during World War II totaled 11 percent of the state's population, more than the national average.

Idahoans purchased millions of dollars' worth of war bonds and, in fact, exceeded the state's quota in each of eight campaigns. Children collected scrap metal, and families raised victory gardens. Many young Idahoans moved west to take jobs in the booming shipyards of the Portland-Vancouver area or in the aircraft plants of the Seattle area.

An air base called Gowen Flying Field was constructed at Boise in late

1940. A second air base was built at Pocatello, and a third at Mountain Home, which is still in use. Several Idaho colleges and universities offered pilot training.

Pocatello had a naval ordnance plant that included a lathe 225 feet long to handle large guns. To test the weapons, a facility was built in the desert near Arco in 1942. Most prominent of all wartime facilities was the Farragut Naval Training Station on Lake Pend Oreille.

When the largest inland naval base in the world opened in August 1942 near Sandpoint, it had the capacity to handle 30,000 recruits at a time in its six self-contained training camps and was for a while the largest city in Idaho. Some 776 buildings were constructed, including a grade school for children of civilian employees and dormitories for single women. "Liberty buses" ran to Coeur d'Alene every hour and less frequently to Sandpoint. There were three passenger trains a day to Spokane. In fifteen months, Farragut trained 293,381 sailors.

79. On Wednesdays and Saturdays a one-hour noon dance was permitted at the Farragut Naval Training Station. Civilian employees, Waves, and occasional guests provided partners for the sailors. Courtesy Museum of North Idaho, Far-2–39.

Japanese-American Relocation

Few Japanese Americans lived in Idaho prior to 1942, but that changed dramatically with the coming of war. Japan's devastating attack on Pearl Harbor heightened prevailing anti-Asian prejudice along the Pacific Coast to create an almost hysterical fear of invasion. In the spring of 1942, federal authorities preemptorily relocated all people of Japanese ancestry living in western portions of Oregon and Washington to inland camps.

One of these was the Minidoka Relocation Center located on a 68,000-acre desert tract near Hunt, a site north of Twin Falls. The camp was a desolate place, hot and dusty in summer and frigid in winter. Surrounded by barbed wire and armed guards, it served as home for ten thousand people mainly from the Portland and Seattle areas, many of them second- and third-generation Japanese Americans. Anyone with as little as one-sixteenth Japanese blood could be incarcerated. In addition to the Minidoka facility, Idaho had a German prisoner of war camp near Paul and conscientious objector camps in McCall and Downey.

Ironically, the twelve hundred Japanese Americans already living in Idaho were not relocated, and as a result some people at risk in other areas moved voluntarily to Idaho to escape internment. What they could not escape was prejudice. When, for instance, Idaho firms hired Japanese workers, the Pocatello Central Labor Union protested: "We request all members of organized labor to refrain from patronizing any and all business establishments employing Japs."[1]

In the fall of 1942, in what was labeled the Retreat from Moscow, the University of Idaho denied admission to six persons of Japanese ancestry born in the United States, although it had initially accepted them as transfer students from the University of Washington. Local citizens created such a furor that two of the women were temporarily housed in jail under protective custody.

Japanese Americans confined to the relocation camp on the Snake River plain sought to fashion an environment as livable as the arid conditions permitted. They planted victory gardens and organized a first-rate baseball team that played against clubs from nearby communities. Many hundreds of internees were permitted to work outside the camp in order to harvest the crops of the inland Northwest. Urban dwellers with no agricultural experience went to work in the potato and sugar beet fields of the Snake River valley to assist Idaho farmers beset by a severe labor shortage.

By October 1945 some twenty-four hundred Japanese Americans worked in the fields of Idaho, northern Utah, eastern Oregon, eastern Washington,

80. Japanese-American farm laborers leaving their camp near Twin Falls to visit town in July 1942. Note the "Rupert Pirates" T-shirt. Courtesy Library of Congress, 11604.

and Montana. Supplementing their labor was that of Mexican nationals, Jamaicans, and German prisoners of war.

Legal challenges to the relocation order reached the United States Supreme Court. But in each case the high court upheld the constitutionality of the removal order. In 1988, however, the United States Congress provided twenty thousand dollars in compensation to each Japanese American who was relocated.

Cold War and the Nuclear Age

When World War II ended, Camp Farragut closed permanently. During the immediate postwar years a part of the former base functioned for a time as Farragut College and Technical Institute. Eventually, however, forests and fields reclaimed most of the area that is now Farragut State Park.

The air base at Mountain Home closed also, but it reopened during the cold war in 1948 as a training facility for a Strategic Air Command photographic unit. After 1953 the Strategic Air Command used it as a station for bombers and refueling planes. Three Titan missile sites were located there

81. One part of the National Reactor Testing Station as it appeared in 1962. Courtesy Idaho State Historical Society, 72–205.22.

from 1960 to 1965. Today the Mountain Home base is part of the Tactical Air Command, which is headquartered in Virginia.

Another legacy of the cold war is the largest permanent federal installation in Idaho: the sprawling nuclear reservation located on a sparsely populated portion of the Snake River plain west of Idaho Falls. It dates from March 20, 1949, when the Atomic Energy Commission (AEC) announced plans to locate a special reactor-testing facility on the site.

By combining land formerly used to test naval ordnance with thousands of additional acres of desert, the AEC created a reservation totaling 870 square miles, or about three-quarters of the land area of Rhode Island. Here the federal government invested millions of dollars to build fifty-two reactors, most of them one-of-a-kind plants that have subsequently been phased out.

Residents of the nearby communities welcomed the National Reactor Testing Station, which provided jobs and created a population boom. The number of people living in Blackfoot doubled during the first decade of the facility's operation, although Idaho Falls probably benefited most. A large number of engineers and nuclear research specialists added a new element to the community's population.

The facility produced the nation's first electricity from nuclear energy in 1951, and on July 17, 1955, Arco became the first city in the world lighted by the atom. In the early 1950s the National Reactor Testing Station developed the first reactor to power submarines, and hundreds of nuclear submarine crewmen still train there every year.

The name of the station was changed to the Idaho National Engineering Laboratory (INEL) in 1974. Currently INEL employs about ten thousand people, both military personnel and civilians, and provides almost 5 percent of the state's jobs. One of INEL's several subcontractors alone employs thirty-five hundred people. The laboratory's budget approached $800 million in 1987, a sum considerably larger than the state government's general budget.

In the early years the facility's scientists considered plans for nuclear-powered railway locomotives and aircraft; now they engage in research projects involving electric vehicles, lasers, and biotechnology. Today, however, not all Idahoans see the atom as a friend, and some fear the site produces and stores wastes that will permanently foul the Snake River aquifer.

Their concerns about pollution are not unfounded. Government documents reveal that between 1957 and 1963 there were intentional atmospheric leaks of radioactive gas. The radiation as measured in curies was four thousand times greater than the amount released during the celebrated Three Mile Island accident in Pennsylvania in 1979. Already one 140-acre landfill is home to 75 percent of all buried transuranic waste in the United States. Various isotopes of plutonium, a deadly man-made element, have been detected about a hundred feet below the ground at one storage site.

Late in 1988, Governor Cecil Andrus halted shipment of nuclear wastes to the site and thereby called national attention to a protective new attitude in Idaho. According to some estimates it will cost billions of dollars to clean up one of the most contaminated sites in the weapons industry.

Entrepreneurial Talent and the Postwar Economy

While in some parts of the West the Second World War created a permanent new manufacturing economy, Idaho continued in its traditional role as a supplier of raw materials and semifinished products. In fact, a smaller percentage of Idahoans held manufacturing jobs in 1946 than in 1940—down from 8.1 to 7.2 percent. However, the cold war and especially the conflict in Korea in the early 1950s brought prosperity to the Coeur d'Alene mining district by increasing the demand for lead and zinc. Pulp and paper production expanded along with mining during the 1950s, and food processing grew in importance. Production boomed as Idaho lumber found a market helping to build the nation's growing suburbs.

Cold war tensions, the rise of suburbia, the "baby boom," and other even less definable phenomena played a role in shaping the Idaho economy since 1945. But that economy also bears the imprint of some highly talented individual entrepreneurs. Boise today is home to more large companies than perhaps any city its size in America, and some of the most prominent of those enterprises still bear the names of the individuals who founded them. Three of them most clearly recall rags-to-riches sagas.

Morrison-Knudsen is a billion-dollar multinational giant that has over the years engaged in heavy construction, shipbuilding, steel fabrication, and a myriad of other activities. This Boise-based firm traces its origin to 1912 and the entrepreneurial talents of Harry Winford Morrison, an Illinois farm boy, and Morris Hans Knudsen, a Danish immigrant. Starting with horses, scrapers, and wheelbarrows valued at six hundred dollars, their general contracting partnership dug canals during the reclamation and irrigation boom of the early twentieth century and built logging roads and a variety of railroad projects.

Morrison-Knudsen gradually extended its range until in the early 1930s it joined with five other construction firms to build Hoover Dam on the Colorado River, the world's largest construction venture to that time. The Boise firm also participated in the construction of the San Francisco–Oakland Bay Bridge and Grand Coulee Dam. Between 1930 and 1940, in fact, Morrison-Knudsen was a partner in the construction of twenty *major* dams. The world war and cold war created many additional projects that required the talents of Morrison-Knudsen. In 1954, a *Time* magazine cover story acclaimed Harry Morrison as "the man who has done more than anyone else to change the face of the earth."[2]

Like Morrison-Knudsen, Joseph A. Albertson's multimillion-dollar grocery and drug enterprise sprang from humble beginnings. Starting as a clerk at a Safeway store in Caldwell in the mid-1920s, Albertson used $5,000 of his savings to open his first store in Boise in 1939. By 1989, Albertsons had expanded from that first facility to include about five hundred outlets in seventeen states throughout the West and Southeast. It is the sixth largest retail food and drug chain in the United States, and Albertson is among the country's wealthiest men. Indicative of how the business has grown is the fact that stock worth $10,000 when the firm went public in 1959 would have

82. Idaho's "Potato King," J. R. Simplot, had already begun to amass a fortune from the vegetable when this photograph was taken in the 1940s. In 1990 *Forbes* magazine estimated his wealth at $660 million, second to Joseph Albertson's $725 million, figures that make them the two wealthiest men in Idaho history. Courtesy Idaho State Historical Society: 77–2.45.

been worth $1.2 million thirty years later and would have paid $103,000 in dividends.

The entrepreneurial drive of Jack Simplot took the form of the J. R. Simplot Company, a constellation of enterprises that range from food processing and chemical fertilizers to mining and ranching. Simplot started in the potato business modestly enough by renting 160 acres of land near Burley. His big boost came when the Second World War created an enormous demand for dehydrated potatoes, onions, and other food products needed to feed the troops. The war made Simplot the "world's biggest potato farmer." MR. SPUD is the apt name on his personalized license plate.

After the war Simplot turned his talents to creating a host of potato products, from instant potatoes to frozen french fries, for the consumer market. Per capita consumption of french fries soared from two pounds in 1960 to fourteen in 1984, and today the Simplot Company supplies the McDonald's restaurant business with over half of its french fries.

But that is only part of the story: when potato growers needed more fertilizer, Simplot hired geologists to explore southeastern Idaho for new phosphate deposits and thereby launched yet another business. In still another example of vertical integration, he acquired timberland to supply the wood needed to build potato boxes.

From one perspective, the years of world war and cold war left only a slight impression on Idaho. With the exceptions of the Mountain Home Air Base and the Idaho National Engineering Laboratory, no permanent military-industrial complex resulted from this period. Yet the nation as a whole changed as a result of the baby boom, the move to suburbia, the growing number of women working outside the home, the rising use of fast and convenience foods, and increased personal spending for recreation and leisure-time activities. These national trends affected Idaho businesses large and small.

CHAPTER 17

Throughout Idaho are men who have settled
in the state and natives who refuse to leave
simply because the side rewards of living
there are greater than the greater money they
might make outside. They like small-towns
and small-city associations, and they like free
space, and they fill their eyes with grandeur
and their ears with the great silence of the
mountains.—from A. B. Guthrie, Jr., "Idaho,"
Holiday (May 1954)

The Contours of
Contemporary Idaho

The four decades from 1945 to 1985 stimulated new growth from Idaho's
historic roots. In many ways Idaho remained a last frontier among the lower
forty-eight states. Not until 1970 did more Idahoans live in urban than in rural
areas, and even then, a pronounced rural character continued to define the
state. Its number one source of income in the mid-1980s was agriculture (as
it had been since statehood), followed by manufacturing, tourism, lumber, and
mining in that order. Employment in manufacturing, however, accounted for
a minuscule one-quarter of 1 percent of the total for the United States.

Yet the events of recent years also revealed another Idaho breaking free of
the old constraints. In the 1970s manufacturing began to challenge agriculture as the chief wealth producer, though much of the manufacturing still
related to food processing. State colleges became universities, though they
were still forced to struggle to gain recognition outside Idaho.

A burst of highway construction culminated in the near completion of a
four-lane interstate system authorized by Congress in 1956. Lewiston finally
realized a century-old dream when a paved highway (now U.S. 12) was completed up the Clearwater Valley and across Lolo Pass to Missoula in 1962.
The route became a funnel for thousands of truckloads of Montana and Dakota grain that poured into Lewiston after it became Idaho's only seaport in
1975. In that year the last of eight dams was completed to make the Snake
and Columbia rivers a highway for barge traffic to Portland.

Boise Means Business[1]

In the mid-1970s Boise ranked briefly as America's sixth fastest-growing city, and Idaho as the fastest-growing state. In 1940 Boise's population was 26,130; by 1980 it had almost quadrupled to 102,160. In 1962, when annexation made Pocatello Idaho's most populous city, Boise changed its charter and took in all the suburbs it could to regain its status as the state's major population center.

Even with all the growth, Boise retained the ambience of a small town through its proximity to the outdoors. A commentator observed in 1975 that a trout stream was located five minutes from the state capitol, and businessmen could easily go duck hunting before work only fifteen minutes away, snow skiing or swimming in a mountain lake only an hour or two away. Even in the early 1990s that juxtaposition had not changed much.

Boise remains an oasis in many respects. A city of trees on an arid plain, it was described thirty years ago as the only city in the nation more than three hundred miles from another city. That was still true in the late 1980s, when Boise also seemed like an oasis of prosperity and enterprise in a state still struggling to recover from the recession that crippled its basic industries earlier in the decade. In America's so-called outback or empty quarter— the states of Idaho, Montana, Wyoming, North Dakota, and South Dakota— Boise continues to be the only city with a population of one hundred thousand or more.

The Idaho capital was not without its problems, however. An overambitious urban renewal program in the mid-1960s ripped through the downtown area, especially the old Chinese district, and left so many parking lots that one critic likened the city to a doughnut because of its disappearing downtown and booming outskirts. But during the 1980s Boise made progress in renovating its remaining historic buildings. At the same time it gained a dramatic new skyline.

Occupying prominent buildings were corporate giants like Morrison-Knudsen, Simplot, Ore-Ida Foods, and Boise Cascade, a diversified forest products giant created in 1957. Boise is now home to 3,150 millionaires and ranks sixth in the nation on a per capita basis as a location for major corporate headquarters. In the interior West where homegrown economic power is rare, Boise is a conspicuous exception.

Why so many such enterprises originated and flourished in Boise is not entirely clear. Luck was part of the equation. A symbiotic relationship was another: Morrison-Knudsen helped with the reclamation projects that made large-scale commercial agriculture possible in southern Idaho and thus contributed at least indirectly to the rise of Simplot's food-processing empire. Joseph Albertson's supermarkets formed the retail end of this informal relationship.

The growth of Boise's corporate giants has not been without setbacks. For a time, none was more dramatic than the reversal suffered by Boise Cascade. With roots that extend back to 1913 and the formation of its predecessor, the Boise Payette Lumber Company, Boise Cascade climbed rapidly from a modest producer of forest products into a high-flying conglomerate with interests in paper manufacturing, real estate, leisure homes, and even Latin American bonds and utilities.

Robert V. Hansberger, the architect of this expansion, argued that all these lines of business were in some way connected to building materials. But the overextended company ran into trouble. In 1972 Hansberger was out, and the company took a $200 million write-off as it shrank to a more manageable size. Under the leadership of John B. Fery, it retreated to its core businesses and prospered once again. In 1989 Boise Cascade ranked as the nation's third largest producer of plywood and its eighth largest paper company.

Not to be overshadowed by Idaho's older and larger firms were high-tech newcomers like Micron Technology, founded in 1978 and now a leading manufacturer of computer memory chips. Much of the initial capital (sixteen million dollars) for the enterprise came from J. R. Simplot; the managerial skills and technical know-how, from the twin brothers Joe and Ward Parkinson and Douglas Pitman.

In 1988 Micron Technology reported an income of $106 million on revenues of $446 million; or, in other words, the firm earned more than the state's venerable sheep industry. The young company survived a ruinous price-cutting war with the Japanese in the mid-1980s that forced it to prune its work force of fourteen hundred by half, and when the decade ended, it was the only enterprise left in the United States whose business depended almost wholly on sales of memory chips to the open market.

Idaho jobs in electronics increased from thirty-nine hundred in 1980 to seventy-one hundred in 1984 and, despite the cutbacks of middecade, climbed to new highs as the state entered the 1990s. The largest electronic employer in the late 1980s was Hewlett Packard, which provided almost four thousand jobs in Boise producing printers and disk drives. This company launched its operation in the capitol city in 1973 with thirty employees; three years later it employed four hundred people.

Boom-and-Bust: Will the Cycle Be Unbroken?

Confidence was in the air in the 1970s when Idaho enjoyed a most satisfying ride up the economic roller coaster. For years a low per capita income had ranked Idaho with the impoverished states of the deep South. But during one of the years of the 1970s, that figure leaped from $3,780 to $4,345, the fourth highest increase of any state. Such growth was, unfortunately, part of a cyclical pattern that Idahoans with any sense of their past knew only too well. As had happened so frequently before, the Gem State's economy came careening back down before the decade ended.

When the downturn of the late 1970s and early 1980s was viewed from a national perspective, it was a recession. But to residents of towns like Potlatch and Wallace, it was nothing less than a great depression that persisted even when the national economy recovered in the mid-1980s. In no industries did the boom-and-bust cycle seem wilder than in timber and mining.

A variety of ills closed sawmills across the Pacific Northwest and caused Idaho's jobless rate to soar in the early 1980s. Only in 1986 did the industry regain its health. Chief causes of trouble in the timber country were the revival of southern pine forests (which Pacific Northwesterners had once dismissed as having the quality of weeds), competition from Canadian imports, a housing slump caused by high interest rates, and a shifting market.

Mining was another of Idaho's extractive industries to experience several difficult years. Silver production boomed during the late 1970s, when Americans, frightened by an inflation rate that reached 18 percent, rushed to buy gold and silver as a hedge against further erosion of the dollar's buying power. But when the rate of inflation dropped during the 1980s, so did the price of silver.

As late as 1982 Idaho produced 37 percent of the nation's silver, but plunging prices coupled with rising labor costs caused several large companies to close their mines rather than operate them at a loss. When Bunker Hill Mine and Smelter, Idaho's second largest employer, halted operations in Kellogg in 1981, it idled two thousand workers.

Five years earlier, Kellogg had been a bustling community of five thousand, hub of the fifty-mile-long Silver Valley where one-quarter of the twenty thousand residents worked in mining. By the mid-1980s Kellogg's population had fallen below three thousand, and fewer than four hundred people remained employed in the valley's mines. As a result of the economic downturn, closed mines and abandoned sawmills were for a time common features of the Idaho landscape.

It was not just Idaho's loggers and miners who lost their jobs. Agriculture

83. When mining was king in Kellogg: the electrolytic zinc plant of the massive Bunker Hill facility. Courtesy Idaho State Historical Society, F752.Sh7.

suffered too, and many observers considered 1985 the worst year for farmers since the Great Depression. Even high-tech enterprises experienced trouble: during a six-month period in 1985, Idaho electronics firms laid off hundreds of employees. The shutdowns inevitably exacted a psychological and social toll measurable in an increase in family-related problems.

Even when the timber industry revived—as it did in the late 1980s, innovative technology that included computers and lasers enabled modern sawmills to employ far fewer hands than they employed only a decade earlier. Such changes forced many workers to make painful and permanent adjustments in their life-style. Never again would it be possible to describe Idaho and the Pacific Northwest as a Sawdust Empire. An era had clearly ended when sawmills closed for good in Potlatch, Coeur d'Alene, and other communities.

In the mining industry too, even when silver prices rebounded, technological changes permanently eliminated hundreds of mine and smelter jobs.[2] For some, it appeared that the Silver Valley had a future only as a ski resort.

Agriculture in Idaho, 1920–1980

	No. of Farms	Average Size (in acres)
1920	42,106	199
1930	41,674	224
1940	43,663	236
1950	41,900	334
1960	36,300	421
1970	28,500	544
1980	24,100	639

Source: *Idaho Blue Book* (1983–86), 234.

Population Growth in Idaho, 1870–1980

	Population	Density (Sq. Mile)	Increase (Percent)	Net Migration (Estimated)
1870	14,999	0.18	———	———
1880	32,610	0.39	117.4	1,700
1890	88,548	1.07	171.5	34,200
1900	161,772	1.96	82.7	39,800
1910	325,594	3.95	101.3	104,100
1920	431,866	5.24	32.6	37,300
1930	445,032	5.40	3.0	−50,600
1940	524,873	6.37	17.9	−20,500
1950	588,637	7.14	12.1	−29,600
1960	667,191	8.10	13.3	−39,300
1970	713,015	8.65	7.0	−42,000
1980	944,127	11.45	32.4	130,000

Source: *Idaho Blue Book* (1983–86), 267.

In fact, several of Idaho's natural resource–based communities turned to tourism for economic salvation.

Riggins was a timber town on the Salmon River until its mill burned in 1982, but river running and outfitting emerged as the community's economic mainstay when the decade ended. In 1985 Kellogg began the slow process of transforming itself from a mining town into a tourist-oriented Bavarian ski village, and its population began to increase a bit. An even more spectacular sign of the times was Duane Hagadone's sixty-million-dollar Coeur d'Alene Resort, which represented an up-to-date blend of big-city life-style and an Idaho setting rich in natural beauty and outdoor attractions. The massive resort is one of the most powerful tourist magnets in northern Idaho.

Given the facts that so many of the Gem State's attractions are still largely unknown outside its borders and that Idaho remains one of the least visited states in the nation, tourism can be expected only to grow ever more significant. It is predicted to become the state's number one industry by the year 2000. In short, the 1980s in many ways witnessed the historic restructuring of the Idaho economy.

Growing Pains: Population and Education Trends

Population trends since World War II mirror the state's economic ups and downs. In 1940 Idaho's population exceeded one-half million for the first time. By 1980 that number had climbed to 944,127. The rate of increase was particularly rapid during the 1970s, by far the largest net in-migration being from California. But then as a result of the economic troubles that plagued the state, the population wobbled around the one million mark during the 1980s. In fact, in middecade Idaho experienced its largest net out-migration in fifteen years as people looked elsewhere for jobs.

Idaho remained the "whitest" state west of the Mississippi River, with only three thousand blacks, six thousand Asians, and ten thousand American Indians recorded in the 1980 census. Hispanic Americans—including about twenty-three thousand of Mexican origin—constituted the Gem State's largest minority group. When the Second World War created a shortage of agricultural labor, the United States government had imported workers directly from Mexico to harvest crops. Between 1943 and 1947 more than forty-seven thousand Mexican males or braceros supplied farm labor in Oregon, Washington, and Idaho. Most lived in an alien culture that subjected them to various forms of exploitation and discrimination.

The migrants complained about living conditions: their housing often amounted to little more than tents in the winter, and their food was often spoiled or dust covered, as was the case in a mess tent in Wilder where strong winds blasted through and seasoned the food with grit. Life in the labor camps was at best Spartan, and braceros were allowed no families in order to encourage them to return to Mexico after the war. Among the three Northwest states, Idaho developed the most notorious reputation for discrimination. Signs in business houses in both Nampa and Caldwell forbade Mexicans to enter. On one occasion, in June 1944, the braceros at Preston went on strike over poor wages.

In the late 1940s a new type of Hispanic labor arrived from Texas and the Southwest and included families drawn north by jobs. Additional families from Mexico permanently changed the minority composition of Idaho and the Pacific Northwest. People of Spanish origin numbered 36,615, or 3.9 percent of Idaho's total population by 1980.

Predominantly Mexican in origin, male, and youthful, Hispanic Americans numbered at least 10 percent of the population in Minidoka and Owyhee counties. Although these were rural counties and people of Mexican origin were often stereotyped as agricultural workers, an ever-increasing number of them found employment in white-collar jobs. Caldwell is today as close to a Hispanic center as Idaho has, and groups like the Idaho Migrant Council have unified many workers striving for a better life.

Idaho's Indian population in 1980 was 10,418, about equal to that in 1800. The Nez Perces are the largest group of Native Americans in the state today. Except for the loss of a Pend d'Oreille or Flathead band to Montana in 1854, and the gain of a Delaware band that settled on an island north of New Plymouth in 1924, Idaho's organized tribes of the mid-1980s were identical to those of 1800.

Today's Indians pursue a variety of life-styles. In 1986 the Kutenai tribe, with assistance from Duane Hagadone, opened a 48-room inn in Bonners Ferry. After the facility had been in operation a year, Best Western motels named the Kootenai River Inn the best in its worldwide association.[3] Some Idaho Indians are also urban professionals, although about two-thirds of them still live on the state's five reservations.

One outstanding fact about Idaho's population has been its relative youth. During the 1980s it ranked second only to Utah in the percentage of residents ten years old or younger (18.7 percent). Population trends, notably the postwar baby boom, were also reflected in education statistics, which, except for the years of the Korean War in the early 1950s, generally showed an increasing number of people attending the state's colleges and universities.

In 1947 the two-year Pocatello branch of the University of Idaho became a

84. The "Kutenai war" in September 1974 called attention to the Indians' request for just compensation from the federal government. Courtesy *Idaho Statesman*.

degree-granting institution, Idaho State College. State-supported institutions experienced a setback in the early 1950s when lack of funds caused the North Idaho College of Education to close temporarily and the Southern Idaho College of Education to close for good. During the euphoric 1960s and early 1970s, it became politically popular to upgrade institutions of higher learning. Probably nothing better illustrates the era's unprecedented expansion than the growth of Boise State University. It was founded in 1932 as a private junior college, developed into a four-year college in 1964, became a state-supported school in 1969, and achieved university status in 1974. Idaho State College in Pocatello became a university in 1963.

85. A classic scene from the 1950s: students pause on the front steps of the Administration Building, North Idaho College. Courtesy Museum of North Idaho, NIC, 1–14.

The state's campus population tended to level off in the mid-1970s, shortly before the economy slumped. As a result, the 1980s will be remembered as years of academic malaise, of recurrent funding crises and drastic retrenchment, of salaries that failed to keep pace with inflation, and of declining faculty morale.

Making matters worse is that instead of one university, three now compete for the state's higher education dollars. Perhaps as a result of this trend, one national commentator observed in 1972 that "no university of exceptional quality exists in the state; the land grant University of Idaho campus at remote Moscow on the northern panhandle suffers from all the problems of trying to operate a respectable university in a backwoods setting."[4] Whether Idaho is to have a "flagship" institution in Moscow or three "crown jewels," equal but basically mediocre and underfunded universities, is a problem few public officials have had the courage to face.

The state's elementary and secondary schools experienced similar cycles. The postwar population boom of the 1950s and 1960s created crowded classrooms and forced school boards to construct new facilities, more than some communities could fully utilize in the late 1970s when the number of school-age children dropped. The cost of public education continued to climb, even as parents and educators worried about declining standards.

Leisure Time

A key feature of life in contemporary Idaho is the increased leisure time available to Americans. Leisure time is big business. It not only provides fuel for the tourist industry but also sustains new forms of popular entertainment, notably outdoor recreation and television.

The postwar years saw Idahoans taking to the outdoors in ever greater numbers. Many families headed to national parks and other natural attractions each summer. It is perhaps ironic that, although Idaho was the first of the three Pacific Northwest states to establish a major state park, it is today the only state in the West without a national park (except for a remote 31,488-acre strip of Yellowstone National Park).[5]

As early as 1908, Senator Weldon Heyburn attempted to have Congress designate Lake Chatcolet, near St. Maries in the northern panhandle, a 7,838-acre national park. He failed, but the area now called Heyburn Park became the Pacific Northwest's first major state park in 1911.

After that time the number of Idaho state parks grew slowly. As late as 1961 there were only a few diverse properties that ranged from Ponderosa Park near McCall to the virtually undeveloped Mary Minerva McCroskey Park north of Potlatch. By comparison, Washington had 70 state parks, and Oregon 140. Not until the Harriman family donated the 4,700-acre Railroad Ranch near Yellowstone Park did the state have the impetus to form a parks department. With the support of Governor Robert Smylie, Idaho's Parks Department was formed in 1965. During the next two years, six new parks were added to the system, which continues to expand slowly.

Widespread public interest in a Sawtooth national park dates back at least to 1911 when Idaho clubwomen first endorsed the idea. Bills to give the scenic area some kind of protection were introduced in Congress: "The proposed Sawtooth National Park embraces a little over one hundred thousand acres and is less than two days journey from the state capital and one day from the nearest railroad point, Ketchum," noted one enthusiast.

Few realize that there is such grand scenery in Idaho as that in the Sawtooth. This range is remarkable for its numerous high peaks, many of them having never been scaled. Socially speaking, mountain climbing is eminently correct, but so far as original enterprise is concerned, there is little room for talk today. One finds that almost all of the great mountains of the world have been "done" by some one ahead; but this is not true in Idaho.[6]

Nothing happened until Congress created the 754,000-acre Sawtooth National Recreation Area in 1972. The core of the preserve is the 216,000-acre Sawtooth wilderness with its three hundred lakes and fifty peaks over ten thousand feet high. Critics today argue that the Sawtooths too closely resemble the Grand Teton Mountains to warrant national park status, and a significant number of Idahoans simply do not want a national park to draw crowds of outsiders to the scenic area. They fear that hordes of tourists might turn the picturesque little town of Stanley into another urban excrescence like West Yellowstone.

Idaho does have a national monument in Craters of the Moon, established in 1924, which could conceivably gain national park status in the future, and the Nez Perce National Historical Park created in 1965 brings together a total of twenty-four historic areas. The Hells Canyon National Recreation Area established in 1976 straddles a sixty-seven-mile-long stretch of the Snake River on the Idaho-Oregon border, and it has also been suggested as a new national park.

In the postwar decades Idahoans not only spent time and money on outdoor pursuits but also on an important new medium of instruction and entertainment: television. The first commercial station did not arrive until 1953, when station KIDO (later KTVB) broadcast to homes in the Boise Valley. Instead of tuning the radio to popular programs like "Amos and Andy" or the Jack Benny show, families in the mid-1950s started watching them on the small black-and-white screens that the inventiveness of Idaho's television pioneer, Philo Farnsworth, made possible.

In those early years, television stations were on the air only in the afternoon and evening hours. The broadcast day gradually lengthened after network programs reached Idaho in 1954 by way of Salt Lake City and Twin Falls. Television was initially available only in the state's major cities, but with the advent of cable television and home satellite receivers in the 1970s and 1980s, even the remotest farm or ranch had access to the fare that television offered.

Idaho's public television system dates from 1969 when the legislature appropriated funds to establish educational stations at the University of Idaho (KUID), Boise State College (KAID), and Idaho State University (KISU). Today

Idaho Public Television is headquartered in Boise and its programs reach much of the state.

Many of the events that determined the contours of contemporary Idaho generated considerable public debate and political controversy. It was in the arena of government that these conflicts were often resolved. Regardless of political persuasion, most Idahoans have faith in the political process, a fact evidenced by one of the top rates of voter turnout in the nation. The next chapter examines the role of political processes in shaping Idaho since World War II.

CHAPTER 18

In the years after World War II a period of
moderate Republican rule [in Idaho] gradually
gave way to two very different and competing
political strains: right-wing Republicanism
and environmental protectionism.—from Neal
R. Peirce and Jerry Hagstrom, *The Book of
America: Inside Fifty States Today* (1984)

Beneath the Capitol Dome
Political Trends, Personalities,
and Controversies since 1945

The men and women who represented Idaho on Capitol Hill and in the Boise
statehouse were for the most part honest and hardworking people. To put
the state's political good fortune in perspective, one need only think of the
South's sizable crop of postwar racist demagogues or the Midwest's red-
baiting senators, Joseph R. McCarthy of Wisconsin and William Jenner of
Indiana. Government and politics in Idaho have also been fortunate to escape
major scandals as well as domination by a single company or industry, unlike
those in neighboring Montana, which were long under the heel of Anaconda
Copper. Idaho politics during the postwar decades remained issue and personality oriented, and some of the key issues related to matters of environment and the natural resources with which the Gem State was so blessed.

Trends: The Triumph of Conservatism?

Democrats held one of Idaho's two United States Senate seats during all but
six years from 1945 to 1981 and the governor's office from 1971 to the present,
but Republicans dominated most legislative sessions. In fact, during the century 1889–1989, the Democratic party has had a majority in both houses of
the legislature a total of only ten years—and not once since 1961.

For most of the middle and late twentieth century, Democrats tended to
be the majority party in counties north of the Salmon River, and Republicans
south of that line, where three-fifths of the population lives. A conspicuous
exception to the Republican south was working-class Pocatello.

But this pattern changed during the 1980s. Organized labor declined in membership and power in its strongholds of Pocatello, Lewiston, and the Silver Valley. In 1982, only 16 percent of the Idaho work force was unionized, down from 25 percent of nonagricultural workers in the 1950s, and this adversely affected the Democratic vote. Seeming to confirm the declining power of organized labor was enactment of the state's first right-to-work law, a controversial measure that survived both a ballot challenge in 1986 and many legal battles.

In Coeur d'Alene and surrounding Kootenai County, on the other hand, an influx of affluent retirees and the closure of several sawmills gave Republican fortunes a boost. Also aiding Republicans was the fact that eleven of fourteen counties in the state's southeast corner were at least half Mormon. Regardless of party, Idaho politics tended to be personality oriented, Populist, and conservative—especially so when viewed from a national perspective.

Since the election of Franklin D. Roosevelt in 1944, only one Democrat has won a *majority* of Idaho votes cast for president: in 1964 Lyndon Johnson beat the conservative Republican candidate, Barry Goldwater, by the slimmest of margins (.92 percent). That was Goldwater's best showing in any non-Southern state except his native Arizona. Four years later George C. Wallace's right-wing American Independent party received 13 percent of Idaho's vote. John G. Schmitz, presidential candidate of the right-wing American party in 1972, received 9.2 percent of the vote in Idaho, a higher percentage than in any other state. In the presidential elections of 1980 and 1984, Ronald Reagan carried Idaho by a landslide (67 percent in 1980 and 72 percent in 1984); George Bush won 63 percent of Idaho's votes in the 1988 presidential election. Only in Utah did these Republicans run better than in Idaho. The mountain West in general is the staunchest Republican territory anywhere in presidential politics.

It is easy now to forget that the Socialist party once scored victories in pre–World War I Nampa, Coeur d'Alene, and Rupert. Earl W. Bowman of Council, a journalist and political maverick, was elected to the Idaho senate in 1914 as a Socialist. And Glen H. Taylor, who represented Idaho in the United States Senate from 1945 to 1951, ran for vice-president of the United States on the left-wing Progressive ticket in 1948. The Socialist John T. Wood was elected mayor of Coeur d'Alene in 1911, though he later underwent such a complete transformation that when he was elected to Congress in the 1950s he distinguished himself as one of the most right-wing officeholders in the state's history.

Conservative or liberal, Idahoans continue to take their civic duty seri-

Idaho's Political Leaders since World War II

United States Senate

First Position

John Thomas (R) 1940–45
Charles C. Gossett (D) 1945–46
Bert H. Miller (D) 1946–49
Henry C. Dworshak (R) 1949–62
Len B. Jordan (R) 1962–73
James A. McClure (R) 1973–91
Larry Craig (R) 1991–

Second Position

Glen H. Taylor (D) 1945–51
Herman Welker (R) 1951–57
Frank Church (D) 1957–81
Steven D. Symms (R) 1981–

House of Representatives

First District

Compton I. White (D) 1933–47
Abe McGregor Goff (R) 1947–49
Compton I. White (D) 1949–51
John T. Wood (R) 1951–53
Gracie Pfost (D) 1953–63
Compton White, Jr. (D) 1963–67
James A. McClure (R) 1967–73
Steven D. Symms (R) 1973–81
Larry Craig (R) 1981–91
Larry La Rocco 1991–

Second District

Henry C. Dworshak (R) 1939–47
John Sanborn (R) 1947–51
Hamer Budge (R) 1951–61
Ralph R. Harding (D) 1961–65
George V. Hansen (R) 1965–69
Orval Hansen (R) 1969–75
George V. Hansen (R) 1975–85
Richard Stallings (D) 1985–

Governor's Office

Charles C. Gossett (D) 1945
Arnold Williams (D) 1945–47
C. A. Robbins (R) 1947–51
Len B. Jordan (R) 1951–55
Robert E. Smylie (R) 1955–67
Don Samuelson (R) 1967–71
Cecil D. Andrus (D) 1971–77
John V. Evans (D) 1977–87
Cecil D. Andrus (D) 1987–

ously. In the elections of 1952, 1956, and 1960, the Gem State ranked first in the nation in voter turnout. Since that time it has remained among the top states: the turnout of Idaho's eligible voters in recent presidential elections was 68 percent in 1980, 60 percent in 1984, and 58 percent in 1988.

Personalities: Thespians and Statesmen

In a state as geographically divided as Idaho, a flamboyant personality often seemed one way for candidates to grab the attention of voters. Long before Ronald Reagan and other actors entered politics, Idaho had Glen H. Taylor, the Singing Cowboy. The ability of the New Deal governor C. Ben Ross to

entertain a crowd so impressed Taylor that he too decided to run for public office. In a typical scenario, he would come to town with his hillbilly band, the Glendora Ranch Gang, play and sing a few songs to attract a crowd, and then preach his message, a program of near socialism and world peace that he toned down as the years went by.

Taylor was a loved and hated man. He ran for office eight times but was elected only once, in 1944, when he won a term in the United States Senate by capturing 51.1 percent of Idaho's vote to defeat the Republican C. A. Bottolfsen. A liberal Democrat, Taylor distinguished himself as a staunch advocate of civil rights and better relations with the Soviet Union. Many people, however, regarded him as nothing more than an opportunist who avidly sought publicity. They cited the time he put on a large Stetson hat and sang and accompanied himself on a guitar on the Capitol steps to call attention to the housing shortage in wartime Washington. To the tune of ''Home on the Range'' Taylor pleaded:

86. Glen Taylor's Glendora Singers. The future United States senator holds a banjo, his wife, Dora, holds a trombone, and between them is their son, Arod (Dora spelled backwards). Courtesy Idaho State Historical Society, 78–207.2.

87. Steven D. Symms (b. 1938) served four terms in the United States House of Representatives after his election in 1972. He was elected to the United States Senate in 1980. Courtesy Senator Steve Symms.

Oh, give us a home
Near the Capitol Dome
With a yard where the children can play—
Just one room or two,
Any old thing will do,
We can't find a pla-a-ce to stay.

More than anything else, it was his teaming up with Henry Wallace on the Progressive ticket in 1948 that tainted Taylor as an incorrigible leftist in the eyes of many Idaho voters. The Progressive party, which Communists

Frank Church

Senator Steve Symms's immediate predecessor was Frank Church, who was elected to the Senate in 1956 at the age of thirty-two, thus becoming one of the youngest people ever to sit in that body. A Boise lawyer who married Chase Clark's daughter, Bethene, he was a gifted orator and pragmatic liberal.

In 1956 Church narrowly survived a primary challenge from his fellow Democrat Glen Taylor (by 170 votes), then went on to defeat handily the ailing Herman Welker in the general election, carrying forty-one of Idaho's forty-four counties. In 1962 he became the first Democratic senator from Idaho to win a second term. Church decided to run for president in 1976. He won primaries in Nebraska, Idaho, Oregon, and Montana as part of his "late, late strategy" but withdrew in favor of Jimmy Carter.

Like his idol, William Borah, he chaired the Senate's prestigious Committee on Foreign Relations and emerged as a major critic of America's interventionist foreign policy. Ironically, after Church became head of the committee in 1978, the assignment turned out to be a monumental headache. His outspoken opposition to American participation in the Vietnam War, his support for a treaty phasing out American control over the Panama Canal (he was floor leader for the controversial matter, which passed the Senate sixty-eight to thirty-two, one vote more than the required two-thirds majority), and his investigation of Central Intelligence Agency misdeeds cost him votes in conservative Idaho.

A liberal Democrat for twenty-four years in a state growing increasingly conservative, Church was narrowly defeated for reelection to a fifth term in 1980 by the Republican congressman Symms. The margin of victory was less than 1 percent of the votes cast. Some commentators maintain that the Reagan landslide helped Symms, especially when President Jimmy Carter conceded at 5:30 P.M. Idaho time (4:30 in the north) while the polls were still open. Church died of cancer in 1984 at the age of fifty-nine.

---

heavily infiltrated at the national level, attracted only five thousand votes in the Gem State; its weak showing probably foreshadowed Taylor's defeat in the Democratic primary in 1950.

Taylor left the Senate and moved to California to become a manufacturer of wigs called Taylor Toppers. Replacing him on Capitol Hill was Herman Welker, a conservative Republican and so strong a backer of Joseph McCarthy's anti-Communist crusade that he earned the nickname Little Joe from Idaho.[1]

Like Taylor, the conservative Republican senator Steve Symms had a talent for grabbing headlines. He once turned up at an anti–gun control news conference packing two revolvers. Symms was a natural politician, upbeat and friendly. His campaign signature was to take a bite out of a Symms Fruit Ranch apple, symbolizing his intent to take a bite out of big government. Like his predecessors Taylor, Borah, and Church, he stood out from the crowd, a trait Idahoans seem to like in their politicians. But unlike Taylor,

88. Senator Frank Church (1924–84) wears the black hat. A man who loved the outdoors, he is responsible for the preservation of much of Idaho's magnificent wilderness land. Courtesy Boise State University Library, Frank Church Papers, Out-059.

Jim McClure
U.S. Senator, Idaho

One of Our Own—One of Our Best

89. James A. McClure (b. 1924) was elected to the United States Senate in 1972 following the retirement of Len B. Jordan. This brochure cover dates from his successful campaign for reelection in 1984. Author's collection.

90. Cecil D. Andrus (b. 1931), governor of Idaho, 1971–77 and 1987–, and the only home-state Idahoan to serve in a presidential cabinet. He was Jimmy Carter's secretary of the interior from 1977 to 1981. Courtesy Governor Cecil D. Andrus.

Symms learned to reach out to middle-of-the-road voters and thus won re-election in 1986 by narrowly beating Governor John V. Evans.

One conspicuous exception to the rule that flamboyance was an asset in Idaho's personality-oriented political culture was the United States senator James McClure. A moderate conservative and a soft-spoken man, he chaired the Energy and Natural Resources Committee during the years from 1981 to 1985 when Republicans were the Senate's majority party. McClure was only the third Idahoan (after Borah and Church) to chair a full Senate committee. Generally he favored the energy industry and the development of resources on federal lands. Even those who opposed McClure on the issues regarded him as an honest and dedicated public servant.

From 1983 until 1987, for the first time in fifty years, Republicans held all six United States Senate seats from the Pacific Northwest. That changed with the election of 1986 when Brock Adams of Washington State, former transportation secretary under President Jimmy Carter, unseated the Republican incumbent Slade Gorton. Two other Carter cabinet officers also emerged winners: the former transportation secretary Neil Goldschmidt was elected governor of Oregon, and Cecil Andrus, Idaho governor from 1971 to 1977 and then secretary of the interior, returned to the governor's office. Describing himself as a problem-solver, Andrus worked closely with the Republican legislature to achieve major funding increases for Idaho education.

When Andrus first won the governorship in 1970, he broke a Republican hold on the office that dated back to 1947. Half of those years belonged to Robert E. Smylie, the only man in Idaho history to serve three consecutive four-year terms as governor. Smylie was a personable and energetic man, a Progressive in the Republican ranks.

In Smylie's first eight years, Idaho built more roads than during any previous twenty-four-year period. The state also trebled its budgetary commitment to education. Educational reform went forward rapidly: the 1,250 school districts that existed in 1947 were reduced to a more realistic 110 by 1962. Smylie's biggest political mistake was backing a sales tax to finance the increased cost and responsibilities of government. The 3 percent tax won voter approval in a referendum, but the conservative Don Samuelson blocked Smylie's quest for a fourth term in the Republican primary of 1966.

Samuelson was so prodevelopment that his opponent in the 1970 election, Cecil Andrus, made protection of the environment a key issue for the first time in an Idaho gubernatorial campaign. A former logger from Clearwater County, Andrus declared, "The most important long-range issue is the protection of our magnificent Idaho environment."[2]

At the center of the campaign was the White Clouds Peak controversy. This beautiful alpine area, located twenty-five miles northwest of Sun Valley, was where the American Smelting and Refining Company of New York (ASARCO) wanted to dig a 740-acre open-pit facility to mine molybdenum, a metal used to harden steel for use in high temperatures, such applications as the space program required. The mine meant jobs, and also it meant the despoliation of a highly scenic area.

Governor Samuelson sprang to the defense of the company saying, "The raw materials are here and should be exploited to the fullest possible extent."[3] Here was a classic statement of the user-oriented mentality that had long held sway in Idaho. Yet in 1970 a significant number of Idahoans were no longer persuaded by the arguments.[4]

Helped by the environmental issue and the rare ability of the usually fractious Democrats to close ranks, Andrus won. Though elected by 52 percent of the vote, he carried only fifteen of Idaho's forty-four counties, mainly those in the panhandle. This was a pattern repeated in his narrow election victory in 1986.

Idaho Democrats have generally not fared well in their quest for seats in the U.S. House of Representatives. Through 1988 fifteen Idaho Republicans have held congressional seats for a total of 115 years; ten Democrats have been seated for a total of 46 years. From 1966 until 1984 not one Democrat was elected from the two congressional districts, and the Republicans that Idaho kept in Congress grew increasingly conservative. Democrats gained both seats in 1990.

In the 1974 primary, Republicans ousted Orval Hansen, an uncommonly bright and studious man with a moderate-to-liberal voting record, in favor of George Hansen, freewheeling Populist champion of far-right causes. Variously described as a knight-errant and the Huey Long of Idaho politics, George the Dragon Slayer, as Hansen once styled himself, served in the House of Representatives for fourteen years and grabbed many headlines. When he went to Tehran in 1979 in an unsuccessful attempt to negotiate with Iranian officials for the release of American hostages, President Carter complained about his meddling in foreign affairs.

George Hansen's undoing was neither his ideology nor his antics but rather his political finances. A court convicted him of violating a 1978 ethics law for failing to report $333,000 in loans and other transactions and sentenced him to five to fifteen years in prison. The House reprimanded him in a 354-to-52 vote of censure. While appealing his conviction he ran for reelection in 1984 against Richard Stallings and lost by a scant 170 votes. Hansen later served six months in prison, while Stallings, a moderate Democrat and history professor at Ricks College, won reelection in the highly conservative district.

No woman has ever served either as governor or as United States senator from Idaho. Only one has been elected to the House of Representatives. That was Gracie Pfost, who served from 1953 to 1962, a total of five terms. She was credited with playing a crucial role in the House passage of the wilderness bill. Her nickname on Capitol Hill was Hells Belle because of her fight against private construction of a dam in Hells Canyon. Defeated in a bid for the Senate, Pfost returned to Washington and took a position with the Federal Home Administration.

Controversies: Dam the Rivers, Pave the Wilderness

Idaho's political life since World War II has been enlivened by numerous issues competing for popular attention. Many, like education, highway construction, and public welfare, arose year after year to bedevil the legislators; others surfaced only briefly and were soon forgotten. Voters approved a state sales tax in 1966, although in 1978 they supported an initiative that limited property taxes to 1 percent of market value. The first land use–planning bill passed in 1975.

No single issue dominated Idaho politics in the years from 1945 to 1990, yet amid the welter of public concerns the question of resource development and the related matter of environmental degradation seemed to generate the most debate. One controversy centered on dams and water resources, another on scenic backcountry like the White Clouds Peak area and eventually on wilderness lands in general, and a third on pollution—nuclear waste at the Idaho National Engineering Laboratory and metals and acid rain in the Coeur d'Alene River valley.

The controversy over damming up the Snake River's scenic Hells Canyon began in 1950 and ultimately ended up in the United States Supreme Court. It pitted private power against public power and both against proponents of preservation, a point of view that arose in the mid-1960s and gradually won the fight. It was the environmental issue that did most to turn a local concern into a national one.

In 1964 the Federal Power Commission granted a license to the Pacific Northwest Power Company—a consortium of privately owned utilities—to construct High Mountain Sheep Dam on the middle Snake River. People interested in public-power development appealed to the United States Supreme Court. Years of debate followed.

The Teton Dam Collapse

No one who lived in Idaho on June 5, 1976, can forget the day the 310-foot-high Teton Dam collapsed. The eighty billion gallons of water it impounded turned into a rampaging maelstrom eight miles across and twenty miles long. It wiped out two-thirds of Rexburg, a city of ten thousand, and flooded other communities. Some three hundred thousand people were forced to flee for their lives.

For a time the flood raised the specter of an ever-enlarging wall of water that would crash into dams all along the Snake River and topple them like dominos, creating an unbelievable catastrophe for the unfortunate people living downstream. People held their collective breath and waited. A critical dam held firm and the threat of further damage diminished, but what actually happened was bad enough: the Teton Dam collapse resulted in a total property loss estimated at five hundred million dollars, and it left fourteen thousand people homeless. Eleven deaths are attributed to the disaster.

In a landmark ruling written in 1967 by the ardent conservationist William O. Douglas, the Supreme Court ordered the Federal Power Commission to hold more hearings on whether any dam should be built at all. A year later, Senators Frank Church and Len B. Jordan of Idaho agreed to a ten-year moratorium on dam construction.

In 1973 Senator Church and his colleague James McClure together with Oregon's Robert Packwood and Mark Hatfield backed a bill that set aside the spectacular 650,000-acre Hells Canyon National Recreation Area. Yet, for at least another decade developers dreamed of building one more dam across the Snake to the north of the protected area.

It was during the 1960s and especially the 1970s that the environment became a key concern for Idaho voters. Perhaps the most divisive environmental issue was what to do with the Gem State's magnificent wilderness lands. "For nearly as long as I can remember, wilderness has been a political hot potato," Senator Steve Symms reported in a newsletter to his constituents in late 1989. As he saw it, proponents of wilderness only wanted to ban humans from government-owned land.

Today Idaho has more congressionally designated wilderness land than any state apart from Alaska and California, a total of approximately 4 million acres including the 2.3 million-acre Frank Church River of No Return Wilderness created in 1980.[5] Many of Idaho's wilderness lovers are convinced that their license plates should bear the legend Wilderness State instead of advertising potatoes.

Interest in the preservation of wilderness land dates back to 1930 when Senator Borah and Governor H. C. Baldridge arranged for the Forest Service

91. Cleaning up a Rexburg street after the Teton Dam collapsed in June 1976. Courtesy *Idaho Statesman*.

to keep a large portion of central Idaho roadless. Working with the state legislature, the Forest Service designated a primitive area in central Idaho the following year. More recently, Senator Frank Church took the concept of preservation a step farther when he sponsored national wilderness legislation.

Church, by seeking a middle ground between developers and preservationists, was viewed as standing up for the environment in a state where in years past *conservation* had been a dirty word and few people objected to any type of timber cutting. Leader of the successful fight to pass the Wilderness Act of 1964, he declared that without wilderness, the world was a cage. Opponents, however, feared that wilderness lands would lock up timber and mineral resources and thereby cost jobs. The issue engendered such strong emotions that opponents hanged Church in effigy during hearings for the Gospel Hump Wilderness.

The setting aside of state and federal land as parks and recreation areas was often justified in economic terms—either the land was worthless as regards minerals and timber, or conversely, it might generate tourist dollars.

But what about wilderness lands? The issue was often reduced to the question whether it was better to log or mine the backcountry for the sake of jobs and profits or to preserve the region's remaining wilderness areas for their own special qualities.

During the 1980s few topics could produce more heated public debates than what to do with Idaho's wilderness lands. Critics charged that locking up so much land was elitist and economically indefensible. Environmentalists responded that the nation needed wild country even if most people only drove to the edge for a quick look. It was wilderness land, they added, that gave Idaho its special character.

One proposal that surfaced in mid-1986 was to build a two-lane paved highway into the heart of the Frank Church River of No Return Wilderness so as to make it more accessible to tourists. To lovers of wilderness the idea made as much sense as crushing Plymouth Rock and distributing the pieces to the fifty states to make history more accessible to schoolchildren.

Another emotionally charged issue was pollution. For decades the south fork of the Coeur d'Alene River transported a dangerous load of zinc, cadmium, and lead from numerous mine tailings to the muddy bottom of seemingly pristine Lake Coeur d'Alene. The lead level in the Coeur d'Alene River delta in the mid-1980s ranged from one thousand to eight thousand parts per million; a normal range was fifteen to twenty parts per million background count. This was perhaps the highest lead level recorded in the United States. As early as 1932 an investigator had recommended construction of settling ponds to deal with the problem, but not until 1968 when mining firms were subjected to heavy pressure from state and federal governments did they take that step.

No less dangerous was the smelter-polluted air that hung above the Silver Valley until the early 1980s. It resulted in the highest levels of sulphur dioxide gas recorded in the United States. As acid rain, the smelter effluents were responsible for denuding the surrounding hillsides. Schoolchildren in Kellogg, where the massive Bunker Hill smelter was located, had abnormally high levels of lead in their blood. Toxic residues so contaminated the Silver Valley that the Environmental Protection Agency placed it on a list of hazardous sites for federally funded cleanup.

Mining, metal-processing, and pulp mill wastes from Montana increasingly fouled the waters of another northern Idaho river, the Clark Fork, which flows into Lake Pend Oreille. Cleanup will necessarily require cooperation between the two states or federal intervention.

In 1990, when Idaho celebrated its centennial, the physical changes that occurred during the first hundred years of statehood were obvious. The wonder is that in the midst of change Idaho had managed to preserve certain desirable qualities, among these its physical beauty, the pleasant ambience of small-town life, the work ethic, and a continuing commitment to issue- and personality-oriented politics.

In the 1990s, as was true a century earlier, natural resources and the environment remained the underlying concerns in many political controversies. In the 1890s, the main question was how to develop nature's abundance, and in the 1990s many people still saw the development of natural resources as the key to Idaho's future prosperity. But now there was a rising chorus of dissenters who wondered whether Idaho needed another dam or facility for processing nuclear waste if that meant degradation of the state's environment.

Compared to my own bulging, booming state
of Arizona, the future of Idaho looks clean,
bright, free, and hopeful. Maybe I'll move.
—from the late Edward Abbey in *National
Geographic Traveler* (July/August 1989)

EPILOGUE
What of the Future?

Idaho remains one of the least known and most puzzling of American states.
It is the "riddle of the Rockies" to many out-of-state commentators.

During the 1980s the national news media typically ignored Idaho except
for the activities of the California expatriate Richard Butler and his Aryan
Nations followers, some of whom engaged in overt violence and criminal
activities to further their cause. Attracted to the Gem State for its isolation
and homogeneous population, Butler built a fortress compound at Hayden
Lake complete with school, guard post, and living quarters. As head of the
Church of Jesus Christ (Christian), he expounded a white supremacist gospel. Despite all the media attention given to Butler and his group, their annual Aryan Congress at Hayden Lake typically drew more reporters and
protesters than participants.

Too often obscured by the glare of unfavorable publicity is the fact that
less than ten miles from Butler's compound is Coeur d'Alene, fast becoming
a world-class resort. Farther north is the trend-setting community of Sandpoint, which holds an annual music festival that attracts nationally recognized artists.

Even in the early 1990s, despite its Fortune 500 giants and high-tech
upstarts, much of Idaho remains a hinterland. Of the state's fifty-three million
acres, only about one-third of 1 percent are urban. The juxtaposition of the
modern metropolis and the hinterland is, in fact, the defining quality of life
in modern Idaho. The accessibility of the hinterland's mountain slopes and

92. Giving the term "Air Mail" a special meaning is Ray Arnold, who still flies out of Cascade to link the people of Idaho's rugged Salmon River country with the outside world. The date of this photograph is May 1981, but it could just as well be 1991. Courtesy *Idaho Statesman*.

pristine rivers from metropolitan centers remains the *key* feature of what residents regard as a desirable life-style.

Concerns about how best to promote the state's economic health contributed to one of the debates that promised to loom larger as Idaho approached the year 2000: in the name of jobs would legislators and other public officials permit lands to be logged off or mined that were better set aside as a wilderness heritage for future generations of Idahoans who are more likely to spend their working lives in offices than in the fields, forests, or mines?

In 1980, 9.8 percent of Idaho's work force engaged in agriculture compared with 42 percent in 1910; .6 percent in mining compared with 61 percent in 1870. At the same time there was a big increase in jobs in trades and services, which together employ about 50 percent of all Idahoans today but employed only 18 percent at the turn of the century. Thanks to innovative developments like the Microelectronics Research Center at the University of Idaho, where in the late 1980s the world's fastest computer chip was designed for the National Aeronautics and Space Administration, Idaho may become as well known for computer memory chips as for chips of the potato variety.

93. The Salmon River valley being transformed by real estate development, June 1974. Courtesy *Idaho Statesman*.

A sense of Idaho's past will help the present generation understand better the kind of state that evolved in recent years when the modern metropolis intersected with a hinterland rich in beauty and natural resources. It is the continuing juxtaposition of hinterland and trend-setting urban area that will likely shape the course of public debate into the twenty-first century.

The number of people who call Idaho home is certain to grow again if the state maintains its health and as more outsiders come to value Idaho's scenic resources and high quality of life in a nation increasingly troubled by decaying cities, pollution, and congestion. Room to roam, the state's enduring work ethic, and the age of jet travel combine to make Idaho especially appealing to business and professional people.

Even as Idaho looks to its economic future, whether it is based on high-tech or tourism or markets along the Pacific rim, it will not be able to ignore one of the persistent problems of the twentieth century, that of the economic instability of its extractive industries. State government during the 1980s clearly mirrored this problem. The Gem State finished the decade with a $63 million surplus in its treasury, although as recently as 1983 it wrestled with a $70 million deficit as the result of an ailing economy.

In addition, public officials will have to resolve the conflict that is inevitable between metropolitan dwellers who regard nonagricultural portions of the hinterland as recreational getaways, and those people who, on the other hand, wish to exploit the hinterland for its natural resources. The future of Idaho could be as exciting as its past.

94. Two children with
their catch around 1919;
the location appears to be
in the vicinity of Redfish
Lake. To the consterna-
tion of historians, such
photographic gems often
lack a specific date or
location.

During the course of re-
searching this book I
sorted through thousands
of images in dozens of
public archives and found
numerous pictures that
lacked even the most ele-
mental identifying notes.
The fault lies with a photographer too trusting to
memory, but the real
loser is history. Courtesy
Library of Congress.

Notes

Chapter 1

1 Former United States Senator James McClure publicly emphasized this point by always using the term "northern Idaho" to describe the panhandle. His was an effort to bring the state's sections closer together. Perhaps he would encourage groups like the North Idaho Chamber of Commerce and North Idaho College to change their names to reflect that concern. See *Oh! Idaho: The Idaho State Magazine* 1 ([1988]): 12–13.

2 *Lewiston Morning Tribune*, Jan. 11, 1989.

3 An acre-foot of water, for those unfamiliar with this important unit of measurement, is the amount of water it takes to cover an acre to the depth of one foot.

4 James H. Hawley, *History of Idaho: Gem of the Mountains* (Chicago: S. J. Clarke, 1920), 1 : 809.

Chapter 2

1 Gary Moulton, ed., *The Journals of the Lewis and Clark Expedition* (Lincoln: University of Nebraska Press, 1988), 5 : 188.

2 Less than a mile actually separated the headwaters of the two rivers, but that was a meaningless fact in terms of canoe travel, for churning waters ran from the Continental Divide to the Snake River.

3 Patrick Gass, *Gass's Journal of the Lewis and Clark Expedition* (1811; rpt. Chicago: A. C. McClurg, 1904), 142.

4   Gass, *Journal*, 145; Moulton, ed., *Journals of the Lewis and Clark Expedition*, 5:209.

5   Moulton, ed., *Journals of the Lewis and Clark Expedition*, 5:223.

6   For further information on the controversies surrounding Sacagawea, see James P. Ronda, *Lewis and Clark among the Indians* (Lincoln: University of Nebraska Press, 1984), 256–59.

Chapter 3

1   As quoted in John S. Galbraith, *The Hudson's Bay Company as an Imperial Factor, 1821–1869* (Berkeley: University of California Press, 1957), 88.

2   As quoted in Galbraith, *The Hudson's Bay Company*, 90.

Chapter 4

1   John Mullan, *Miners' and Travelers' Guide to Oregon, Washington, Idaho, Montana, Wyoming, and Colorado* (New York: Wm. M. Franklin, 1865), 12.

2   W. J. McConnell, *Early History of Idaho* (Caldwell: Caxton, 1913), 120.

Chapter 5

1   Except where noted, the history of Idaho's early mining booms is distilled from the following sources: Hiram T. French, *History of Idaho* (Chicago: Lewis Publishing, 1914), 1:26–39; John Hailey, *The History of Idaho* (Boise: Syms-York, 1910), 29–48; James H. Hawley, *History of Idaho*, 1:9–134; McConnell, *Early History of Idaho*, 55–99; and Merrill D. Beal and Merle W. Wells, *History of Idaho* (New York: Lewis Historical Publishing, 1959), 1:280–316.

2   A. J. Cain, United States Indian agent, posted this notice: "The settlement made at the junction of the Snake and Clearwater rivers is in violation of United States Law and cannot be permitted under any circumstances." It did not stop the tide of humanity from flooding onto Nez Perce land. See Gene Mueller, *Lewiston: A Pictorial History* (Lewiston: Lewiston Chamber of Commerce, 1986), 15.

3   Thomas Donaldson, *Idaho of Yesterday* (Caldwell: Caxton, 1941), 26.

4   A good summary account of the creation of Idaho is in Beal and Wells, *History of Idaho*, 1:325–58.

Chapter 6

1   McConnell, *Early History of Idaho*, 190–91.

2   As quoted in Merle W. Wells, "Caleb Lyon's Indian Policy," *Pacific Northwest Quarterly* 61 (October 1970): 200.

Chapter 7

1 Carrie Adell Strahorn, *Fifteen Thousand Miles by Stage* (1911; rpt. Lincoln: University of Nebraska Press, 1988), 1 : 79.

2 *Lewiston Teller* as quoted in " 'She Will Strike about There . . .': Steamboating in Hell's Canyon," *Idaho Yesterdays* 1 (Summer 1957), 3.

3 The *Mary Moody* sailed from Pend Oreille City (near modern Bayview) across the lake and up the Clark Fork River as far as Noxon Rapids to transport goods and miners to the Montana diggings.

4 Even more recently, in the late 1980s the Montana Rail Link took over train service on the old Northern Pacific main line from Sandpoint to Laurel, Montana, near Billings.

5 *An Illustrated History of North Idaho* (Chicago: Western Historical Publishing, 1903), 106.

Chapter 8

1 The Sunshine Mine would also be the site of a terrible disaster: on May 2, 1972, fire claimed the lives of ninety-one men. It was one of the worst underground hard-rock mine fires in United States history.

2 As quoted in Hailey, *History of Idaho*, 175.

Chapter 9

1 McConnell, *Early History of Idaho*, 138–39.

2 McConnell, *Early History of Idaho*, 72.

3 In addition to Boise, only Pocatello exceeded 2,500 people. Moscow came close with 2,484 residents, Lewiston with 2,425, and Wallace with 2,265.

Chapter 10

1 As quoted in Betty Derig, "Celestials in the Diggings," *Idaho Yesterdays* 16 (Fall 1972): 1.

2. See Margaret Lauterbach, "A Plentitude of Senators," *Idaho Yesterdays* 21 (Fall 1977), 2–8, for a discussion of this strange episode.

3 Idaho, Washington, and probably several other states permitted women to vote in certain school elections during the years before they won the right to vote in primary and general elections.

Chapter 11

1 Mark Wyman, "Frontier Journalism," *Idaho Yesterdays* 17 (Spring 1973): 36.

2 As quoted in Ronald W. Taber, "Vardis Fisher of Idaho, March 31, 1895–July 9, 1968," *Idaho Yesterdays* 12 (Fall 1968): 5.

3   Strahorn, *Fifteen Thousand Miles*, 2:49–50.

4   At about the same time, the Northern Pacific line opened a small hotel in Hope, where passengers occasionally stayed a few days to hunt and fish on Lake Pend Oreille.

5   C. E. Flagg as quoted in French, *History of Idaho*, 1:527.

6   Nicholas Point, *Wilderness Kingdom: Indian Life in the Rocky Mountains, 1840–1847; The Journals and Paintings of Nicholas Point, S. J.*, trans. Joseph P. Donnelly (New York: Holt, Rinehart and Winston, 1967), 181.

Chapter 12

1   Cleveland, who ran for president on the Democratic party's gold platform, received but two write-in votes in Idaho.

2   *Fifth Biennial Report, Commissioner of Immigration, Labor and Statistics, 1907–1908* (Boise: State of Idaho, [1909]), 138.

3   As quoted in James Montgomery, *Liberated Woman: A Life of May Arkwright Hutton* (Fairfield, Wash: Ye Galleon Press, 1974), 58.

4   Pettibone was acquitted in January 1908, and Moyer was eventually released without having to stand trial.

Chapter 13

1   Strahorn, *Fifteen Thousand Miles*, 2:45.

2   Union Pacific Railroad, *The Resources and Attractions of Idaho* (Chicago: Rand McNally, 1889), 19–20.

3   As quoted in Hubert Howe Bancroft, *History of Washington, Idaho, and Montana, 1845–1899* (San Francisco: History Company, 1890), 579.

4   As quoted in Hawley, *History of Idaho*, 1:292–293.

5   William E. Smythe, *The Conquest of Arid America* (1905; rpt. Seattle: University of Washington Press, 1969), 191.

Chapter 14

1   David Glaser, "Migration in Idaho's History," *Idaho Yesterdays* 11 (Fall 1967): 25.

2   Annie Pike Greenwood, *We Sagebrush Folks* (1934; rpt. Moscow: University of Idaho Press, 1988), 253.

3   Jack Donohue, "Joining North and South Idaho," *New West* 10 (April 1919): 46.

4   Frank Church, "Borah the Statesman," *Idaho Yesterdays* 9 (Summer 1965): 3.

5   Robert James Maddox, *William E. Borah and American Foreign Policy* (Baton Rouge: Louisiana State University Press, 1969), xiii.

Chapter 15

1 As quoted in Richard L. Neuberger, *Our Promised Land* (1938; rpt. Moscow: University of Idaho Press, 1989), 34.

2 As quoted in *Seventh Biennial Report of Commissioner of Immigration, Labor and Statistics* [of Idaho], *1911–1912* (Caldwell: Caxton, 1912), 174.

Chapter 16

1 As quoted in David Glaser, "Migration in Idaho's History," *Idaho Yesterdays* 11 (Fall 1967): 29.

2 "The Earth Mover," *Time* 63 (May 3, 1954): 86.

Chapter 17

1 L. J. Davis, "Unlikely, but Boise Means Big Business," *New York Times Magazine*, June 11, 1989, pp. 24–25, 70, 72.

2 In 1988 about fifteen hundred people were employed in the mines of the Coeur d'Alene district. And for the first time since the slump began, the number of people working in Idaho's timber industry had climbed back to the fifteen thousand mark.

3 *Christian Science Monitor*, Dec. 19, 1988.

4 Neal R. Peirce, *The Mountain States of America: People, Politics, and Power in the Eight Rocky Mountain States* (New York: Norton, 1972), 143.

5 Some people argue that Idaho gained a national park in 1965 with creation of the Nez Perce National Historical Park. This is supposed to be Idaho's equivalent to better-known national parks like Yellowstone, Yosemite, and Mesa Verde, but not everyone agrees.

6 Jean Conley Smith as quoted in French, *History of Idaho*, 1:535.

Chapter 18

1 Eleven months after the election Welker was dead of a massive brain tumor, an ailment unknown to voters in 1956, who assumed that his memory lapses and slurred speech were caused by alcohol.

2 Randy Stapilus, *Paradox Politics: People and Power in Idaho* (Boise: Ridenbaugh Press, 1988), 17.

3 As quoted in Peirce, *The Mountain States of America*, 151.

4 By the early 1970s a move was afoot in Congress to create Sawtooth Recreation Area and National Park. The legislation passed after the national park portion was dropped.

5 The Republican Senator James McClure shepherded a bill through Congress in 1984 renaming the area for Frank Church, his former Democratic colleague who was dying of cancer.

Suggestions for Further Reading

Chapter 1

Attebery, Louie W. *Idaho Folklife: Homesteads to Headstones*. Salt Lake City: University of Utah Press, 1985.

Bancroft, Hubert Howe. *History of Washington, Idaho, and Montana, 1845–1889*. San Francisco: History Company, 1890. Vol. 31 of *The Works of Hubert Howe Bancroft*.

Beal, Merrill D., and Merle W. Wells. *History of Idaho*. 3 vols. New York: Lewis Historical Publishing, 1959.

The Compact Atlas of Idaho. Moscow: University of Idaho Center for Business Development and Research and Cart-O-Graphics Laboratory, 1983.

Conley, Cort. *Idaho for the Curious: A Guide*. Cambridge, Idaho: Backeddy Books, 1982. This guidebook is keyed to Idaho highways and provides excellent capsule histories.

Etulain, Richard W., and Merwin Swanson. *Idaho History: A Bibliography*. Pocatello: Idaho State University Press, 1979.

[Fisher, Vardis.] *Idaho: A Guide in Word and Picture*. Caldwell, Idaho: Caxton, 1937. The first of the nation's many Works Progress Administration guides, it remains a classic.

Idaho Almanac. Boise: Executive Office of the Governor and Idaho Division of Tourism and Industrial Development, 1977.

Idaho: An Illustrated History. Boise: Idaho State Historical Society, 1976.

Idaho Blue Book. Boise: Secretary of State, published biennially since 1969. The most valuable source of information about contemporary Idaho.

Idaho State Historical Society "Reference Series." Several hundred, mostly one- or two-page typed essays on a wide variety of Idaho topics, many written by Merle Wells. An invaluable source of history, available at the Idaho State Historical Society research library in Boise.

Idaho Yesterdays. A quarterly journal published since 1957 by the Idaho State Historical Society that is necessary to the study of Idaho history.

Kimerling, A. Jon, and Philip L. Jackson, eds. *Atlas of the Pacific Northwest*. 7th ed. Corvallis: Oregon State University Press, 1985.

Lovin, Hugh T. "Sage, Jacks, and Snake Plain Pioneers." *Idaho Yesterdays* 22 (Winter 1979): 13–15, 18–24.

Martin, Boyd A. "Idaho: The Sectional State." In *Politics in the American West*, ed. Frank H. Jonas, 180–200. Salt Lake City: University of Utah Press, 1969.

Meinig, D. W. *The Great Columbia Plain: A Historical Geography, 1805–1910*. Seattle: University of Washington Press, 1968.

Nelson, Milo G., and Charles A. Webbert, eds. *Idaho Local History: A Bibliography with a Checklist of Library Holdings*. Moscow: University Press of Idaho, 1976.

Peterson, F. Ross. *Idaho, a Bicentennial History*. New York: Norton, 1976.

———. "Idaho at a Crossroads: History Charts the Course." *Idaho Yesterdays* 30 (Fall 1986): 2–8.

Rouyer, Alwyn R. *The Idaho Political Handbook*. Moscow: Bureau of Public Affairs Research, University of Idaho, 1980.

Stratton, David H. "Hells Canyon: The Missing Link in Pacific Northwest Regionalism," *Idaho Yesterdays* 28 (Fall 1984): 2–9.

Swanson, Earl H., Jr. "The Snake River Plain." *Idaho Yesterdays* 18 (Summer 1974): 2–11.

Walker, Eugene H. "The Geologic History of the Snake River Country of Idaho." *Idaho Yesterdays* 7 (Summer 1963): 18–31.

Wells, Merle W., and Arthur A. Hart. *Idaho: Gem of the Mountains*. Northridge, Calif.: Windsor, 1985. An illustrated history.

Wuerthner, George. *Idaho Mountain Ranges*. Helena, Mont.: American Geographic, 1986.

Chapter 2

[Appleman, Roy E.] *Lewis and Clark: Historic Places Associated with Their Transcontinental Exploration (1804–06)*. Washington, D.C.: Department of the Interior, 1975.

Crowder, David L. "Nineteenth-Century Indian-White Conflict in Southern

Idaho." *Idaho Yesterdays* 23 (Summer 1979): 13–18.

Fahey, John. *The Kalispel Indians*. Norman: University of Oklahoma Press, 1986.

Josephy, Alvin M., Jr. *The Nez Perce Indians and the Opening of the Northwest*. New Haven: Yale University Press, 1965.

———. "Origins of the Nez Perce People." *Idaho Yesterdays* 6 (Spring 1962): 2–13.

Lavender, David. *The Way to the Western Sea: Lewis and Clark across the Continent*. New York: Harper & Row, 1988.

Liljeblad, Sven. "The Indians of Idaho." *Idaho Yesterdays* 4 (Fall 1960): 22–28.

———. "Indian Peoples of Idaho." In *History of Idaho*, Merrill D. Beal and Merle W. Wells, 1:29–59. New York: Lewis Historical Publishing, 1959.

Madsen, Brigham D. *The Bannock of Idaho*. Caldwell, Idaho: Caxton, 1958.

———. *The Lemhi: Sacajawea's People*. Caldwell, Idaho: Caxton, 1980.

———. *The Northern Shoshoni*. Caldwell: Caxton, 1980.

Moulton, Gary E., ed. *The Journals of the Lewis and Clark Expedition*. Lincoln: University of Nebraska Press, 1983–; volumes 1–.

Peebles, John J. "On the Lolo Trail: Route and Campsites of Lewis and Clark." *Idaho Yesterdays* 9 (Winter 1965–66): 2–15.

———. "The Return of Lewis and Clark." *Idaho Yesterdays* 10 (Summer 1966): 16–27.

———. "Rugged Waters: Trails and Campsites of Lewis and Clark in the Salmon River Country." *Idaho Yesterdays* 8 (Summer 1964): 2–17.

Rees, John. "The Shoshoni Contribution to Lewis and Clark." *Idaho Yesterdays* 2 (Summer 1958): 2–13.

Ronda, James P. *Lewis and Clark among the Indians*. Lincoln: University of Nebraska Press, 1984.

Ruby, Robert H., and John A. Brown. *Indians of the Pacific Northwest*. Norman: University of Oklahoma Press, 1981.

———. *The Spokane Indians: Children of the Sun*. Norman: University of Oklahoma Press, 1970.

Stewart, Omer C. "Shoshoni History and Social Organization." *Idaho Yesterdays* 9 (Fall 1965): 2–5, 28.

Taber, Ronald W. "Sacagawea and the Suffragettes." *Pacific Northwest Quarterly* 58 (1967): 7–13.

Trafzer, Clifford E., and Richard D. Scheuerman. *Renegade Tribe: The Palouse Indians and the Invasion of the Inland Pacific Northwest*. Pullman: Washington State University Press, 1986.

Walker, Deward E., Jr. *Indians of Idaho*. Moscow: University Press of Idaho, 1978.

———. *Myths of Idaho Indians*. Moscow: University Press of Idaho, 1980.

Chapter 3

"The Adventures of Alexander Ross in the Snake Country." *Idaho Yesterdays* 14 (Spring 1970): 8–15.

Carriker, Robert C. "Direct Successor to DeSmet: Joseph M. Cataldo, S.J., and Stabilization of the Jesuit Indian Missions of the Pacific Northwest, 1877–1893." *Idaho Yesterdays* 31 (Spring/Summer 1987): 8–12.

Chittenden, Hiram Martin. *The American Fur Trade of the Far West*. 2 vols. 1935. Reprint. Lincoln: University of Nebraska Press, 1986.

Clark, Ella E. "The Old Mission." *Idaho Yesterdays* 15 (Fall 1971): 18–27.

Cline, Gloria Griffen. *Peter Skene Ogden and the Hudson's Bay Company*. Norman: University of Oklahoma Press, 1974.

Coates, Lawrence G. "Mormons and Social Change among the Shoshoni, 1853–1900." *Idaho Yesterdays* 15 (Winter 1972): 2–11.

———. "The Spalding-Whitman and Lemhi Missions: A Comparison." *Idaho Yesterdays* 31 (Spring/Summer 1987): 38–46.

Crowder, David L. "Nineteenth-Century Indian-White Conflict in Southern Idaho." *Idaho Yesterdays* 23 (Summer 1979): 13–18.

Culverwell, Albert H. "The Fascinating Pleasures of the Far-Famed Spokane House." *Idaho Yesterdays* 14 (Spring 1970), 2–7.

De Smet, Pierre Jean. *Oregon Missions and Travels over the Rocky Mountains in 1845–46*. 1847. Reprint. Fairfield, Wash.: Ye Galleon Press, 1978.

Drury, Clifford M. *Henry Harmon Spalding: Pioneer of Old Oregon*. Caldwell, Idaho: Caxton, 1936.

"Fort Boise: From Imperial Outpost to Historic Site." *Idaho Yesterdays* 6 (Spring 1962): 14–16, 33–39.

"Fort Hall, 1834–1856." *Idaho Yesterdays* 12 (Summer 1968): 28–31.

Galbraith, John S. *The Hudson's Bay Company as an Imperial Factor, 1821–1869*. Berkeley: University of California Press, 1957.

Hafen, LeRoy R., ed. *Mountain Men and Fur Traders of the Far West: Biographical Sketches*. 1965–72. Reprint. Lincoln: University of Nebraska Press, 1982. A condensation of a ten-volume set.

Haines, Francis D., Jr. "François Payette." *Idaho Yesterdays*. 8 (Winter 1964–65): 12–21.

———. "François Payette, Master of Fort Boise." *Pacific Northwest Quarterly* 47 (1956): 57–61.

Hayden, Willard C. "The Battle of Pierre's Hole." *Idaho Yesterdays* 16 (Summer 1972): 2–11.

Hopwood, Victor G., ed. *David Thompson: Travels in Western North America, 1784–1812.* Toronto: Macmillan of Canada, 1971.

Irving, Washington. *Astoria; or, Anecdotes of an Enterprize beyond the Rocky Mountains.* 1836. Reprint. Boston: Twayne, 1976.

Lavender, David. *Land of Giants: The Drive to the Pacific Northwest, 1750–1950.* 1958. Reprint. Lincoln: University of Nebraska Press, 1979.

Nash, John D. "Salmon River Mission of 1855: A Reappraisal." *Idaho Yesterdays* 11 (Spring 1967): 22–31.

Parker, Samuel. *Journal of an Exploring Tour beyond the Rocky Mountains.* 1838. Reprint. Minneapolis, Minn.: Ross & Haines, 1967.

Point, Nicholas. *Wilderness Kingdom: Indian Life in the Rocky Mountains: 1840–1847; The Journals and Paintings of Nicholas Point, S.J.* Trans. Joseph P. Donnelly. New York: Holt, Rinehart and Winston, 1967.

Prucha, Francis Paul. "Two Roads to Conversion: Protestant and Catholic Missionaries in the Pacific Northwest." *Pacific Northwest Quarterly* 79 (1988): 130–37.

Robinson, Willard B. "Frontier Architecture: Father Ravalli and the Design of the Coeur d'Alene Mission of the Sacred Heart." *Idaho Yesterdays* 3 (Winter 1959–60): 2–6.

Ross, Alexander. *Adventures of the First Settlers on the Oregon or Columbia River, 1810–1813.* 1904. Reprint. Lincoln: University of Nebraska Press, 1986.

Saum, Lewis O. *The Fur Trader and the Indian.* Seattle: University of Washington Press, 1965.

Schoenberg, Wilfred P. "The Bishops Blanchet and Their Role in the Whitman Massacre." *Idaho Yesterdays* 31 (Spring/Summer 1987): 3–7.

Spalding, Henry H., and Asa Bowen Smith. *The Diaries and Letters of Henry H. Spalding and Asa Bowen Smith Relating to the Nez Perce Mission, 1838–1842.* Ed. Clifford M. Drury. Glendale, Calif.: Arthur H. Clark, 1958.

Thompson, A. W. "New Light on Donald Mackenzie's Post on the Clearwater, 1812–1813." *Idaho Yesterdays* 18 (Fall 1974): 22–32.

Thompson, Erwin N. "Joseph M. Cataldo and Saint Joseph's Mission." *Idaho Yesterdays* 18 (Summer 1974): 19–29.

Townsend, John Kirk. *Across the Rockies to the Columbia.* Lincoln: University of Nebraska Press, 1978. Abridged reprint of 1839 version called *Narrative of a Journey across the Rocky Mountains to the Columbia River.*

Tuohy, Donald R. "Horseshoes and Handstones: The Meeting of History and Prehistory at the Old Mission of the Sacred Heart." *Idaho Yesterdays* 2 (Summer 1958): 20–27.

[Wells, Merle W.] "The Adventures of Alexander Ross in the Snake Country." *Idaho Yesterdays* 14 (Spring 1970): 8–15.

Wells, Merle W. "'A House for Trading': David Thompson on Pend d'Oreille Lake." *Idaho Yesterdays* 3 (Fall 1959): 22–26.

Whitman, Narcissa. *Narcissa Prentiss Whitman, My Journal, 1836*. Ed. Lawrence Dodd. Fairfield, Wash.: Ye Galleon Press, 1982.

Wishart, David J. *The Fur Trade of the American West, 1807–1840: A Geographical Synthesis*. Lincoln: University of Nebraska Press, 1979.

Chapter 4

Barkan, Frances B., ed. *The Wilkes Expedition: Puget Sound and the Oregon Country*. Olympia: Washington State Capital Museum, 1987.

Bartlett, Richard A. *Great Surveys of the American West*. Norman: University of Oklahoma Press, 1962.

Burns, Robert Ignatius. *The Jesuits and the Indian Wars of the Northwest*. 1966. Reprint. Moscow: University of Idaho Press, [1985].

"Caleb Lyon's Bruneau Treaty." *Idaho Yesterdays* 13 (Summer 1969): 16–19, 32.

Clark, Malcolm, Jr. *Eden Seekers: The Settlement of Oregon, 1818–1862*. Boston: Houghton Mifflin, 1981.

Crowder, David L. "Nineteenth-Century Indian-White Conflict in Southern Idaho." *Idaho Yesterdays* 23 (Summer 1979): 13–18.

———. *Tendoy: Chief of the Lemhis*. Caldwell, Idaho: Caxton, 1969.

Dozier, Jack. "Coeur d'Alene Country: The Creation of the Coeur d'Alene Indian Reservation in North Idaho." *Idaho Yesterdays* 6 (Fall 1962): 2–7.

Drury, Clifford M. "Lawyer, Head Chief of the Nez Perce, 1848–1875." *Idaho Yesterdays* 22 (Winter 1979): 2–12.

Faragher, John Mack. *Women and Men on the Overland Trail*. New Haven: Yale University Press, 1979.

Frémont, John C. *The Exploring Expedition to the Rocky Mountains*. 1945. Reprint. Washington, D.C.: Smithsonian Institution Press, 1988.

Goetzmann, William H. *Army Exploration in the American West, 1803–1863*. 1959. Reprint. Lincoln: University of Nebraska Press, 1979.

———. *Exploration and Empire: The Explorer and Scientist in the Winning of the American West*. 1966. Reprint. New York: Norton, 1978.

———. *New Lands, New Men: America and the Second Great Age of Dis-*

covery. New York: Viking, 1986.

Hayden, Willard C. "The Hayden Survey." *Idaho Yesterdays* 16 (Spring 1972): 20–25.

Irving, Washington. *The Adventures of Captain Bonneville, U.S.A., in the Rocky Mountains and the Far West*. Ed. Edgeley W. Todd. 1837. Reprint. Norman: University of Oklahoma Press, 1986.

Joseph. *Chief Joseph's Own Story*. 1879. Reprint. Fairfield, Wash.: Ye Galleon Press, 1972.

Liljeblad, Sven. "Epilogue: Indian Policy and the Fort Hall Reservation." *Idaho Yesterdays* 2 (Summer 1958): 15–16.

McGregor, Alexander Campbell. "The Economic Impact of the Mullan Road on Walla Walla, 1860–1883." *Pacific Northwest Quarterly* 65 (1974): 118–29.

Madsen, Brigham D. *The Northern Shoshoni*. Caldwell, Idaho: Caxton, 1980.

Richards, Kent D. *Isaac I. Stevens: Young Man in a Hurry*. Provo: Brigham Young University Press, 1979.

Ruby, Robert H., and John A. Brown. *A Guide to the Indian Tribes of the Pacific Northwest*. Norman: University of Oklahoma Press, 1986.

Stanton, William. *The Great United States Exploring Expedition of 1838–1842*. Berkeley: University of California Press, 1975.

Taylor, Arthur S., and William M. McKinney. "An Accurate Observer: William Hoffman's View of Idaho in 1853." *Idaho Yesterdays* 8 (Summer 1964): 20–25.

Unruh, John D., Jr. *The Plains Across: The Overland Emigrants and the Trans-Mississippi West, 1840–60*. Urbana: University of Illinois Press, 1979.

Viola, Herman J. *Exploring the West*. Washington, D.C.: Smithsonian Books, 1987.

Chapter 5

Angelo, C. Aubrey. "Impressions of the Boise Basin in 1863." *Idaho Yesterdays* 7 (Spring 1963): 4–13.

Arrington, Leonard J. *Great Basin Kingdom: Economic History of the Latter-day Saints, 1830–1900*. 1958. Reprint. Lincoln: University of Nebraska Press, 1966.

———. "The Mormon Settlement of Cassia County, Idaho, 1873–1921." *Idaho Yesterdays* 23 (Summer 1979): 36–46.

Arrington, Leonard J., and Davis Bitton. *The Mormon Experience: A History of the Latter-day Saints*. New York: Knopf, 1979.

Arrington, Leonard J., and Richard Jensen. "Pioneer Portraits: Lorenzo Hill Hatch." *Idaho Yesterdays* 17 (Summer 1973): 2–8.

Beal, Merrill D. "Cache Valley Pioneers." *Idaho Yesterdays* 4 (Spring 1960): 2–7.

———. *A History of Southeastern Idaho*. Caldwell, Idaho: Caxton, 1942.

Bitton, Davis. "Blackfoot: The Making of a Community, 1878–1910." *Idaho Yesterdays* 19 (Spring 1975): 2–15.

———. "Peopling the Upper Snake: The Second Wave of Mormon Settlement in Idaho." *Idaho Yesterdays* 23 (Summer 1979): 47–52.

Bird, Annie Laurie. "Idaho's First Territorial Governor." *Idaho Yesterdays* 10 (Summer 1966): 8–15.

Bowditch, Barbara. "Pioneer Portraits: Charles C. Rich." *Idaho Yesterdays* 7 (Fall 1963): 18–20.

Davis, William E. "George Forman, the Great Pedestrian." *Idaho Yesterdays* 10 (Spring 1966): 2–11. Firsthand impressions of the Boise Basin rush.

Deutsch, Herman J. "The Evolution of the International Boundary in the Inland Empire of the Pacific Northwest." *Pacific Northwest Quarterly* 51 (1960): 63–79.

"Fabulous Florence!" *Idaho Yesterdays* 6 (Summer 1962): 22–31.

"Idaho's Centennial: How Idaho Was Created in 1863." *Idaho Yesterdays* 7 (Spring 1963): 44–58.

Limbaugh, Ronald H. *Rocky Mountain Carpetbaggers: Idaho's Territorial Governors, 1863–1890*. Moscow: University Press of Idaho, 1982.

May, Dean L. "Mormon Cooperatives in Paris, Idaho, 1869–1896." *Idaho Yesterdays* 19 (Summer 1975): 20–30.

Oviatt, Alton B. "Pacific Coast Competition for the Gold Camp Trade of Montana." *Pacific Northwest Quarterly* 56 (1965): 168–76.

Paul, Rodman W. "The Mormons of Yesterday and Today." *Idaho Yesterdays* 19 (Fall 1975): 2–7.

Pierce, E. D. *The Pierce Chronicle: Personal Reminiscenses of E. D. Pierce as transcribed by Lou A. Larrick*. Ed. J. Gary Williams and Ronald W. Stark. Moscow, Idaho: Idaho Research Foundation, n.d.

Poulsen, Ezra J. "Parisian Life . . . Western Style." *Idaho Yesterdays* 8 (Spring 1964): 2–9.

Reitzes, Lisa B. *Paris: A Look at Idaho Architecture*. Boise: Idaho State Historic Preservation Office, 1981.

Rich, A. McKay. "The Two Montpeliers." *Idaho Yesterdays* 3 (Winter 1959–60): 8–14.

Romig, Robert L. "Stamp Mills in Trouble: Quartz Miners Learned the Hard

Way on the South Boise Ledges." *Pacific Northwest Quarterly* 44 (1953): 166–76.

Simmonds, A. J. "Southeast Idaho as a Pioneer Mormon Safety Valve." *Idaho Yesterdays* 23 (Winter 1980): 20–30.

Simon-Smolinski, Carole. *Journal 1862: Timothy Nolan's Account of His Riverboat and Overland Journey to the Salmon River Mines, Washington Territory*. Clarkston, Wash.: Northwest Historical Consultants, 1983. A fictional account solidly grounded in the history of the Clearwater rush.

Throckmorton, Arthur L. *Oregon Argonauts: Merchant Adventurers on the Western Frontier*. Portland: Oregon Historical Society, 1961. Discusses the relationship between Idaho's 1860s gold rushes and Portland's merchants.

Wells, Donald N. "Farmers Forgotten: Nez Perce Suppliers of the North Idaho Gold Rush Days." *Idaho Yesterdays* 2 (Summer 1958): 29–32.

Wells, Merle W. *Anti-Mormonism in Idaho, 1872–92*. Provo: Brigham Young University, 1978.

———. *Gold Camps and Silver Cities: Nineteenth Century Mining in Central and Southern Idaho*. Moscow: Idaho Department of Lands/Bureau of Mines and Geology, 1983.

———. "The Long Wait for Statehood: Why It Took Washington 36 Years and Idaho 26 Years to Achieve Their Goals." *Columbia: The Magazine of Northwest History* 2 (Fall 1988): 18–23.

———. "Territorial Government in the Inland Empire." *Pacific Northwest Quarterly* 44 (1953): 80–87.

———. "Walla Walla's Vision of a Greater Washington." *Idaho Yesterdays* 10 (Fall 1966): 20–31.

Wunder, John R. "Tampering with the Northwest Frontier: The Accidental Design of the Washington/Idaho Boundary." *Pacific Northwest Quarterly* 68 (1977): 1–12.

Chapter 6

Alexander, Thomas G. "Mason Brayman and the Boise Ring." *Idaho Yesterdays* 14 (Fall 1970): 21–27.

Beal, Merrill D. *"I Will Fight No More Forever": Chief Joseph and the Nez Perce War*. Seattle: University of Washington Press, 1963.

Bean, Kristina Kay. "Self-Evident: The Civil War and Idaho Immigration." *Idaho Yesterdays* 32 (Fall 1988): 30–34.

Brown, Mark H. *The Flight of the Nez Perce*. 1967. Reprint. Lincoln: University of Nebraska Press, 1982.

Burns, Robert Ignatius. *The Jesuits and the Indian Wars of the Northwest*.

1966. Reprint. Moscow: University of Idaho Press, [1985?].

Crowder, David L. "Nineteenth-Century Indian-White Conflict in Southern Idaho." *Idaho Yesterdays* 23 (Summer 1979): 13–18.

———. *Tendoy: Chief of the Lemhis*. Caldwell, Idaho: Caxton, 1969.

Dakis, Ruth, and Mike N. Dakis. "Vigilantes on Trial." *Idaho Yesterdays* 12 (Winter 1968): 6–12.

DeLorme, Roland L. "Crime and Punishment in the Pacific Northwest Territories: A Bibliographic Essay." *Pacific Northwest Quarterly* 76 (1985): 42–51.

Dozier, Jack. "1885: A Nez Perce Homecoming." *Idaho Yesterdays* 7 (Fall 1963): 22–25.

Haines, Francis. "The Nez Perce Tribe versus the United States." *Idaho Yesterdays* 8 (Spring 1964): 18–15.

"Idaho's Centennial: How Idaho Was Created in 1863." *Idaho Yesterdays* 7 (Spring 1963): 44–58.

Johannsen, Robert W. *Frontier Politics and the Sectional Conflict: The Pacific Northwest on the Eve of the Civil War*. Seattle: University of Washington Press, 1955.

Josephy, Alvin M., Jr. *The Nez Perce Indians and the Opening of the Northwest*. New Haven: Yale University Press, 1965.

Limbaugh, Ronald H. "The Case of the Three Musicians," *Idaho Yesterdays* 4 (Winter 1960–61): 2–7.

———. *Rocky Mountain Carpetbaggers: Idaho's Territorial Governors, 1863–1890*. Moscow: University Press of Idaho, 1982.

———. "Territorial Elites and Political Power Struggles in the Far West, 1865–1890." In *The Changing Pacific Northwest: Interpreting Its Past*. Ed. David H. Stratton and George A. Frykman. Pullman: Washington State University Press, 1988.

Madsen, Brigham D. *Chief Pocatello, the "White Plume."* Salt Lake City: University of Utah Press, 1986.

———. *The Northern Shoshoni*. Caldwell, Idaho: Caxton, 1980.

———. *The Shoshoni Frontier and the Bear River Massacre*. Salt Lake City: University of Utah Press, 1985.

Mather, R. E., and F. E. Boswell. *Hanging the Sheriff: A Biography of Henry Plummer*. Salt Lake City: University of Utah Press, 1987. This revisionist account challenges the view that Plummer was a desperado who was hanged for good reason.

Nez Perce Country: A Handbook for the Nez Perce National Historical Park. Washington, D.C.: U.S. Department of the Interior, 1983.

Ostrogorsky, Michael. "Fort Boise and the 'New Confederacy': The Early Years." *Idaho Yesterdays* 22 (Winter 1979): 25–31.

———. "Fort Boise and the 'New Confederacy': Vigilantes, Indians, and Copperheads." *Idaho Yesterdays* 23 (Spring 1979): 18–24.

Pomeroy, Earl S. *The Territories and the United States, 1861–1890: Studies in Colonial Administration.* 1947. Reprint. Seattle: University of Washington, 1969.

Ruby, Robert H., and John A. Brown. *A Guide to the Indian Tribes of the Pacific Northwest.* Norman: University of Oklahoma Press, 1986.

Schlicke, Carl P. *General George Wright: Guardian of the Pacific Coast.* Norman: University of Oklahoma Press, 1988.

"Territorial Governors of Idaho." *Idaho Yesterdays* 7 (Spring 1963): 14–23.

Trafzer, Clifford E., and Richard D. Scheuerman. *Renegade Tribe: The Palouse Indians and the Invasion of the Inland Pacific Northwest.* Pullman: Washington State University Press, 1986.

Waite, Robert. "Necessary to Isolate the Female Prisoners: Women Convicts and the Women's Ward in the Old Idaho Penitentiary." *Idaho Yesterdays* 29 (Fall 1985): 2–15.

Walker, Deward E., Jr. *Conflict and Schism in Nez Perce Acculturation: A Study of Religion and Politics.* Moscow: University of Idaho Press, 1985.

Wells, Merle W. "Caleb Lyon's Indian Policy." *Pacific Northwest Quarterly* 61 (1970): 193–200.

———. "Idaho and the Civil War." *Rendezvous* 11 (Fall 1976): 9–26.

———. "The Idaho-Montana Boundary." *Idaho Yesterdays* 12 (Winter 1968–69): 6–9.

———, ed. "S. R. Howlett's War with the Idaho Legislature, 1866–1867." *Idaho Yesterdays* 20 (Spring 1976): 20–27.

"A Year without a Code," *Idaho Yesterdays* 25 (Spring 1981): 13.

Yeckel, Carl. "The Sheepeater Campaign." *Idaho Yesterdays* 15 (Summer 1971): 2–9.

Chapter 7

Athearn, Robert G. *Union Pacific Country.* Chicago: Rand McNally, 1971.

Beal, Merrill D. "The Story of the Utah Northern Railroad, Part I." *Idaho Yesterdays* 1 (Spring 1957): 3–10.

———. "The Story of the Utah Northern Railroad, Part II." *Idaho Yesterdays* 1 (Summer 1957): 16–23.

Bolino, August C. "The Big Bend of the Northern Pacific." *Idaho Yesterdays* 3 (Summer 1959): 5–10.

Butler, W. Daniel. "The Camas Prairie Railroad and Its Larger Railroad Owners." *Idaho Yesterdays* 26 (Winter 1983): 2–8.

———. "Passenger Service on the Camas Prairie Railroad." *Idaho Yesterdays* 27 (Spring 1983): 31–40.

Carrey, John, Cort Conley, and Ace Barton. *Snake River of Hells Canyon*. Cambridge, Idaho: Backeddy Books, 1979.

Fahey, John, *Inland Empire: D. C. Corbin and Spokane*. Seattle: University of Washington Press, 1965. A story of railroad building in northern Idaho.

———. *The Inland Empire: Unfolding Years, 1879–1929*. Seattle: University of Washington Press, 1986. Especially the chapter called "The Railroads: Beneficent, Malignant, Fickle."

Freeman, Otis W. "Early Wagon Roads in the Inland Empire." *Pacific Northwest Quarterly* 45 (1954): 125–30.

Greene, Sally. "Operator—Could You Please Ring? A History of Rural Telephone Service to Kendrick and Juliaetta, Idaho." *Idaho Yesterdays* 31 (Fall 1987): 2–10.

Hailey, John. *The History of Idaho*. Boise: Syms-York, 1910. Emphasizes transportation in early Idaho.

Hofsommer, Don L. "Hill's Dream Realized: The Burlington Northern's Eight-Decade Gestation." *Pacific Northwest Quarterly* 79 (1988): 138–46.

Hult, Ruby El. *Steamboats in the Timber*. Caldwell, Idaho: Caxton, 1953. Steamboating in northern Idaho.

Huntley, James L. *Ferryboats in Idaho*. Caldwell, Idaho: Caxton, 1979.

Jackson, W. Turrentine. *Wells Fargo and Co. in Idaho Territory*. Boise: Idaho State Historical Society, 1984.

Jones, Larry R. "Staging to the South Boise Mines." *Idaho Yesterdays* 29 (Summer 1985): 19–25.

Lewty, Peter J. *To the Columbia Gateway: The Oregon Railway and the Northern Pacific, 1879–1884*. Pullman: Washington State University Press, 1987.

McIntosh, Clarence F. "The Chico and Red Bluff Route: Stage Lines from Southern Idaho to the Sacramento Valley, 1865–1867." *Idaho Yesterdays* 6 (Fall 1962): 12–15, 18–19.

Meinig, D. W. *The Great Columbia Plain: A Historical Geography, 1805–1910*. Seattle: University of Washington Press, 1968. Especially chapter 9: "Strategy: Settlers and Railroads, 1870–90."

Meyer, Bette E. "The Pend Oreille Routes to Montana, 1866–1870." *Pacific Northwest Quarterly* 72 (1981): 76–83.

Mills, Randall V. *Stern-Wheelers up Columbia: A Century of Steamboating in the Oregon Country.* 1947. Reprint. Lincoln: University of Nebraska Press, 1977.

Myers, Rex C. "The Gilmore and Pittsburgh: Lemhi Valley's Railroad." *Idaho Yesterdays* 15 (Summer 1971): 18–23.

Riegger, Hal. *The Camas Prairie: Idaho's Railroad on Stilts.* Edmonds, Wash.: Pacific Fast Mail, 1986.

Schwantes, Carlos A. "The Milwaukee Road's Pacific Extension: 1909–1929: The Photographs of Asahel Curtis." *Pacific Northwest Quarterly* 72 (1981): 30–40.

Simon-Smolinski, Carole. *Clearwater Steam, Steel, and Spirit.* Clarkston, Wash.: Northwest Historical Consultants, 1984.

Strahorn, Carrie Adell. *Fifteen Thousand Miles by Stage.* 1911. Reprint. Lincoln: University of Nebraska Press, 1988.

Winther, Oscar O. *The Old Oregon Country: A History of Frontier Trade, Transportation, and Travel.* 1950. Reprint. New York: Kraus, 1969.

Wood, John V. *Railroads through the Coeur d'Alenes.* Caldwell, Idaho: Caxton, 1983.

Chapter 8

Arrington, Leonard J. *Beet Sugar in the West: A History of the Utah-Idaho Sugar Company, 1891–1966.* Seattle: University of Washington Press, 1966.

———. "From Panning Gold to Nuclear Fission: Idaho's Economic Development, 1860–1960." *Idaho Yesterdays* 6 (Summer 1962): 2–10.

Attebery, Louie W. "Celts and Other Folk in the Regional Livestock Industry." *Idaho Yesterdays* 28 (Summer 1984): 21–29.

Barrett, Glen W., "Banks, Bankers, and Bank Robbers." *Idaho Yesterdays* 19 (Fall 1975): 8–13.

———. "Colonel E. A. Wall: Mines, Miners, and Mormons." *Idaho Yesterdays* 14 (Summer 1970): 2–11.

———. "Enos Andrew Wall: Mine Superintendent and Inventor." *Idaho Yesterdays* 15 (Spring 1971): 24–31.

———. "When Big Money Came to Owyhee." *Idaho Yesterdays* 13 (Spring 1969): 2–9, 22–29.

Beal, Merrill D. "Rustlers and Robbers: Idaho Cattle Thieves in Territorial Days." *Idaho Yesterdays* 7 (Spring 1963): 24–28.

Bolino, August C. "The Role of Mining in the Economic Development of Idaho Territory." *Oregon Historical Quarterly* 59 (1958): 116–51.

Cook, R. G. "Senator Heyburn's War against the Forest Service." *Idaho Yes-*

terdays 14 (Winter 1970–71): 12–15.

Davis, James W., and Nikki Balch Stilwell. *Aristocrat in Burlap: A History of the Potato in Idaho.* Boise: Idaho Potato Commission, 1977.

Day, Henry L. "Mining Highlights of the Coeur d'Alene District." *Idaho Yesterdays* 7 (Winter 1963–64): 2–9.

Fahey, John. "Big Lumber in the Inland Empire: The Early Years, 1900–1930." *Pacific Northwest Quarterly* 76 (1985): 95–103.

———. *The Inland Empire: Unfolding Years, 1879–1929.* Seattle: University of Washington Press, 1986.

Forsling, O. E. "Sheep to Cheyenne." *Idaho Yesterdays* 8 (Summer 1964): 26–32.

Greever, William S. *Bonanza West: The Story of the Western Mining Rushes, 1848–1900.* 1963. Reprint. Moscow: University of Idaho Press, [1985?].

Grover, David H. *Diamondfield Jack: A Study in Frontier Justice.* Reno: University of Nevada Press, 1968.

Hidy, Ralph W. "Lumbermen in Idaho: A Study in Adaptation to Change in Environment." *Idaho Yesterdays* 6 (Winter 1962): 2–17.

Hidy, Ralph W., Frank Ernest Hill, and Allan Nevins. *Timber and Men: The Weyerhaeuser Story.* New York: Macmillan, 1963.

Kensel, W. Hudson. "The Early Spokane Lumber Industry, 1871–1910." *Idaho Yesterdays* 12 (Spring 1968): 25–31. Lumber in the inland Pacific Northwest.

———. "Inland Empire Mining and the Growth of Spokane, 1883–1905." *Pacific Northwest Quarterly* 60 (1969): 84–97.

Livingston-Little, Dallas E. "The Bunker Hill and Sullivan." *Idaho Yesterdays* 7 (Spring 1963): 34–43.

———. *An Economic History of North Idaho, 1800–1900.* Los Angeles: Journal of the West, 1965.

McClenahan, Judith. "Call and See the Elephant." *Idaho Yesterdays* 11 (Fall 1967): 11–13. Wyatt Earp and the Coeur d'Alene gold rush.

McFadden, Thomas G. "Banking in the Boise Region: The Origins of the First National Bank of Idaho." *Idaho Yesterdays* 11 (Spring 1967): 2–17.

McGregor, Alexander Campbell. *Counting Sheep: From Open Range to Agribusiness on the Columbia Plateau.* Seattle: University of Washington Press, 1982.

Major, Kris. "The Yankee Fork Dredge and Its Community." *Idaho Yesterdays* 32 (Summer 1988): 22–34.

May, Dean L., and Jenny Cornell. "Middleton's Agriminers: The Beginnings of an Agricultural Town." *Idaho Yesterdays* 28 (Winter 1985): 2–11.

Oliphant, J. Orin. *On the Cattle Ranges of the Oregon Country*. Seattle: University of Washington Press, 1968.

Paul, Rodman W. *Mining Frontiers of the Far West, 1848–1880*. New York: Holt, Rinehart and Winston, 1963.

Petersen, Keith C. *Company Town: Potlatch, Idaho, and the Potlatch Lumber Company*. Pullman: Washington State University Press, 1987.

Peterson, Richard H. "Simeon Gannett Reed and the Bunker Hill and Sullivan: The Frustrations of a Mining Investor." *Idaho Yesterdays* 23 (Fall 1979): 2–8.

Smalley, Eugene V. "The Great Coeur d'Alene Stampede of 1884." *Idaho Yesterdays* 11 (Fall 1967): 2–10.

Space, Ralph S. "The Race for Clearwater Timber." *Idaho Yesterdays* 17 (Winter 1974): 2–5.

Spence, Clark C. "The Boom of the Wood River Mines." *Idaho Yesterdays* 23 (Summer 1979): 4–12.

Young, James A., and B. Abbott Sparks. *Cattle in the Cold Desert*. Logan: Utah State University Press, 1985. Although it emphasizes Nevada, the book includes material on Idaho's cattle industry.

Chapter 9

Arrington, Leonard J. "The Promise of Eagle Rock: Idaho Falls, Idaho, 1863–1980." *Rendezvous* 18 (Spring 1983): 2–17.

Attebery, Jennifer Eastman. "Courthouse Architecture in Idaho, 1864–1940." *Idaho Yesterdays* 31 (Fall 1987): 11–15.

———. "Domestic and Commercial Architecture in Caldwell." *Idaho Yesterdays* 23 (Winter 1980): 2–11.

———. "The Square Cabin: A Folk House Type in Idaho." *Idaho Yesterdays* 26 (Fall 1982): 25–31.

Boyce, Ronald R. "The Mormon Invasion and Settlement of the Upper Snake River Plain in the 1880s: The Case of Lewisville, Idaho." *Pacific Northwest Quarterly* 78 (1987): 50–58.

Chaffee, Eugene B. "Boise: The Founding of a City." *Idaho Yesterdays* 7 (Summer 1963): 2–7.

Crowder, David L. *Rexburg, Idaho: The First One Hundred Years, 1883–1983*. Rexburg: D. Crowder, 1983.

Derig, Betty. "Bullionaire Society." *Idaho Yesterdays* 1 (Winter 1957–58): 7–10, 20. Early Silver City.

Gittins, H. Leigh. *Pocatello Portrait: The Early Years, 1878 to 1928*. Moscow: University Press of Idaho, 1983.

Hart, Arthur A. "Architectural Styles in Idaho: A Rich Harvest." *Idaho Yesterdays* 16 (Winter 1972–73): 2–9.

———. *Historic Boise: An Introduction to the Architecture of Boise, Idaho, 1863–1938.* Boise: Historic Boise, 1985.

Mueller, Gene. *Lewiston: A Pictorial History.* Lewiston: Lewiston Chamber of Commerce, 1986.

Neil, J. Meredith. *Saints and Odd Fellows: A Bicentennial Sample of Idaho Architecture.* Boise: Boise Gallery of Art Association, 1976.

Petersen, Keith C. "The Boosters of Moscow." *Idaho Yesterdays* 31 (Fall 1987): 24–32.

Reitzes, Lisa B. *Paris: A Look at Idaho Architecture.* Boise: Idaho State Historic Preservation Office, 1981.

Wells, Merle W. *Boise: An Illustrated History.* Woodland Hills, Calif.: Windsor Publications, 1982.

West, Elliott. "Five Idaho Mining Towns: A Computer Profile." *Pacific Northwest Quarterly* 73 (1982): 108–20.

Whiting, Henry, II, with Robert G. Waite, *Teater's Knoll: Frank Lloyd Wright's Idaho Legacy.* Midland, Mich.: Northweed Institute Press, 1987.

Wright, Patricia, and Lisa B. Reitzes, *Tourtellotte and Hummel of Idaho: The Standard Practice of Architecture.* Logan: Utah State University Press, 1987.

Chapter 10

Bennett, Dana. "Mormon Polygamy in Early Southeastern Idaho. *Idaho Yesterdays* 28 (Spring 1984): 24–30.

Bieter, Pat. "Reluctant Shepherds: The Basques in Idaho." *Idaho Yesterdays* 1 (Summer 1957): 10–15.

Cox, Thomas R. "Tribal Leadership in Transition: Chief Peter Moctelme of the Coeur d'Alenes." *Idaho Yesterdays* 23 (Spring 1979): 2–9, 25–31.

Derig, Betty. "Celestials in the Diggings." *Idaho Yesterdays* 16 (Fall 1972): 2–23.

Dozier, Jack. "The Coeur d'Alene Land Rush, 1909–1910." *Pacific Northwest Quarterly* 53 (1962): 145–50.

Etulain, Richard W. "Basque Beginnings in the Pacific Northwest." *Idaho Yesterdays* 18 (Spring 1974): 26–32.

Gay, E. Jane. *With the Nez Perces: Alice Fletcher in the Field, 1889–92.* Lincoln: University of Nebraska Press, 1981.

Gibbs, Granville H. "Mormonism in Idaho Politics, 1880–1890." *Utah Historical Quarterly* 21 (1953): 285–305.

Graff, Leo W., Jr. *The Senatorial Career of Fred T. Dubois of Idaho, 1890–1907*. New York: Garland Publishing, 1988.

Hart, I. W., ed. *Proceedings and Debates of the Constitutional Convention of Idaho, 1889*. Caldwell, Idaho: Caxton, 1912.

Hulse, James W. "Idaho versus Nevada: The 1887 Struggle between Nevada's Senator and Idaho's Governor." *Idaho Yesterdays* 29 (Fall 1985): 26–31.

Larson, T. A. "Idaho's Role in America's Woman Suffrage Crusade." *Idaho Yesterdays* 18 (Summer 1974): 2–15.

———. "The Woman's Rights Movement in Idaho." *Idaho Yesterdays* 16 (Spring 1972): 2–15, 18–19.

Limbaugh, Ronald H. *Rocky Mountain Carpetbaggers: Idaho's Territorial Governors, 1863–1890*. Moscow: University Press of Idaho, 1982.

Lyman, E. Leo. "A Mormon Transition in Idaho Politics." *Idaho Yesterdays* 20 (Winter 1977): 2–11, 24–29.

Mark, Joan. *A Stranger in Her Native Land: Alice Fletcher and the American Indians*. Lincoln: University of Nebraska Press, 1988. Of special interest are the chapters on Idaho.

Morrill, Allen C., and Eleanor D. Morrill. "The Measuring Woman and the Cook." *Idaho Yesterdays* 7 (Fall 1963): 2–15. Alice Fletcher's work among the Nez Perce Indians.

Owens, Kenneth D. "Pierce City Incident." *Idaho Yesterdays* 3 (Fall 1959): 8–13.

Scott, Mary Katsilometes. "The Greek Community in Pocatello, 1890–1941." *Idaho Yesterdays* 28 (Fall 1984): 29–36.

Simmonds, A. J. "Idaho's Last Colony: Northern Cache Valley under the Test Oath, 1872–1896." *Idaho Yesterdays* 32 (Summer 1988): 2–14.

Sims, Robert C. "The Japanese American Experience in Idaho." *Idaho Yesterdays* 22 (Spring 1978): 2–10.

Stratton, David H. "The Snake River Massacre of Chinese Miners, 1887." In *A Taste of the West: Essays in Honor of Robert G. Athearn,"* Ed. Duane A. Smith, 109–29. Boulder, Colo.: Pruett Publishing, 1983.

Thompson, Dennis L. "Religion and the Idaho Constitution." *Pacific Northwest Quarterly* 58 (1967): 169–78.

Todd, A. C. "Cousin Jack in Idaho." *Idaho Yesterdays* 8 (Winter 1964–65): 2–11.

Wells, Merle W. *Anti-Mormonism in Idaho, 1872–92*. Provo: Brigham Young University Press, 1978.

———. "Law in the Service of Politics: Anti-Mormonism in Idaho Territory.

Idaho Yesterdays 25 (Spring 1981): 33–43.

———. "Origins of Anti-Mormonism in Idaho, 1872–1880." *Pacific Northwest Quarterly* 47 (1956): 107–16.

———. "Politics in the Panhandle: Opposition to the Admission of Washington and North Idaho, 1886–1888." *Pacific Northwest Quarterly* 46 (1955): 79–89.

———. "Walla Walla's Vision of a Greater Washington." *Idaho Yesterdays* 11 (Fall 1966): 20–31.

Wunder, John. "The Courts and the Chinese in Frontier Idaho." *Idaho Yesterdays* 25 (Spring 1981): 23–32.

Chapter 11

Arrington, Leonard J., and Jon Haupt. "The Mormon Heritage of Vardis Fisher." *Brigham Young University Studies* 18 (Fall 1977): 27–47.

Barrett, Glen. *Boise State University: Searching for Excellence, 1932–1984.* Boise: Boise State University, 1984.

Cox, Thomas R. *The Park Builders: A History of State Parks in the Pacific Northwest.* Seattle: University of Washington Press, 1988.

Day, Louise. "My Chautauqua." *Idaho Yesterdays* 13 (Fall 1969): 2–5.

Gibbs, Rafe. *Beacon for Mountain and Plain: Story of the University of Idaho.* Moscow: University of Idaho, 1962.

Gilliard, Fred. "Early Theater in the Owyhees." *Idaho Yesterdays* 17 (Summer 1973): 9–15.

———. "Pioneer Dramatists in the Boise Basin." *Idaho Yesterdays* 19 (Winter 1976): 2–9.

Knight, Oliver. "The *Owyhee Avalanche:* The Frontier Newspaper as a Catalyst in Social Change." *Pacific Northwest Quarterly* 58 (1967): 74–81.

McFarland, Ronald E., and William Studebaker, eds. *Idaho's Poetry: A Centennial Anthology.* Moscow: University of Idaho Press, 1988.

Maguire, James H., ed. *The Literature of Idaho: An Anthology.* Boise: Hemingway Western Studies Publications, Boise State University, 1986.

Paul, Rodman W. "When Culture Came to Boise: Mary Hallock Foote in Idaho." *Idaho Yesterdays* 20 (Summer 1976): 2–12.

Petersen, Keith C. *This Crested Hill: An Illustrated History of the University of Idaho.* Moscow: University of Idaho Press, 1987.

Rhodes-Jones, Carolyn. "An Evolving View of the Landscape: Trappers, Tourists, and the Great Shoshone Falls." *Idaho Yesterdays* 23 (Summer 1979): 19–27.

Staggers, Kermit L. "Coeur d'Alene Junior College, 1933–1939." *Idaho Yes-*

terdays 22 (Summer 1978): 18–26.

Taber, Ronald W. "Vardis Fisher of Idaho, March 31, 1895–July 9, 1968." *Idaho Yesterdays* 12 (Fall 1968): 2–8.

Woodward, Tim. *Tiger on the Road: The Life of Vardis Fisher, a Biography of a Literary Maverick.* Caldwell, Idaho: Caxton, 1989.

Wyman, Mark. "Frontier Journalism." *Idaho Yesterdays* 17 (Spring 1973): 30–36.

Chapter 12

Bonney, Richard J. "The Pullman Strike of 1894: Pocatello Perspective." *Idaho Yesterdays* 24 (Fall 1980): 23–28.

Conlin, Joseph R. "The Haywood Case: An Enduring Riddle." *Pacific Northwest Quarterly* 59 (1968): 23–32.

Dubofsky, Melvyn. "James H. Hawley and the Origins of the Haywood Case." *Pacific Northwest Quarterly* 58 (1967): 23–32.

Fahey, John. "Coeur d'Alene Confederacy." *Idaho Yesterdays* 12 (Spring 1968): 2–7.

———. *The Days of the Hercules.* Moscow: University Press of Idaho, 1978.

———. "Ed Boyce and the Western Federation of Miners." *Idaho Yesterdays* 25 (Fall 1981): 18–30.

Gaboury, William J. *Dissension in the Rockies: A History of Idaho Populism.* New York: Garland Publishing, 1988.

Glaser, David. "Migration in Idaho's History." *Idaho Yesterdays* 11 (Fall 1967): 22–31.

Graff, Leo W., Jr. "Fred T. Dubois and the Silver Issue, 1896." *Pacific Northwest Quarterly* 53 (1962): 138–44.

Grover, David H. *Debaters and Dynamiters: The Story of the Haywood Trial.* Corvallis: Oregon State University Press, 1964.

Hart, Patricia, and Ivar Nelson. *Mining Town: The Photographic Record of T. N. Barnard and Nellie Stockbridge from the Coeur d'Alenes.* Seattle: University of Washington Press, 1984.

Hawley, James H. "Steve Adams' Confession and the State's Case against Bill Haywood." *Idaho Yesterdays* 7 (Winter 1963–64): 16–27.

Jensen, Vernon H. *Heritage of Conflict: Labor Relations in the Nonferrous Metals Industry up to 1930.* 1950. Reprint. New York: Greenwood Press, 1968.

Kissane, Leedice. "Steve Adams, the Speechless Witness." *Idaho Yesterdays* 4 (Fall 1960): 18–21.

Kizer, Benjamin H. "May Arkwright Hutton." *Pacific Northwest Quarterly* 57

(1966): 49–56.

Kolb, Harold H., Jr. "Industrial Millstone." *Idaho Yesterdays* 16 (Summer 1972): 28–32. The Western Federation of Miners.

Lingenfelter, Richard E. *The Hardrock Miners: A History of the Mining Labor Movement in the American West, 1863–1893.* Berkeley: University of California Press, 1974.

Magnuson, Richard G. *Coeur d'Alene Diary: The First Ten Years of Hardrock Mining in North Idaho.* Portland: Binford & Mort, 1968..

Montgomery, James W. *Liberated Woman: A Life of May Arkwright Hutton.* Fairfield, Wash.: Ye Galleon Press, 1974.

Schwantes, Carlos A. "The History of Pacific Northwest Labor History." *Idaho Yesterdays* 28 (Winter 1985): 23–35.

———. "Law and Disorder: The Suppression of Coxey's Army in Idaho." *Idaho Yesterdays* 25 (Summer 1981): 10–15, 18–26.

Smith, Robert Wayne. *The Coeur d'Alene Mining War of 1892: A Case Study of an Industrial Dispute.* 1961. Reprint. Gloucester, Mass.: Peter Smith, 1968.

Thiessen, D. G., and Carlos A. Schwantes. "Industrial Violence in the Coeur d'Alene Mining District: The Visual Record." *Pacific Northwest Quarterly* 78 (1987): 83–90.

Thomason, Frank. "The Bellevue Stranglers." *Idaho Yesterdays* 13 (Fall 1969): 26–32. A study of labor unrest in the Wood River valley during the 1880s.

Wells, Merle W. "Fred T. Dubois and the Idaho Progressives." *Idaho Yesterdays* 4 (Summer 1960): 24–30.

White, W. Thomas. "Railroad Labor Protests, 1894–1917: From Community to Class in the Pacific Northwest." *Pacific Northwest Quarterly* 75 (1984): 13–21.

Wyman, Mark. *Hard Rock Epic: Western Miners and the Industrial Revolution, 1860–1910.* Berkeley: University of California Press, 1979.

Chapter 13

Arrington, Leonard J. "Irrigation in the Snake River Valley: An Historical Overview." *Idaho Yesterdays* 30 (Spring/Summer 1986): 3–11.

Athearn, Robert G. "The Oregon Short Line." *Idaho Yesterdays* 13 (Winter 1969–70): 2–18.

Buckendorf, Madeline. "Life and Death of a Small Town: The Case of Montour, Idaho." *Idaho Yesterdays* 33 (Summer 1989): 8–24.

Casner, Nicholas. "'Two-Gun Limbert': The Man from the Sawtooths."

Idaho Yesterdays 32 (Spring 1988): 2–11.

Coate, Charles. "Federal-Local Relationships on the Boise and Minidoka Projects, 1904–1926." *Idaho Yesterdays* 25 (Summer 1981): 2–9.

Cook, Rufus G. "Pioneer Portraits: Weldon B. Heyburn." *Idaho Yesterdays* 10 (Spring 1966): 22–26.

———. "The Political Suicide of Senator Fred T. DuBois of Idaho." *Pacific Northwest Quarterly* 60 (1969): 193–98.

Fletcher, Marvin. "Army Fire Fighters." *Idaho Yesterdays* 16 (Summer 1972): 12–15.

Gertsch, W. Darrell. "Water Use, Energy, and Economic Development in the Snake River Basin." *Idaho Yesterdays* 23 (Summer 1979): 58–72.

Gittins, H. Leigh. *Pocatello Portrait: The Early Years, 1878 to 1928*. Moscow: University Press of Idaho, 1983.

Hibbard, Don. "Chicago 1893: Idaho at the World's Columbian Exposition." *Idaho Yesterdays* 24 (Summer 1980): 24–29.

Hult, Ruby El. *Northwest Disaster: Avalanche and Fire*. Portland: Binfords & Mort, 1960.

Jones, Shawn. "The Road to Jackpot," *Idaho Yesterdays* 33 (Spring 1989): 2–12. A history of gambling in Idaho.

Knight, Oliver. "Robert E. Strahorn, Propagandist for the West." *Pacific Northwest Quarterly* 59 (1968): 33–45.

Lovin, Hugh T. "The Carey Act in Idaho, 1895–1925: An Experiment in Free Enterprise Reclamation." *Pacific Northwest Quarterly* 78 (1987): 122–33.

———. "Free Enterprise and Large-Scale Reclamation on the Twin Falls–North Side Tract, 1907–1930." *Idaho Yesterdays* 29 (Spring 1985): 2–14.

———. "How Not to Run a Carey Act Project: The Twin Falls–Salmon Falls Creek Tract, 1904–1922." *Idaho Yesterdays* 30 (Fall 1986): 9–15, 18–24.

———. "Sage, Jacks, and Snake Plain Pioneers." *Idaho Yesterdays* 22 (Winter 1979): 13–15, 18–24.

Murphy, Paul L. "Early Irrigation in the Boise Valley." *Pacific Northwest Quarterly* 44 (1953): 177–84.

Neil, J. Meredith. "A Forgotten Alternative: Reclamation by the States." *Idaho Yesterdays* 9 (Winter 1965–66): 18–21.

Perry, Barbara E. "Arrowrock Dam Is Built." *Idaho Yesterdays* 29 (Spring 1985): 15–23.

Petersen, Keith C. *Company Town: Potlatch, Idaho, and the Potlatch Lumber Company*. Pullman: Washington State University Press, 1987.

Peterson, F. Ross, and W. Darrell Gertsch. "The Creation of Idaho's Lifeblood: The Politics of Irrigation." *Rendezvous* 11 (Fall 1976): 53–61.

Putman, Edison K. "Travail at the Turn of the Century: Efforts at Liquor Control in Idaho." *Idaho Yesterdays* 33 (Spring 1989): 13–19, 22–24.

Reisner, Marc. *Cadillac Desert: The American West and Its Disappearing Water*. New York: Viking, 1986.

Spencer, Betty Goodwin, *The Big Blowup: The Northwest's Great Fire*. Caldwell, Idaho: Caxton, 1956.

Wegars, Priscilla. "'Inmates of Body Houses': Prostitution in Moscow, 1885–1910." *Idaho Yesterdays* 33 (Spring 1989): 25–37.

Wells, Merle W. *Boise: An Illustrated History*. Woodland Hills, Calif.: Windsor Publications, 1982.

Williams, Marjorie. "The Rainmakers' Reign." *Idaho Yesterdays* 27 (Winter 1984): 24–36.

Worster, Donald. *Rivers of Empire: Water, Aridity, and the Growth of the American West*. New York: Pantheon Books, 1985.

Chapter 14

Arrington, Leonard J. "The Influenza Epidemic of 1918–1919 in Southern Idaho." *Idaho Yesterdays* 33 (Fall 1988): 19–29.

Ashby, LeRoy. *The Spearless Leader: Senator Borah and the Progressive Movement in the 1920s*. Urbana: University of Illinois Press, 1972.

Barrett, Gwynn, and Leonard Arrington. "The 1921 Depression: Its Impact on Idaho." *Idaho Yesterdays* 15 (Summer 1971): 10–15.

Borah, Mary. *Elephants and Donkeys: The Memoirs of Mary Borah as Told to Mary Louise Perrine*. Moscow: University Press of Idaho, 1976.

Cooper, John Milton. "William E. Borah, Political Thespian." *Pacific Northwest Quarterly* 56 (1965): 145–53.

Greenwood, Annie Pike. *We Sagebrush Folks*. 1934. Reprint. Moscow: University of Idaho Press, 1988.

Johnson, Claudius O. *Borah of Idaho*. 1936. Reprint. Seattle: University of Washington Press, 1967.

Lovin, Hugh T. "Disloyalty, Libel, and Litigation: Ray McKaig's Ordeal, 1917–1920." *Idaho Yesterdays* 27 (Summer 1983): 13–14, 18–24.

———. "The Farmer Revolt in Idaho, 1914–1922." *Idaho Yesterdays* 20 (Fall 1976): 2–15.

———. "Idaho and the 'Reds,' 1919–1926." *Pacific Northwest Quarterly* 69 (1978): 107–15.

———. "Moses Alexander and the Idaho Lumber Strike of 1917: The Wartime Ordeal of a Progressive." *Pacific Northwest Quarterly* 66 (1975): 115–22.

————. "The Nonpartisan League and Progressive Renascence in Idaho, 1919–1924." *Idaho Yesterdays* 32 (Fall 1988): 2–15.

————. "The Red Scare in Idaho, 1916–1918." *Idaho Yesterdays* 17 (Fall 1973): 2–13.

————. "World War Vigilantes in Idaho, 1917–1918." *Idaho Yesterdays* 18 (Fall 1974): 2–11.

McKenna, Marian C. *Borah*. Ann Arbor: University of Michigan Press, 1961.

Maddox, Robert James. *William E. Borah and American Foreign Policy*. Baton Rouge: Louisiana State University Press, 1969.

Malone, Michael P. *C. Ben Ross and the New Deal in Idaho*. Seattle: University of Washington Press, 1970. Contains material on Idaho in the 1920s.

Ruckman, Jo Ann. "'Knit. Knit, and Then Knit': The Women of Pocatello and the War Effort of 1917–1918." *Idaho Yesterdays* 26 (Spring 1982): 26–36.

Sims, Robert C. "Idaho's Criminal Syndicalism Act: One State's Response to Radical Labor." *Labor History* 15 (1974): 511–29.

Wells, Merle W. "Fred T. Dubois and the Nonpartisan League in the Idaho Election of 1918." *Pacific Northwest Quarterly* 56 (1965): 17–29.

Chapter 15

Arrington, Leonard J. "Idaho and the Great Depression." *Idaho Yesterdays* 13 (Summer 1969): 2–8.

Arrington, Leonard J., and Gwynn W. Barrett. "Stopping a Run on a Bank: The First Security Bank of Idaho and the Great Depression." *Idaho Yesterdays* 14 (Winter 1970–71): 2–11.

Austin, Judith. "The CCC in Idaho: An Anniversary View." *Idaho Yesterdays* 27 (Fall 1983): 13–17.

Fisher, Vardis. *Idaho: A Guide in Word and Picture*. Caldwell, Idaho: Caxton, 1937.

Glaser, David. "Migration in Idaho's History." *Idaho Yesterdays* 11 (Fall 1967): 22–31.

"Hard Times in Idaho between the Great Wars, 1920–1941," *Rendezvous* 20 (Fall 1984). The articles in this issue emphasize the social history of the Great Depression in Idaho.

Lowitt, Richard. *The New Deal and the West*. Bloomington: Indiana University Press, 1984.

Malone, Michael P. *C. Ben Ross and the New Deal in Idaho*. Seattle: University of Washington Press, 1970.

————. "C. Ben Ross: Idaho's Cowboy Governor." *Idaho Yesterdays* 10 (Winter 1966–67): 2–9.

————. "The New Deal in Idaho." *Pacific Historical Review* 38 (1969): 293–310.

Neuberger, Richard L. *Our Promised Land*. New York: Macmillan, 1938. A lively account of Idaho and the Pacific Northwest during the 1930s.

[Norwood, Gus]. *Columbia River Power for the People: A History of Policies of the Bonneville Power Administration*.

Portland: Bonneville Power Administration, [ca. 1981].

Oppenheimer, Doug, and Jim Poore. *Sun Valley: A Biography*. Boise: Beatty Books, 1976.

Sims, Robert C. "James P. Pope, Senator from Idaho." *Idaho Yesterdays* 15 (Fall 1971): 9–15.

Swanson, Merwin R. "The Civil Works Administration in Idaho." *Idaho Yesterdays* 32 (Winter 1989): 2–10.

————. "The New Deal in Pocatello." *Idaho Yesterdays* 23 (Summer 1979): 53–57.

————. "Pocatello's Business Community and the New Deal." *Idaho Yesterdays* 21 (Fall 1977): 9–15.

Taber, Ronald W. "Vardis Fisher and the *Idaho Guide:* Preserving Culture for the New Deal." *Pacific Northwest Quarterly* 59 (1968): 68–76.

————. "Vardis Fisher of Idaho, March 31, 1895–July 9, 1968." *Idaho Yesterdays* 12 (Fall 1968): 7–8.

Tollefson, Gene. *BPA and the Struggle for Power at Cost*. Portland: Bonneville Power Administration, [1987].

Watters, Ron. "The Long Snowshoe: Early Skiing in Idaho." *Idaho Yesterdays* 23 (Fall 1979): 18–25.

Young, George C., and Frederic J. Cochrane. *Hydro Era: The Story of the Idaho Power Company*. Boise: Idaho Power Company, 1978.

Chapter 16

Barrett, Glen W. "Reclamation's New Deal for Heavy Construction: M-K in the Great Depression." *Idaho Yesterdays* 22 (Fall 1978): 21–27.

Daniels, Roger. *Asian America: Chinese and Japanese in the United States since 1850*. Seattle: University of Washington Press, 1988. Especially see chapter 6: "Asian Americans and World War II."

Davis, William E. "Portrait of an Industrialist." *Idaho Yesterdays* 11 (Summer 1967): 2–7. J. R. Simplot.

"The 'Good War' in Retrospect: Memories of World War II." *Rendezvous* 22 (Spring 1987). This series of essays emphasizes social aspects of World War II in Idaho.

Nash, Gerald D. *The American West Transformed: The Impact of the Second World War*. Bloomington: Indiana University Press, 1985.

Ourada, Patricia K. "Reluctant Servants: Conscientious Objectors in Idaho during World War II." *Idaho Yesterdays* 31 (Winter 1988): 2–14, 15–23.

Schwantes, Carlos A., ed. *The Pacific Northwest in World War II*. Manhattan, Kans.: Sunflower University Press, 1986.

Sims, Robert C. "'A Fearless, Patriotic, Clean-Cut Stand': Idaho's Governor Clark and Japanese-American Relocation in World War II." *Pacific Northwest Quarterly* 70 (1979): 75–81.

———. "The Japanese American Experience in Idaho." *Idaho Yesterdays* 22 (Spring 1978): 2–10.

Sone, Monica. *Nisei Daughter*. 1953. Reprint. Seattle: University of Washington Press, 1979. Especially chapter 10 on life in Camp Minidoka.

Chapter 17

Cox, Thomas R. *The Park Builders: A History of State Parks in the Pacific Northwest*. Seattle: University of Washington Press, 1988.

Gamboa, Erasmo. "Braceros in the Pacific Northwest: Laborers on the Domestic Front, 1942–1947," *Pacific Historical Review* 55 (1987): 378–98.

Garnsey, Morris. *America's New Frontier: The Mountain West*. New York: Knopf, 1950.

Gertsch, W. Darrell. "Contours of Change: Water Resource Allocation and Economic Stability in the Snake River Basin." *Idaho Yesterdays* 30 (Spring/Summer 1986): 12–19.

Morgan, Neil. *Westward Tilt: The American West Today*. New York: Random House, 1963. Especially chapter 13, "Mountain North: Idaho, Montana, Wyoming."

Ourada, Patricia K. *Migrant Workers in Idaho*. [Boise: n.p., 1980]

Petersen, Keith C., and Mary E. Reed. "'For All the People, Forever and Ever': Virgil McCroskey and the State Parks Movement." *Idaho Yesterdays* 28 (Spring 1984): 2–15.

Boise Magazine (1983 to date) and *Oh! Idaho* (1988 to date) are both good sources of information on contemporary Idaho.

Chapter 18

Ashby, LeRoy. "Frank Church Goes to the Senate: The Idaho Election of 1956." *Pacific Northwest Quarterly* 78 (1987): 17–31.

Ashworth, William. *Hells Canyon: The Deepest Gorge on Earth*. New York: Hawthorn Books, 1977.

Church, F. Forrester. *Father and Son: A Personal Biography of Senator Frank Church of Idaho by His Son*. Boston: Faber and Faber, 1985.

Gunther, John. *Inside U. S. A.* New York: Harper & Brothers, 1947. See chapter 7, "Two Freshmen from the Mountain Slopes."

Hagstrom, Jerry. *Beyond Reagan: The New Landscapes of American Politics*. New York: Penguin, 1988.

Jordan, Grace E. *The Unintentional Senator*. Boise: Syms-York, 1972. An account of Len B. Jordan.

Peirce, Neal R. *The Mountain States of America: People, Politics, and Power in the Eight Rocky Mountain States*. New York: Norton, 1972.

Peirce, Neal R., and Jerry Hagstrom. *The Book of America: Inside Fifty States Today*. New York: Warner Books, 1984.

Peterson, F. Ross. *Prophet without Honor: Glen H. Taylor and the Fight for American Liberalism*. Lexington: University Press of Kentucky, 1974.

Pratt, William C. "Glen H. Taylor: Public Image and Reality." *Pacific Northwest Quarterly* 60 (1969): 10–16.

Short, Brant. "Socialism in Minidoka County, 1912–1916." *Idaho Yesterdays* 26 (Summer 1982): 30–38.

Stapilus, Randy. *Paradox Politics: People and Power in Idaho*. Boise: Ridenbaugh Press, 1988.

Taylor, Glen H. *The Way It Was with Me*. Secaucus, N.J.: Lyle Stuart, 1979.

Recent Contributions to Idaho History

Attebery, Jennifer Eastman. *Building Idaho: An Architectural History*. Moscow: University of Idaho Press, 1991.

Beck, Richard J. *100 Famous Idahoans*. Moscow: Richard J. Beck, 1989. Biographical sketches of well-known Idahoans.

Colson, Dennis C. *Idaho's Constitution: The Tie that Binds*. Moscow: University of Idaho Press, 1991.

Fahey, John. *Hecla: A Century of Western Mining*. Seattle: University of Washington Press, 1990. History of the Hecla Mining Company in northern Idaho.

Harthorn, Sandy, and Kathleen Bettis. *One Hundred Years of Idaho Art, 1850–1950*. Boise Art Museum, 1990.

Renk, Nancy F. "Off to the Lakes: Vacationing in North Idaho during the Railroad Era, 1885–1917." *Idaho Yesterdays* 34 (1990): 2–15.

Wilfong, Cheryl. *Following the Nez Perce Trail: A Guide to the Nee-Me-Poo National Historic Trail, with Eyewitness Accounts*. Corvallis: Oregon State University Press, 1990.

Index